T0301404

The People's Own Landscape

Social History, Popular Culture, and Politics in Germany
Geoff Eley, Series Editor

Series Editorial Board
Kathleen Canning, University of Michigan
David F. Crew, University of Texas, Austin
Atina Grossmann, The Cooper Union
Alf Lüdtke, University of Erfurt, Germany / Hanyang University, Seoul, Korea
Andrei S. Markovits, University of Michigan

Recent Titles
The People's Own Landscape: Nature, Tourism, and Dictatorship in East Germany
    Scott Moranda
Envisioning Socialism: Television and the Cold War in the German Democratic Republic
    Heather L. Gumbert
German Colonialism Revisited: African, Asian, and Oceanic Experiences
    Nina Berman, Klaus Mühlhahn, and Patrice Nganang, Editors
Becoming a Nazi Town: Culture and Politics in Göttingen between the World Wars
    David Imhoof
Germany's Wild East: Constructing Poland as Colonial Space
    Kristin Kopp
Colonialism, Antisemitism, and Germans of Jewish Descent in Imperial Germany,
    Christian S. Davis
Africa in Translation: A History of Colonial Linguistics in Germany and Beyond,
    1814–1945, Sara Pugach
Between National Socialism and Soviet Communism: Displaced Persons in
    Postwar Germany, Anna Holian
Dueling Students: Conflict, Masculinity, and Politics in German Universities, 1890–1914,
    Lisa Fetheringill Zwicker
The Golem Returns: From German Romantic Literature to Global Jewish Culture,
    1808–2008, Cathy S. Gelbin
German Literature on the Middle East: Discourses and Practices, 1000–1989,
    Nina Berman
Franz Radziwill and the Contradictions of German Art History, 1919–45,
    James A. van Dyke
Weimar through the Lens of Gender: Prostitution Reform, Woman's Emancipation, and
    German Democracy, Julia Roos
Murder Scenes: Normality, Deviance, and Criminal Violence in Weimar Berlin, Sace Elder
Changing Places: Society, Culture, and Territory in the Saxon-Bohemian Borderlands,
    1870 to 1946, Caitlin E. Murdock
After the Nazi Racial State: Difference and Democracy in Germany and Europe, Rita Chin,
    Heide Fehrenbach, Geoff Eley, and Atina Grossmann
Work, Race, and the Emergence of Radical Right Corporatism in Imperial Germany,
    Dennis Sweeney
The German Patient: Crisis and Recovery in Postwar Culture,
    Jennifer M. Kapczynski

For a complete list of titles, please see www.press.umich.edu

The People's Own Landscape

*Nature, Tourism, and Dictatorship
in East Germany*

SCOTT MORANDA

THE UNIVERSITY OF MICHIGAN PRESS
Ann Arbor

For Grandma

Copyright © by Scott Moranda 2014
All rights reserved

This book may not be reproduced, in whole or in part, including illustrations, in any form (beyond that copying permitted by Sections 107 and 108 of the U.S. Copyright Law and except by reviewers for the public press), without written permission from the publisher.

Published in the United States of America by
The University of Michigan Press
Manufactured in the United States of America
♾ Printed on acid-free paper

2017   2016   2015   2014   4   3   2   1

A CIP catalog record for this book is available from the British Library.

Library of Congress Cataloging-in-Publication Data

Moranda, Scott.
    The people's own landscape : nature, tourism, and dictatorship in East Germany / Scott Moranda.
        pages   cm. — (Social history, popular culture, and politics in Germany)
    Includes bibliographical references and index.
        ISBN 978-0-472-11913-4 (cloth : acid-free paper) — ISBN 978-0-472-02972-3 (ebook)
        1. Tourism—Germany (East)—History.   2. Landscapes—Germany (East)—History.
3. Land use—Germany (East)—History.   4. Nature—Effect of human beings on—Germany
(East)—History.   5. Ecology—Germany (East)—History.   6. Political culture—Germany
(East)—History.   7. Dictatorship—Social aspects—Germany (East)—History.   8. Germany
(East)—Social conditions.   9. Germany (East)—Environmental conditions.   10. Germany
(East)—Politics and government.   I. Title.
G155.G3M67   2013
914.310487—dc23
2013035567

Contents

Abbreviations

Abt.	Abteilung, or Department
Abt. JKS	Abteilung Jugendfragen, Körperkultur und Sport, or Department for Youth Questions, Physical Culture and Sport
BArch	Bundesarchiv in Berlin-Lichterfelde, or Federal Archive in Berlin-Lichterfelde
BfT	Büro für Territorialplanung, or Office for Territorial Planning
DAL	Deutsche Akademie der Landwirtschaftswissenschaften, or German Academy of the Agricultural Sciences
DTSB	Deutscher Turn und Sportbund, or German Gymnastics and Sports League
DWBO	Deutscher Verband für Wandern, Bergsteigen und Orientierungslauf der DDR, or German Association for Hiking, Mountain Climbing, and Orienteering
DWBV	Deutscher Wanderer- und Bergsteigerverband, or German Association for Hiking and Mountain Climbing
FDGB	Freie Deutsche Gewerkschaftsbund, or Free German Trade Union
FDJ	Freie Deutsche Jugend, or Free German Youth
GDR	German Democratic Republic, or Deutsche Demokratische Republik (DDR)
GNU	Gesellschaft für Natur und Umwelt, or Society for Nature and Environment
ILN	Institut für Landesforschung und Naturschutz, or Institute for Regional Research and Nature Protection
IUCN	International Union for the Conservation of Nature
IUPN	International Union for the Protection of Nature
KarchMZ	Kreisarchiv Marienberg-Zschopau, or County Archive Marienberg-Zschopau

KFW   Kirchliche Forschungsheim Wittenberg, or Church Re-
               search Institute in Wittenberg
KTW   Komitee für Touristik und Wandern, or Committee for Tour-
               ism and Hiking
MfU   Ministerium für Umweltschutz, or Ministry for Environ-
               mental Protection
MLF   Ministerium für Land und Forstwirtschaft, or Ministry for
               Agriculture and Forestry
NuH   Natur und Heimatfreunde, or Nature and Heimat Friends
RdB   Rat des Bezirks, or district council
RdK   Rat des Kreises, or county council
RdS   Rat der Stadt, or city council
SAPMO-BArch   Stiftung Archiv der Parteien und Massenorganisationen der
               DDR im Bundesarchiv, or Foundation Archives of the Par-
               ties and Mass Organizations of the GDR in the Federal Ar-
               chives
SäStArchD   Sächsisches Hauptstaatsarchiv Dresden, or Saxon State Ar-
               chive in Dresden
SED   Sozialistische Einheitspartei Deutschland, or Socialist Unity
               Party
SKLN   Ständige Kommission für Landschaftspflege und Natur-
               schutz, or Standing Committee for Landscape Care and Na-
               ture Protection
StaarchEhr   Stadtarchiv Ehrenfriedersdorf, or City Archive Ehrenfrie-
               dersdorf
Stasi   Ministerium für Staatssicherheit, or Ministry for State Secu-
               rity
VEB   Volkseigener Betrieb, or People's Enterprise
VStFB   Verwaltungsleitung Staatliche Forswirtschaftsbetriebe, or
               Supervising Administration for State Forestry Enterprises
ZK der SED   Zenralkomitee der SED, or Central Committee of the SED

Acknowledgments

This book has been long in the making and thus owes a debt to many people. I especially want to thank my mom for all of her love and support. She eventually became a high school German teacher, but she was serving in the American military in West Berlin when I was born. The Federal Archive in Berlin-Lichterfelde, where much of the research for this book took place, was in fact a former American military base where she worked for a time.

Research for my dissertation, which I revised into this manuscript, was made possible by a Fulbright grant from August 2001 to August 2002. I also owe debts of gratitude to the German Academic Exchange Service (or DAAD), the Zentrum für Zeithistorische Forschung Potsdam, and a Summer Research Grant from the State University of New York College at Cortland, for funding later research and writing trips to Berlin, Potsdam, and Chemnitz.

This project and the winding road it followed owe much to many of my former advisors and professors. At Carleton College, I learned a great deal from Diethelm Prowe and Julie Klassen. At the University of Wisconsin–Madison, Rudy Koshar remained patient with me in the early years and provided key support as my dissertation evolved. I also thank Alison Frank, David Sorkin, Bill Cronon, Suzanne Desan, Laird Boswell, and Nancy Langston.

Archives used for this book include the Bundesarchiv in Berlin-Lichterfelde, the Sächsisches Staatsarchiv Chemnitz, and the Sächsisches Hauptstaatsarchiv Dresden. Local archives and libraries in Saxony and the Erzgebirge included the Kreisarchiv Marienberg-Zschopau, the Geyer Turmmuseum, and the Stadtarchiv Ehrenfriedersdorf. I also benefited from the collections on environmental movements at the tiny eco-Archiv in Hofgeismar associated with the Arbeiterkultur und Ökologie e.V., the Archiv der DDR-Opposition at the Robert-Havemann-Gesellschaft in Berlin, and the Umweltbibliothek in Neubrandenburg. Finally, veterans of East German tourism organizations came to my aid. Joachim Schindler, Wolfgang Bagger, and Bernhard Fisch all welcomed me into their homes and provided access to their papers.

At SUNY Cortland, Don Wright, Randi Storch, and Lisi Krall have taught me a lot. Life in Germany would not have been the same without Heather, Peter, Kovar, and Hard Painting Man. Thanks also go to all my Madison friends, especially Nikki and Eric. Most important, I offer heartfelt thanks to Deirdre for all her love and support over the years.

In highly revised form, parts of chapters 1, 3, and 5 appeared in articles previously published. For chapter 1, material is reprinted from "East German Nature Tourism, 1949–1961: In Search of a Common Destination," in *Turizm: The Russian and East European Tourist under Capitalism and Socialism*, edited by Anne E. Gorsuch and Diane Koenker. Copyright © 2006 by Cornell University. Used by permission of the publisher, Cornell University Press.

For chapter 3, material is reprinted from "Camping in East Germany: Making 'Rough' Nature More Comfortable," in *Pleasures in Socialism: Leisure and Luxury in the Eastern Bloc*, edited by David Crowley and Susan E. Reid. Copyright © 2010 by Northwestern University. Used by permission of the publisher, Northwestern University Press.

For chapter 5, material is reprinted from "Nature as a Scarce Consumer Commodity: Vacationing in Communist East Germany," in *From Heimat to Umwelt: New Perspectives on German Environmental History*, edited by Frank Zelko and Stephen J. Scala, GHI Bulletin Supplement 3. Copyright © 2006 by German Historical Institute. Used by permission of the publisher, German Historical Institute.

Introduction

Twentieth-century communism promised to build a new world and fashion new men and women to inhabit it, and in a manner of speaking, German communists were wildly successful. Right down to its chemical structure, Germany between the Iron Curtain and the Oder-Neisse line had been made anew. Under sulfurous skies, sickly trees choked on the emissions of coal-fired industry, and by the 1970s, entire forests in the southern mountains appeared to be dying. In Halle, children fell victim to lung, throat, and nose illnesses, sometimes multiple times in a month's time.[1] On the whole, 80 percent of East Germany's surface water was "polluted" or "heavily polluted" by the beginning of the 1980s. According to historian Arvid Nelson, the groundwater near the city of Bitterfeld had a pH level of 1.9 by 1989, placing it somewhere between battery acid and vinegar. Elsewhere, native heath plants gave way to invasive sand grasses as ash pollution made soils less acidic.[2]

Such ecological turmoil was perhaps not all too surprising in a state with such far-reaching economic and social goals. Beginning as the Soviet Occupation Zone in 1945 and designated the German Democratic Republic (GDR) in 1949, this was a state constructed from thin air to eradicate the ills of social inequality and laissez-faire inefficiency. According to its own ideology, all of Europe's social and environmental ills had their roots in the liberal capitalist order. As an alternative, the ruling Socialist Unity Party (SED) offered what has since been identified as socialist modernism. Katherine Pence and Paul Betts define socialist modernism as "precisely the regime's more comprehensive project of social engineering that qualified it as fundamentally modern, one that set its sights on the full scale makeover of the state, society, material culture, and citizens alike."[3] As did other regimes in the Soviet bloc, East Germany practiced democratic centralism (one-party rule) and celebrated state planning, with a particular focus on heavy industry and collectivized industrial agriculture as tools to boost production and create a workers' paradise. Fervor for steel factories, tractors, and chemicalization gripped economic planners who either ignored environmental consequences or lightly brushed them off as symptoms of earlier capitalist greed. Party leaders also demanded the mental and physical transformation of Germans into self-sacrificing socialist personalities characterized by relentless optimism, physical fitness, and a willingness to sacrifice for the collective. This molding of socialist personalities demanded a thorough reengineering of urban and rural spaces, which previously had bred defeatism, racism, and individualism. From its very beginning, East German leaders thus demanded radical interventions into built and natural environments that had tremendous consequences for consumer pleasures and ecological integrity.

The People's Own Landscape investigates this radical remaking of nature, doing so from an unexpected perspective. In the following, I tell the intertwined histories of tourism and landscape planning. Many East Germans, not surprisingly, questioned the GDR's utopian and destructive agenda. Historians interested in East German environmental issues devote most of their attention to a small but important group of 1980s environmental, peace, and antinuclear activists organized within the Protestant church.[4] The protagonists of this book, however, are not inconsequential or trivial to understanding East Germany's environmental history. Most East Germans vacationed within the natural landscapes found inside the GDR's borders—places such as the Baltic seashore, mountain forests, or Mecklenburg lakeshores. Tourism offered opportunities for social engineering, but it also brought East Germans into intimate contact with polluted landscapes and thus can help us understand popular attitudes toward a ruling regime with a disastrous environmental record. As the geographer Barbara Bender has written, "Landscape is never inert; people engage with it, re-work it, appropriate and contest it. It is part of the way in which identities are created and disputed, whether as individual, group, or nation-state."[5] In this sense, I argue that vacationers worked both with and against the SED in the remaking of landscapes. Tourism, more than agriculture or other uses of the land, required the ruling party to interact with and sometimes respond to popular wishes and concerns about the countryside and its appearance. An investigation into tourism thus provides an opportunity to think about environmental change and land use from the perspectives of many different East Germans, including planners, vacationers, and local residents.

Undemocratic SED rule marked by incompetence and corruption doomed the environment, but the behavior of totalitarian rulers alone cannot explain the environmental history of the GDR. This book contends that many everyday East Germans initially accepted and sometimes embraced the necessity of an authoritarian regime for managing economic development so as to prevent social disorder. They shared, in other words, the dream of a therapeutic regime that could control, plan, and improve nature (and also human nature) to provide comfort, plenty, and pleasure. This dream was a reaction to a distinct German history of hunger, disorder, and displacement (a topic revisited later in this introduction). Not all Germans agreed on the form that this therapeutic regime took (many despised Marxism and the SED), but they agreed that the state played an important role in fixing disorder and that touristic pleasures and nature outings belonged to a better future. A mainstream consensus shared by the SED and its subjects (Marxists and non-Marxists alike) helps explain the immense pressure placed on the land and its resources, as well as the types of reforms that unsatisfied East Germans imagined. To be clear, I am not suggesting that a consensus existed about Stalinism, single-party rule, or the militarized police state; the mainstream consensus identified in this book formed very specifically around the notion that natural landscapes could be manipulated or developed by authoritarian experts for the benefit of the average consumer. Participants in this consensus did not endorse the most extreme Marxist-Leninist schemes to conquer nature, but they believed that well-informed experts could balance landscape health with exuberant, perhaps limitless, economic growth. Anthropocentric concerns dominated; material abundance, many believed, depended on developing the landscape carefully.

To better investigate the existence and significance of such a consensus, I sought out sources that could provide insight into the lives and aspirations of everyday citizens and lower-level bureaucrats. State offices and mass organizations left behind mountains of paperwork. With so many official sources organized according to the GDR's bureaucratic structure, it can be easy to write incredibly detailed histories of individual institutions. While such histories have great value, *The People's Own Landscape* attempts to identify stories that crossed institutional and organizational boundaries, as individual reformers sought to create alliances among sympathetic planners in different agencies. Another way to avoid dry institutional history is to explore county and district archives, as central directives often looked different from a local perspective. A history of vacationing also requires historians to find sources that illuminate more than institutional inertia. Even when sources came from the state and party archives, the most useful ones help us understand tourists as they saw themselves. These sources include letters of complaint, public opinion surveys, photographs, market research, local newspapers, and reports prepared by the managers of recreation areas where the give and take between central planning and everyday reality is most visible to the historian.

This book, while not ignoring top-level economic planners or 1980s environmentalists, focuses in particular on two broad categories of East Germans who experienced and influenced their state's environmental history on a daily basis. First, I introduce members of what I have labeled the "conservation bloc," which included experts in architecture, medicine, leisure, sport, and social hygiene who were interested in planning and preserving rural landscapes for the public's benefit. These men (and they were mostly men) came from a variety of political backgrounds, but they included dedicated Marxists as well as middle-class individuals who had embraced National Socialism in the 1930s. They shared with the SED a wariness of capitalism, of Americanization, of consumerism, and of popular culture, all of which they understood as unproductive, disorderly, and potentially destructive of both nature and society. Because they identified the unenlightened masses as a problem, they were receptive to a paternalist, authoritarian program of educating and disciplining popular behavior. Second, I investigate the very consumers feared by conservationists—in this case, East German vacationers who traveled within East German borders. In this study, I focus in particular on the cross section of citizens that owned vehicles, visited bungalow or camping sites, and could opt out of the hotels operated by the state trade union (the FDGB, or Freie Deutsche Gewerkschaftsbund). Many of these vacationers were urban, white-collar workers in the ever-expanding bureaucracy who benefited more than most East Germans from technological changes and economic growth within the SED regime. East Germany's population shifted gradually in the 1960s and 1970s from the countryside to the cities and increasingly into jobs in civil service or the "tertiary sector" (from 12.4 percent of the population in 1950 to 21.6 percent in 1989).[6] The new "service class" included many young men and women from former working-class families who experienced upward mobility with new opportunities for higher education in the 1950s and 1960s and who earned up to 40 percent more than factory workers by the 1980s.[7] While the "service class" is key to this study, other East Germans vacationed at campgrounds; these tourists included highly skilled workers and specialized craftsmen. Income, moreover, did not always determine membership within this group, as state subsidies for leisure, food, and rent lessened gaps between classes. In addition, connections (especially for families with Western relatives or for handymen who could trade supplies or repairs for favors) helped certain individuals from other social backgrounds to obtain camping equipment or building supplies for a bungalow.[8] Two social groups most likely but not completely excluded from this cross section of East German vacationers were retirees who subsisted on very limited incomes and political noncomformists who often found themselves blacklisted from certain career paths or denied certain consumer or leisure pleasures.[9]

While enamored with statism, the conservation bloc differed from the SED in key ways and pointedly embraced outdoor recreation, or *Erholung*, as a means to push the regime to protect landscapes. Both the SED and the conservation bloc understood tourism as productive; it was meant to restore labor productivity and educate citizens morally and politically. Marxists throughout Eastern Europe hoped productive leisure would replace the trivial pleasures of capitalist tourist practices.[10] Despite their affection for authority and productive leisure, this conservation bloc cared much more for landscape protection than the SED did. For these planners, an orderly and wisely used countryside was essential to the project of social engineering and long-term productivity. Landscape protection and social change required a strong, interventionist regime, but the SED had unleashed haphazard economic development and agricultural industrialization that had terrible consequences for the land. Since the SED insisted that it cared about leisure, material living standards, and public health, the conservation bloc argued, it needed to protect natural spaces where healthy outdoor tourism could be practiced.

When the conservation bloc linked dreams of material abundance to landscape protection, they accrued short-term benefits but long-term headaches. The SED promised better living standards, partly guaranteed by productive workers reinvigorated from their nature excursions. Thus, conservationists argued, material prosperity required landscape preserves. In this way, conservation remained relevant. By linking landscape health to material prosperity, however, these conservationists chained themselves to a doctrine of multiple use where various land uses were managed but never excluded. They could not identify a factory or a campground as too great a threat to the land without appearing unsympathetic to economic prosperity and better living standards. Of course, SED censorship kept them wedded to multiple use. Nonetheless, their own faith in scientific planning also made them overconfident in their ability as technical experts to accommodate numerous land uses.

East Germany's nature tourists, for their part, increasingly expected the state to fulfill its "social contract"—in this case, its repeated promises to provide equally shared economic abundance and, more specifically, to manage and protect tourist infrastructure and rural landscapes for the benefit of all consumers. While the conservation bloc presented *Erholung* as an opportunity to improve popular behavior and push the SED to acknowledge the need for landscape planning, these consumers in the 1960s and 1970s understood *Er-*

holung not as path to collective enlightenment but as the right to individual nature pleasures. By the 1970s, private pleasures such as those found in campgrounds and bungalows had become quite central to mainstream assumptions about social justice and economic growth in the GDR. As Paul Betts argues, engagement with the state increasingly evolved into a private affair, as the regime and citizens negotiated over private comforts and pleasures owed them by the paternalistic state. East Germans even used the courts and other state institutions as means to demand their rights to private pleasures and comforts. The SED, in fact, increasingly acknowledged the importance of these private property rights, which came to be understood in East Germany by the 1970s as a right to peace, quiet, and privacy within one's personal property. East Germans inside and outside the state bureaucracy shared the assumption that socialist dictatorship must "provide for—and protect—a decent private life for citizens."[11]

The book therefore investigates the conflicts and negotiations between vacationers, landscape planners, and economic (SED) authorities over how to use or not to use the countryside to create an alternative, healthier modernity. For a time, all three found common ground, which was a faith not only in authority but also in limitless economic growth. Even when in conflict with each other over details, few East Germans before the late 1970s questioned the notion of limitless growth made possible by strong central planning. For a time at least, all three groups believed that modern technology and authoritarian planning could solve the dilemmas of industrial modernity to create an alternative future of equally shared consumer abundance without overly sacrificing nature. The SED's vision of socialist modernization established that common ground, but the various actors in this story shared and shaped its values. As such, many different actors became complicit in the transformations of East German nature in the 1960s and 1970s, with the countryside being not simply a victim of or an escape from SED dictatorship; instead, the countryside evolved into a world created (or, from some points of view, destroyed) by both authorities and consumers, even though the regime shared a greater share of the power and agency in the process. While the SED often understood critiques of economic growth as outright attacks on Marxism, censorship alone cannot explain popular enthusiasm for growthism. Few stepped boldly outside this mainstream consensus. Vacationers voiced frustration, for example, about pollution and scarcity. Yet they differed little from conservation critics who believed that abundance, social equality, and healthy landscapes could be reconciled if the state just fulfilled its promises of scientific planning. They rarely wondered if a growth agenda and conservation were irreconcilable.

I will argue that this common ground began to fracture in the 1970s due in part to new ideas about the limits of nature that became quite common in Western Europe but also to an erosion of consensus that had specific East German roots. From at least 1965, the SED embarked on an accelerated program to appease consumer desires and shore up its political legitimacy. Earlier, conservationists had seen authoritarianism as a useful tool, and since authoritarian regimes usually fear for their political legitimacy, conservationists used those fears to argue for better planning and control of land use. Unfortunately for conservationists, the SED's political fears led to initiatives that encouraged unplanned touristic use of the countryside. As a result, opportunities for conservationists and landscape planners to make their voices heard only seemed to dwindle. Instead of working with conservationists to control tourism, the regime increasingly seemed to ally with tourists against conservation. By the 1980s, frustrations about mindless tourists cluttering landscape preserves led some conservationists to gravitate toward new environmental movements critical of both authoritarianism and consumerism.

For their part, vacationers increasingly accused the SED of betraying a "social contract" with its citizens by failing to live up to its promises to dole out private pleasures. The SED allowed social inequalities to multiply, in particular failing to ensure equal access to nature. Dying forests and air pollution in vacationlands compounded these problems. Popular demands for *Erholung* began to contribute in the 1970s to a unique popular environmentalism expressed in petitions and letters to newspapers. Vacationing East Germans, I argue, framed their environmental complaints within a larger set of demands for greater material comforts. Vacationers desired access to recuperative green spaces to be enjoyed by family and friends. The state's inability to manage the countryside (either to protect it from pollution or to equally distribute vacation spots) offended their understanding of social justice. In many ways, vacationers desired a "light green society," defined by Michael Bess as a society with "a consumer economy that incorporates many elements of ecological thinking, while continuing to offer shoppers an explosively proliferating gamut of products and services."[12] Disgruntled conservationists and their new allies in the church-based environmental movements did not ally easily with the grumbling East German mainstream to topple the dictatorship. Organized environmentalists usually rejected the "light green" environmental critique voiced by many vacationers. In other words, they tried to tell East Germans famously frustrated with an anemic economy and consumer scarcity that they should actually consume even less.

The People's Own Landscape thus contributes to the continuing debate about the relationship between state and society in East Germany and in the Soviet bloc. My history of environmental policy pays particular attention to a mainstream consensus about limitless growth and state planning. This direction leads me to question historical interpretations that artificially separate the SED state from broader East German society and identify them as enemies without any common interests. Tentative consensus did not mean universal agreement, however. One of the central assertions of this book is that a semi-public, if distorted, discussion about nature did exist in the GDR and that the language and parameters of that discussion changed over time. The "state" did not eliminate all discussion and debate within its governing institutions, but "society" also did not always reach universal agreement in its criticisms of the state, as when an anticonsumerist environmentalism emerged as a backlash to what activists saw as a dangerous "mainstream consensus."[13]

Environmental histories of East Germany, for their part, usually accentuate the separation of state and society. Arvid Nelson, for example, tells a story of decline—bleak and plodding collapse marked by passive, relentless suffering on the part of people and plants. Blame rests on the "top-down" control exerted by economic planners in the SED, who departed from traditional forestry and agricultural practices in Germany.[14] Nelson's evidence fits well with other histories of the environment of the Soviet bloc, where beleaguered scientists and preservationists struggled to preserve "little corners of freedom."[15] Elsewhere, David Blackbourn situates GDR environmental policy within a longer history of Germany's conquest of nature, but he also stresses the regime's repression of nature enthusiasm as the regime mimicked Soviet plans to transform nature.[16] For all these books' valuable contributions, they ignore the connections between environmental and social policy in the GDR that complicate a story of ruthless exploitation. A focus on tragic discontinuity also ignores the similarities of East German state planning to earlier periods of German history. Most important, they downplay moments of contingency. Sometimes, East Germany's conflicting policy goals and uneven economic expansion inadvertently spared some physical environments from overuse or pollution. At many steps along the way, conservationists and landscape planners did not just suffer at the hands of the SED; they also engaged with the regime. Conservationists often found authoritarian planning alluring, and they believed that they could reform economic planning to better reflect their concerns about the chaotic economic and environmental consequences of development.[17] The divide between SED and conservationists, in other words, was not always as clear as Nelson implies.

Much as environmental historians do, histories of popular outdoor recreation in East Germany largely separate society and state into two very different and opposing worlds. In these cases, little attention is paid to how tourism led to interaction between authorities and consumers. In the social histories of East Germany's so-called niche society, or *Nischengesellschaft,* many corners of the East German countryside became idyllic retreats from the tyranny of Stalinism. Garden plots, campgrounds, and bungalows served as a colorful escape from the gray and bleak reality of politics and smokestacks. Moreover, these retreats served as islands of historical "continuity" surrounded by spaces radically remade by a regime hell-bent on transforming every little bit of everyday life.[18] In other accounts, the political meaning of these niches is more ambiguous. Paulina Bren, for instance, argues that Czech authorities cherished dacha life as a distraction from political activism and as a means to manipulating popular opinion.[19]

The most recent histories of tourism in socialist Eastern Europe complicate the relationship between state and society. In his history of the FDGB Feriendienst (the state trade union's travel service), Christopher Görlich provides a thorough chronology of the organization as it responded to the various twists and turns in SED policy. Rejecting totalitarianism theory or notions of an East German niche society, he identifies vacations as a terrain for negotiation between state and citizen. He primarily argues that travel planners abandoned their goal of political education and utopian social revolution. Instead, the Feriendienst became a "socialist Neckermann" focused on customer service barely distinguishable from the Neckermann travel agency in the Federal Republic. Görlich asserts that "Adventure and amusement overtook the spaces that utopia could no longer claim."[20] In other words, socialism became increasingly irrelevant as the regime fought to secure its legitimacy by satisfying consumer demands. The two negotiating parties in Görlich's narrative do not share any common expectations or visions.

While Görlich focuses on one tourism agency, another recent contribution to the study of East German state and society has more to say about the relationship of leisure to environmentalism. Jan Palmowski writes about East Germany's attempt to foster loyalty to a new "Socialist Heimat" and turn East Germans away from their historical allegiances to regional Heimat (the German word for "homeland") or German national identities rooted in local culture and landscape. According to Palmowski, top-down attempts to cultivate a Socialist Heimat culture did partially succeed. Even when engaging in Heimat cultural activities, however, East German enthusiasts gave Socialist Heimat local meanings that often undermined the SED's hopes of creating a new East German national identity. Drawing on James C. Scott's notion of public and private transcripts, Palmowski argues that East Germans stopped resisting Socialist Heimat in their "public transcripts" and often benefited from the SED's investment in cultural activities such as hiking, coin collecting, or local history writing. Palmowski then argues that most East Germans continued, in their private transcripts, to celebrate local culture at the expense of any notion of a larger Socialist Heimat. While he is skeptical of how "consciously" East Germans could switch between public and private transcripts, he nonetheless gives the impression that Heimat enthusiasts learned to live dual identities. Underneath the public transcript, continuities in regional Heimat culture could be identified, surviving more or less despite the SED's attempts to create something new. When focusing on the enthusiasts organized within the local clubs of the Kulturbund (Culture League), Palmowski's thesis rings most true.[21]

My focus on a conservation bloc crossing institutional boundaries and on vacationers outside the Kulturbund and the Feriendienst suggests a different story than those told by Görlich and Palmowski. Focusing on these groups, the divide between public and private transcripts seems to crumble. The Feriendienst's change over time from a tool of a utopian regime into a "socialist Neckermann" is evident in *The People's Own Landscape*, but that transformation is not the central driving force of this book's narrative. The focus of this book, instead, is on the common ground shared by certain everyday Germans and the authorities in charge of East Germany's socialist modernist project. Here, Eli Rubin's discussion of centrifugal forces in East German culture is helpful. He writes that "state power influenced everyday life and was also affected by the demands of ordinary East Germans, so that the result became a confluence, a sharing of values, that created a unique culture, something purely East German, a combination of state and society but representing the power of neither over the other."[22] It is important to remember, however, that the mainstream consensus central to this book's argument was shaped by the imbalance of power within the GDR. It is vital to never forget the SED's oversight of all aspects of public and private life. Indeed, the SED's heavy hand was especially evident in the censorship and punishment of overly vocal conservation critics discussed throughout this book. As Rubin stresses, the "mainstream culture" created by his "centrifugal forces" was anything but benign or normal. As I argue here, the imbalance of power even sometimes appealed to certain groups within East Germany, whether planners or vacationers. While there is much to be said for Mary Fulbrook's argument that East Germans experienced everyday life in often normal ways not altogether different from other welfare states in Europe, normality there was very much defined by the dangerous allure of authority.[23]

My history of nature tourism thus complicates narratives of repression and resistance and insists that the increasingly prominent dissident politics of the 1980s reflected the erosion of consensus as much or more than an expression of long-held animosities toward communism. A gray area always existed where conservationists allied with the dictatorship in projects of social control and where average citizens joined state industries, or People's Enterprises, in contributing to the destruction of open space. The state dominated rural landscapes just as they controlled People's Enterprises, but workers and consumers altered those workspaces and natural spaces through their demands for material abundance. The countryside thus became the "people's own landscape" not because it served as a refuge from the regime but because its creation depended on the contributions of both a powerful regime and its less powerful subjects. Many nonconformists and outsiders, of course, did take principled stands against the regime and its environmental policies. As I researched the newsletters of Protestant environmental organizations of the 1980s, however, I found dissidents at their most interesting when they commented on their fellow citizens. As evident in the critiques leveled at everyday East German consumer desires, these nonconformists understood themselves as outsiders struggling not just against the state but against a mainstream consensus about economic growth, material pleasures, and social priorities.

In a sense, nonconformists rebelled against what historians Michael Geyer and Konrad Jarausch have described as the "German average consumer" who wanted "not a market culture, but a potent authority to guarantee subsistence."[24] Much as Geyer and Jarausch have sought to explain longer continuities in the history of German consumption, the history told in this book reveals important continuities with earlier periods in German conservation history. Similarities with and influences from the Soviet Union and other Eastern European states can be found throughout this history of East German nature tourism and conservation, and I will comment more on these in the book's conclusion. Nonetheless, East German conservation efforts are best understood when situated in the longer histories of German encounters with capitalist modernity. Importantly, the efforts of East Germany's conservation bloc built on a statism prevalent among conservationists since the late nineteenth century. While sharpened and transformed by totalitarian communism, the admiration for an authoritarian state planning that could overcome the deficiencies of laissez-faire capitalism was not new. *The People's Own Landscape* thus departs, in part, from historians who have emphasized the GDR's radical departure from German conservation traditions.

Historical continuity becomes especially apparent if East German history is situated within a longer history of German anxieties about scarcity and abundance. Gaining access to natural resources, disciplining consumer or leisure behavior, and managing land use all boiled down to a basic question: How could Germans accrue wealth, avoid scarcity and hunger, and obtain happiness without unleashing social chaos?[25] Late nineteenth-century capitalism and its associated New Imperialism teased participants with dreams of incredible wealth and prosperity, but many Germans feared that their nation did not have enough access to natural resources, especially in a world dominated by the British Empire. In this context, Imperial Germany undertook a variety of technological schemes to increase productivity at home even while securing greater access to materials overseas.[26] Fritz Haber and Carl Bosch, for example, provided a solution to Germany's reliance on South American nitrates by developing a chemical process to industrially produce nitrogen fertilizers.[27] In Germany's colonies, officials worked to coerce free labor and encourage cotton monocultures to provide the home country with a reliable source of industrial-grade cotton.[28] In most of these cases, the goal was to conquer and control nature to make it more reliable for markets.[29]

On the one hand, abundance created increasing unease among Germany's economic and political elite. Revolutions in communication and transportation meant that Germans had access to new ideas and leisure, all of which might prove distracting or detrimental to the economic order. At home and in the colonies, Wilhelmine sociologists and state authorities worked out various schemes to stabilize the labor market. They, for example, promoted the colonization of eastern Germany by German peasants meant to bring order and civilization to an area dominated by Polish speakers identified as socially and economically disruptive and fretted over the reliability of non-white labor in African colonies.[30] Fears of social disorder and revolution in Germany's cities inspired social hygienists to intervene in working-class lives to improve diet, living conditions, and physical culture. Social Darwinists and eugenicists, for their part, insisted that disorderly urban landscapes threatened racial health,.[31]

On the other hand, hunger continued to haunt German imaginations well into the twentieth century. Near-famine conditions dominated Germany during World War I and again threatened after World War II. World War I disrupted global distribution networks and, more important, domestic agricultural production, so that black markets and rationing became a part of everyday life.[32] After World War II, key moments of early Cold War history revolved around occupation responses to a food crisis.[33] Starvation (preventing or causing it) also informed German military policy during those wars, further reinforcing the connections between war, politics, and hunger.[34] As a result, the politics of food remained central to twentieth-century German history, with Germans demanding that authorities provide enough to eat. The juxtaposition of these fears of hunger with periods of immense but disorienting abundance perhaps marks German history as distinct from the history of Eastern Europe and the Soviet Union.

National Socialism responded to the off and on threats of scarcity and abundance with a racial empire in Eastern Europe. Nazi economic planners, in particular, understood history and political conflict as a racial struggle over scarce natural resources. The invasion of Eastern Europe promised the new Nazi empire access to expansive agricultural and mineral resources.[35] The National Socialists urgently pushed for empire in part because they feared racial degeneration due to the social tensions and health crises brought on by rapid urbanization and overcrowding within Germany's shrinking borders.[36] With control of the Soviet Union's grain and oil, Hitler dreamed of an autarkic empire independent of global markets and resource dependency. At the same time, the Third Reich offered workers new tourist opportunities through the Strength through Joy program, which meant to improve social order by improving the racial health of urban Germans and erasing class inequalities.[37]

After World War II, Konrad Adenauer's Federal Republic sought postfascist solutions to scarcity and disorder through economic hyperexpansion. Anxieties about abundance did not disappear, of course. The Christian Democrats still sought to discipline consumption and even censored elements of popular culture that, in their eyes, reflected the immorality, instability, and tyranny of life under National Socialism and Bolshevism.[38] To avoid scarcity, the Federal Republic entered into the European Common Market and drew on food supplies and natural resources from across Western Europe and the world. In 1955, for example, West Germany imported "six times more [tropical] fruit, three to four times more coffee, and four times more cocoa per head than East Germany."[39] At the same time, West Germany's social market economy embarked on an incredibly intense exploitation of natural resources at home, including an expansion of industrial agriculture that drastically transformed rural landscapes and polluted soil and waterways. West German conservationists spread alarm about an incredible loss of open space, and the environmental consequences of the *Wirtschaftswunder* (economic miracle) became increasingly difficult to ignore. Raymond Dominick has even insisted that West Germany, at least up to 1970, caused more environmental damage than East Germany.[40] Certainly, post-1989 media coverage of the GDR and its pollution problems diverted attention from the West's immense enviromental sins. At the very least, the Federal Republic's environmental impact spread further and wider than East Germany's as it drew on natural resources from the Middle East and Latin America.[41]

Hoping to prove its superiority to the West in improving material living standards, the GDR embarked on its own program of hyperindustrialization. Blaming capitalist inefficiencies and greed for hunger and resource shortages, socialist states loudly rejected Malthusian warnings of resource shortages and linked such thinking to the National Socialist racial conquest of Eastern Europe. Instead, Marxists insisted that scientific planning and technological innovation, in the service of the working class, could help socialist states transform nature and create endless abundance.[42] This disdain for Malthusianism and faith in central planning had its roots in Karl Marx's own writings. Interestingly, Marx initially offered protoenvironmental critiques of excessive resource exploitation. We know, for instance, that he happened to be an avid reader of Justus von Liebig's publications on soil fertility and the metabolism of economies—that is, the flow of nutrients and energy into and out of an ecosystem or economy (whether human or otherwise). In the third volume of *Das Kapital*, Marx complained of London's shortsighted waste of human excrement, which could be used as fertilizer.[43] Marx even noted that capitalism was not self-sustaining, because it robbed soil of its nutrients without replacing them—only surviving by exploiting Ireland or South America for nutrient substitutes.[44] Yet Marx (or at least many of his followers) seemed to imply that social revolution gave you a "get out of jail free" card—limitless growth could be possible with better scientific planning. Once the abolition of capitalism put an end to class exploitation, humankind would be free to exploit the land and would no longer be a slave to nature.[45] In particular, Marxists embraced a modernization theory that demanded the destruction of tradition. Marx himself referred to "the idiocy of rural life" and described peasants and the petite bourgeoisie as relics of a bygone era.[46] Following Marx, communist regimes routinely dismissed the everyday knowledge shared by farmers about soil conditions, local growing conditions, and weather patterns. Outdated and irrational rural knowledge, for these modernizers, hindered the state's university-trained experts from providing abundance.[47]

As German regimes (from Bismarck to Ulbricht) grappled with scarcity and abundance, nature conservationists and landscape architects actively joined in the discussion, as chapter 2 of this book will explore in more detail. Nineteenth-century nature preservationists worried that unrestrained growth destroyed cultural landscapes key to integrating the urban masses into a national community, while Weimar landscape planners insisted that liberal capitalism unleashed social disorder even as it wasted scarce resources. Rather than rejecting modern industrialization outright, however, many preservationists placed great faith in authoritarian planning as a means to ensuring unending prosperity while avoiding both social disorder and environmental decay. Noting this affection for authoritarianism, some historians emphasize continuities between the landscape plans of the National Socialists and the Socialist Unity Party. Rather than a brown-red continuum, I argue that this faith in centralized authoritarian planning should be understood as part of a broader tradition within both democratic and authoritarian regimes. Rather than just a Soviet imposition or a totalitarian aberration, East German landscape planning's efforts to preserve social order and ensure future abundance were part of a longer German conversation about food security, natural resource scarcities, and capitalist instability.[48]

Landscape planning in East Germany, for all its particularity, also reflected broader European traditions of managing nature for human happiness. For instance, Italian conservationists argued that nature tended toward degeneracy and collapse if not for human intervention.[49] David Blackbourn has wonderfully illustrated the Enlightenment desire for order and conquest, seen, for example, in Frederick the Great's early modern attempts to drain and reorganize the Oder wetlands into a more productive and governable landscape. Blackbourn's work complements a wider literature on scientific foresters who insisted that forests fell into unproductive disrepair if they were not scientifically managed by experts.[50] German Marxism fit squarely within these traditions of landscape management. Building on Enlightenment tradition, Marxists argued that it was a lack of planning in the age of liberal capitalism that had encouraged nature to fester and decay unchecked, thus increasing the poverty of the working classes. Or, as the Soviets put it, socialist societies were now free to "correct nature's mistakes," which got in the way of human needs.[51]

Even outside Europe, conservationists dreamed of ways to manage economic growth in order to overcome scarcity while avoiding social disorder. In the United States, early conservationists voiced widespread concerns about uncontrolled commercialism and consumerism. In the writings of John Muir and Henry David Thoreau, wilderness preservation positioned itself as a spiritual salvation of Americans lost in an orgy of commercial materialism. Frederick Jackson Turner's Frontier Thesis reflected many fears and concerns similar to those expressed by German preservationists worried about the loss of national values and social order in the face of industrial modernity.[52] American and British conservationists also joined their German counterparts in embracing the state as a tool to control unruly capitalism. On the one hand, conservationists sought to regulate self-interested and shortsighted capitalists. On the other hand, they often set their sights on the poor, who they believed continued an unenlightened exploitation of natural resources that promoted both ecological and social disorder. In different cases at home and abroad, conservationists demanded that Adirondack poor, southern African Americans, or South Asian peasants abandon subsistence practices that were supposedly threatening to forests.[53]

At the same time, an investigation of East German environmental history reveals important divergences from general trends in German, European, and global conservation history. Due to its unique position as an outpost of Soviet power with rather arbitrary boundaries, East Germany attempted industrial hyperexpansion in a small state with less-than-promising access to natural resources and trade networks.[54] Within the tight confines of East Germany, the negative social and ecological by-products of rapid economic expansion could not be exported easily to faraway lands and thus easily disrupted central planning and rational landscape care. Moreover, the regime was profoundly unpopular when compared with Adenauer's West Germany or Hitler's Third Reich. The regime brutally repressed potential political enemies, but it also faced a persistent need to appease the public and secure its legitimacy. Concerns about political legitimacy meant that, especially in the 1960s and 1970s, careful regulations of land use had to be ignored in order to increase the food supply or to provide leisure to workers in key industries. While the regime therefore promised order and stability, its very political survival demanded that the state ignore many of the promises. In addition, World War II and the Holocaust further encouraged the SED to break radically from German tradition. Blaming bourgeois capitalism and romantic traditionalism for mass murder, the SED sought to eliminate middle-class social movements. Landscape planners and nature preservationists thus struggled to win the respect of SED authorities, who persecuted them as romantic nationalists. The specific ways that the GDR repressed tourist and conservation traditions will be explored in depth in the first and second chapters of this book.

A brief comparison with West Germany highlights the important discontinuities of East German conservation. Tainted by association with Nazism, conservationists in West Germany also sought to modernize and scientificize their language and policies. At first, conservationists engaged in projects not so different from those proposed in the East. For example, they began to work with spatial planning experts to create healthy recreation districts and to prevent the gobbling up of open space on the edges of West Germany's growing cities. In the West, however, preservationists had the luxury of clinging to older notions of preservation, even if some adopted the modern language of spatial planning. West German conservationists thus publicly debated many different preservation strategies in the 1950s and 1960s, while members of the East German conservation bloc had to discard out of hand many rhetorical strategies that the SED considered overly traditional, romantic, or fascist.[55]

The discontinuities of East German history should not, however, overshadow striking twentieth-century continuities. Jarausch and Geyer's "German average consumer" still profoundly influenced East Germany's history of consumption, tourism, and land use.[56] East German "average consumers" expected authorities to plan land use in ways that provided abundance without unleashing chaos and instability (in the land, in social relations, and in the stores). Even the growing disillusionment of the 1970s built off this mainstream consensus. In this context, the West Germany of the 1970s perhaps offered a greater break from these longer continuities that marked Germany's history of statism, consumer politics, and conservation. According to many sociologists, the 1970s witnessed the birth of a postmaterialist society in the Federal Republic of Germany.[57] As West Germany became a fully formed consumer society, a vocal group of citizens expressed increasing misgivings about growthism, top-down scientific planning, and ecological sustainability. East Germany's church-based activists did join their Western counterparts in questioning consumerism and materialism more radically. For their part, though, the new "service class" in East Germany did not easily abandon its dreams of material riches (and green spaces) guaranteed by the state. By 1989, however, the average (East) German consumer's faith in potent authority finally did exhaust itself. Disillusionment led some to question materialism in more radical ways. Of course, historians recognize that not all West Germans were "postmaterialists." Sandra Chaney, for example, cautions us that West Germany actually evolved into a "light green society" that combined consumer pleasures and ecological awareness.[58] In this sense, East Germans not involved in organized environmental activism actually may have sought to exchange potent authority for a democratic "light green society" rather than altogether abandoning dreams of unlimited abundance.

NOTES

1. Nathan Stoltzfus, "Public Space and the Dynamics of Environmental Action: Green Protest in the German Democratic Republic," *Archiv für Sozialgeschichte* 43 (2003): 390.

2. Arvid Nelson, *Cold War Ecology: Forests, Farms, and People in the East German Landscape, 1945–1989* (New Haven: Yale University Press, 2005), 156.

3. Paul Betts and Katherine Pence, introduction to *Socialist Modern: East German Everyday Culture and Politics*, ed. Paul Betts and Katherine Pence (Ann Arbor: University of Michigan Press, 2008), 8.

4. On East German environmental activists in the 1980s, see Mary Fulbrook, *Anatomy of a Dictatorship: Inside the GDR, 1949–1989* (Oxford: Oxford University Press, 1995), 225–36; Jost Hermand, *Grüne Utopien in Deutschland: Zur Geschichte des ökologischen Bewusstseins* (Frankfurt am Main: Fischer, 1991); Axel Goodbody, "'Es Stirbt das Land an seinen Zwecken': Writers, the Environment, and the Green Movement in the GDR," *German Life and Letters* 47, no. 3 (July 1994): 325–36; Merrill E. Jones, "Origins of the East German Environmental Movement," *German Studies Review* 16, no. 2 (May 1993): 235–64; Christian Halbrock, "Beginn einer eigenständigen Umweltbewegung in der DDR," in *Störenfried: DDR-Opposition, 1986–1989* (Berlin: BasisDruck, 1992), 43–51.

5. Barbara Bender, "Introduction: Landscape—Meaning and Action," in *Landscape: Politics and Perspectives*, ed. Barbara Bender (Oxford: Berg, 1995), 3.

6. Mary Fulbrook, *The People's State: East German Society from Hitler to Honecker* (New Haven: Yale University Press, 2005), 35.

7. Fulbrook (2005), 36, 229.

8. Fulbrook (2005), 229–31.

9. Fulbrook (2005), 45.

10. On East German tourism and comparisons to West Germany, see Hasso Spode, *Goldstrand und Teutonengrill: Kultur- und Sozialgeschichte des Tourismus in Deutschland 1945 bis 1989*, Institut für Tourismus—FU Berlin, Berichte und Materialien 15 (Berlin: W. Moser, Verlag für Universitäre Kommunikation, 1996). On Eastern European tourism, see Anne E. Gorsuch and Diane Koenker, eds., *Turizm: The Russian and East European Tourist under Capitalism and Socialism* (Ithaca: Cornell University Press, 2006), 14; Diane P. Koenker, "Travel to Work, Travel to Play: On Russian Tourism, Travel, and Leisure," *Slavic Review* 62, no. 4 (Winter 2003): 657–65.

11. Betts (2010), 172, 174–89.

12. Michael Bess, *The Light-Green Society: Ecology and Technological Modernity in France, 1960–2000* (Chicago: University of Chicago Press, 2003), 240–41.

13. This book's conceptualization of "state" and "society" in the GDR builds upon recent works that raise important questions about the nature of dictatorship in East Germany. These include Betts and Pence (2008); Eli Rubin, *Synthetic Socialism: Plastics and Dictatorship in the German Democratic Republic* (Chapel Hill: University of North Carolina Press, 2008); Andrew Port, *Conflict and Stability in the German Democratic Republic* (Cambridge: Cambridge University Press, 2007); Paul Betts, *Within Walls: Private Life in the German Democratic Republic* (Oxford: Oxford University Press, 2010). For summaries of East German historiography, see Scott Moranda, "Towards a More Holistic History? Historians and *East German* Everyday Life," *Social History* 35, no. 3 (August 2010): 330–39; Corey Ross, *The East German Dictatorship: Problems and Perspectives in the Interpretation of the GDR* (London: Arnold, 2002); Catherine Epstein, "East Germany and Its History since 1989," *Journal of Modern History* 75, no. 3 (September 2003): 634–66; Konrad H. Jarausch, "Beyond Uniformity: The Challenge of Historicizing the GDR," in *Dictatorship as Experience: Towards a Socio-cultural History of the GDR*, ed. Konrad H. Jarausch (New York: Berghahn Books, 1999), 3–14; Sandrine Kott, "Everyday Communism: New Social History of the German Democratic Republic." *Contemporary European History* 13, no. 2 (2004): 233–47; Geoff Eley, "The Unease of History: Settling Accounts with the East German

Past," *History Workshop Journal* 57 (2004): 175–201. Key discussions of GDR historiography from German scholars include Thomas Lindenberger, ed., *Herrschaft und Eigen-Sinn in der Diktatur: Studien zur Gesellschaftsgeschichte der DDR* (Cologne: Böhlau, 1999); Thomas Lindenberger, "Everyday History: New Approaches to the History of the Post-war Germanies," in *Divided Past: Rewriting Post-war German History*, ed. Christoph Klessmann (Oxford: Berg, 2001), 11–42; Martin Sabrow, *Geschichte als Herrschaftsdiskurs: Der Umgang mit der Vergangenheit in der DDR* (Cologne: Böhlau, 2000).

14. Before East Germany's archives became available in the 1990s, Raymond Dominick relied on secondary accounts to briefly comment on the GDR. He describes a regime that "obliterated the longstanding conservation organizations" and created a Nature and Heimat Friends that "docilely accepted the enforced spirit of enthusiasm for labor and economic growth that dominated East Germany." He concludes, "Thus there is some doubt whether the eastern zone had an environmental movement during the time period treated in this book" (Raymond H. Dominick, *The Environmental Movement in Germany: Prophets and Pioneers, 1871–1971* [Bloomington: Indiana University Press, 1992], x). On East German environmental history, see Nelson (2005), as well as Raymond Dominick, "Capitalism, Communism, and Environmental Protection: Lessons from the German Experience," *Environmental History* 3, no. 3 (July 1998): 311–32; David Blackbourn, *The Conquest of Nature: Water, Landscape, and the Making of Modern Germany* (New York: W. W. Norton, 2006); Charles Maier, *Dissolution: The Crisis of Communism and the End of East Germany* (Princeton: Princeton University Press, 1997); Nikola Knoth, "'Ich war Bergmann, was wird nun?' Die Niederlausitzer Braunkohlenregion aus umwelthistorischer Sicht," *WerkstattGeschichte* 3 (1992): 27–32; Nikola Knoth,"Eine 'grüne' SED? Aus dem Protokoll einer ZK-Sekretariatssitzung," *Beiträge zur Geschichte der Arbeiterbewegung* 35, no. 4 (1993): 72–79.

15. On Eastern Europe, see Roger Manser, *Failed Transitions: The Eastern European Economy and Environment since the Fall of Communism* (New York: New Press, 1993); Joan DeBardeleben, *The Environment and Marxism-Leninism: The Soviet and East German Experience* (Boulder: Westview, 1985). On the Soviet Union, see Douglas R. Weiner, *Models of Nature: Ecology, Conservation, and Cultural Revolution in Soviet Russia* (Bloomington: University of Indiana Press, 1988; reprint, Pittsburgh: University of Pittsburgh Press, 2000); Douglas R. Weiner, *A Little Corner of Freedom: Russian Nature Protection from Stalin to Gorbachev* (Berkeley: University of California Press, 1999); Brian Bonhomme, "A Revolution in the Forests? Forest Conservation in Soviet Russia, 1917–1925," *Environmental History* 7, no. 3 (2002): 411–34; Murray Feshbach and Alfred Friendly, *Ecocide in the USSR: Health and Nature under Siege* (New York: Basic Books, 1992); Boris Komarov, *The Destruction of Nature in the Soviet Union* (White Plains, N.Y.: M. E. Sharpe, 1980).

16. Blackbourn (2006), 335–45.

17. The literature on landscape planning in East Germany includes Regine Auster, *Landschaftstage: Kooperative Planungsverfahren in der Landschaftsentwicklung—Erfahrungen aus der DDR*, Forum Wissenschaft Studie 38 (Marburg: Bund demokratischer und Wissenschaftlerinnen Wissenschaftler Verlag, 1996); Regine Auster, ed., *Naturschutz in den Neuen Bundesländern—ein Rückblick* (Berlin: Verlag für Wissenschaft und Forschung, 2001); Regine Auster und Hermann Behrens, eds., *Natur-*

schutz in den Neuen Bundesländern—ein Rückblick (Berlin: Verlag für Wissenschaft und Forschung, 1999); Hermann Behrens, *Von der Landesplanung zur Territorialplanung: Zur Entwicklung der räumlichen Planung in der SBZ/DDR von 1945 bis Anfang der 60er Jahre*, Forum Wissenschaft Studien 41 (Bund demokratischer und Wissenschaftlcrinnen Wissenschaftler Verlag: Marburg, 1997); Hermann Behrens and Jens Hoffmann, eds., *Umweltschutz in der DDR: Analysen und Zeitzeugenberichte,* vols. 1–3 (Munich: oekom verlag, 2007); Franz-Josef Brüggemeier and Jens Ivo Engels, eds., *Natur—und Umweltschutz nach 1945: Konzepte, Konflikte, Kompetenzen* (Frankfurt am Main: Campus Verlag, 2005); Bernd Kreuter, ed., *Naturschutz hat Geschichte: Grussworte und Festrede des Bundespräsidenten anlässlich der Eröffnung des Museums zur Geschichte des Naturschutzes am 12. März 2002; Beiträge der Fachtagung "Naturschutz hat Geschichte vom 13. März 2002* (Essen: Klartext Verlag, 2003).

18. Günter Gaus, *Wo Deutschland liegt* (Munich: Hoffmann und Campe, 1983), 156. See also Stefan Wolle, *Die heile Welt der Diktatur: Alltag und Herrschaft in der DDR 1971–1989* (Berlin: Ch. Links, 1998), 219–21.

19. Paulina Bren, "Weekend Getaways: The *Chata*, the Tramp, and the Politics of Private Life in Post-1968 Czechoslovakia," in *Socialist Spaces: Sites of Everyday Life in the Eastern Bloc*, ed. David Crowley and Susan E. Reid (Oxford: Berg, 2002), 127. Spode makes a similar point about East Germany in Spode (1996), 19.

20. Christopher Görlich, *Urlaub vom Staat: Tourismus in der DDR* (Cologne: Böhlau, 2012).

21. Jan Palmowski, *Inventing a Socialist Nation: Heimat and the Politics of Everyday Life in the GDR, 1945–1990* (Cambridge: Cambridge University Press, 2009).

22. Rubin (2008), 9–10.

23. Fulbrook (2005). Fulbrook notes that the GDR "came to appear quite 'normal,' taken for granted, among large numbers of its citizens" (2). Jan Palmowski (2009) also discusses this debate about normality or normalization. See also Esther von Richthofen, "Normalisierung der Herrschaft? Staat und Gesellschaft in der DDR 1961–1979; Kulturelle Massenarbeit in Betrieben und Massenorganisationen im Bezirk Potsdam," in *Das war die DDR: DDR-Forschung im Fadenkreuz von Herrschaft, Aussenbeziehungen, Kultur und Souveränität*, ed. Heiner Timmermann (Münster: LIT Verlag, 2005), 573–591.

24. Konrad Hugo Jarausch and Michael Geyer, *Shattered Past: Reconstructing German Histories* (Princeton: Princeton University Press, 2003), 284.

25. The following narrative of abundance and scarcity builds on Jarausch and Geyer (2003) but also draws from additional contributions to the material and economic history of Germany made by scholars in recent years.

26. On German economic interactions with the global economy, see Sebastian Conrad, *Globalisation and the Nation in Imperial Germany* (Cambridge: Cambridge University Press, 2010). For introductions to the recent flurry of scholarship on German imperialism, see Shelley Baranowski, *Nazi Empire: German Colonialism and Imperialism from Bismarck to Hitler* (Cambridge: Cambridge University Press, 2011); Sebastian Conrad and Sorcha O'Hagan, *German Colonialism: A Short History* (Cambridge: Cambridge University Press, 2012).

27. On Haber and Bosch, see Thomas Hager, *The Alchemy of Air: A Jewish Genius, a Doomed Tycoon, and the Scientific Discovery That Fed the World but Fueled the Rise*

of Hitler (New York: Harmony Books, 2008). A global overview of energy and artificial fertilizers can be found in Vaclav Smil, *Enriching the Earth: Fritz Haber, Carl Bosch, and the Transformation of World Food Production* (Cambridge, Mass.: MIT Press, 2004).

28. Andrew Zimmerman, *Alabama in Africa: Booker T. Washington, the German Empire, and the Globalization of the New South* (Princeton: Princeton University Press, 2010).

29. See Blackbourn (2006) for his thesis about the conquest of nature.

30. Zimmerman (2010) provides a very enlightening overview of German attempts to control labor. See also Thomas Rohkrämer, *Eine andere Moderne? Zivilisationskritik, Natur und Technik in Deutschland 1880–1933* (Paderborn: Schöningh, 1999).

31. On social hygiene and eugenics in Germany, see Atina Grossman, *Reforming Sex: The German Movement for Birth Control and Abortion Reform, 1920–1950* (Oxford: Oxford University Press, 1995); Michael Schwartz, *Sozialistische Eugenik: Eugenische Sozialtechnologien in Debatten und Politik der deutschen Sozialdemokratie, 1890–1933* (Bonn: Dietz, 1995); Paul Weindling, *Health, Race, and German Politics between National Unification and Nazism, 1870–1945* (Cambridge: Cambridge University Press, 1989); Richard Evans, *Death in Hamburg: Society and Politics in the Cholera Years, 1830–1910* (Oxford: Oxford University Press, 1987); Daniel S. Nadav, *Julius Moses (1868–1942) und die Politik der Sozialhygiene in Deutschland* (Gerlingen: Bleicher, 1985); Bernhard Herrmann, *Arbeiterschaft, Naturheilkunde, und der Verband Volksgesundheit 1880–1918* (Frankfurt am Main: Peter Lang, 1990); Eva Barloesius, *Naturgemässe Lebensführung: Zur Geschichte der Lebensreform um die Jahrhundertwende* (Frankfurt am Main: Campus Verlag, 1997); Heinrich Weder, *Sozialhygiene und Pragmatische Gesundheitspolitik in der Weimarer Republik am Beispiel des Sozial und Gewerbehygnikers Beno Chajes, 1880–1938* (Husum: Matthiesen Verlag, 2000); Franz Walter, Viola Denecke, and Cornelia Regin, eds., *Sozialistische Gesundheits und Lebensreform Verbände* (Bonn: Friedrich Ebert Stiftung, 1991); Gisela Bock, *Zwangssterilisation im nationalsozialismus* (Opladen: Westdeutscher Verlag, 1986).

32. Belinda J. Davis, *Home Fires Burning: Food, Politics, and Everyday Life in World War I Berlin* (Chapel Hill: University of North Carolina Press, 2000).

33. Ulrich Kluge, *Vierzig Jahre Agrarpolitik in der Bundesrepublik Deutschland* (Hamburg: P. Parey, 1989); Paul Steege, *Black Market, Cold War: Everyday Life in Berlin, 1946–1949* (New York: Cambridge University Press, 2007). For Cold War food policy outside Europe, see Nick Cullather, *The Hungry World: America's Cold War Battle against Poverty in Asia* (Cambridge, Mass.: Harvard University Press, 2010).

34. See Jarausch and Geyer (2003), especially 269–313.

35. See Blackbourn (2006); Thomas Lekan, *Imagining the Nation in Nature: Landscape Preservation and German identity, 1885–1945* (Cambridge: Harvard University Press, 2003). See also Baranowski (2011) and the literature on the Nazi empire, including Mark Mazower, *Hitler's Empire: How the Nazis Ruled Europe* (New York: Penguin, 2008); Timothy Snyder, *Bloodlands: Europe between Hitler and Stalin* (New York: Basic Books, 2010); Benjamin Madley, "From Africa to Auschwitz: How German South West Africa Incubated Ideas and Methods Adopted and Developed by the Nazis in Eastern Europe," *European History Quarterly* 35, no. 3 (July 2005): 429–464; Vejas G. Liu-

levicius, *The German Myth of the East* (New York: Oxford University Press, 2009); Wendy Lower, *Nazi Empire-Building and the Holocaust in Ukraine* (Chapel Hill: University of North Carolina Press, 2007).

36. On landscape architecture and its planning of the German East, see Thomas Zeller, *Strasse, Bahn, Panorama: Verkehrswege und Landschaftsveränderung in Deutschland von 1930 bis 1990* (Frankfurt am Main: Campus Verlag, 2000); Joachim Wolschke-Bulmahn and Gert Gröning, *Liebe zur Landschaft: Drang nach Osten* (Munich: Minerva, 1986); Gert Gröning, ed., *Planung in Polen im Nationalsozialismus* (Berlin: Hochschule der Künste, 1996).

37. Shelley Baranowski, *Strength through Joy: Consumerism and Mass Tourism in the Third Reich* (Cambridge: Cambridge University Press, 2004).

38. For example, see Uta G. Poiger, *Jazz, Rock, and Rebels: Cold War Politics and American Culture in a Divided Germany* (Berkeley: University of California Press, 2000).

39. Mark Landsman, *Dictatorship and Demand: The Politics of Consumerism in East Germany* (Cambridge, Mass.: Harvard University Press, 2005), 147.

40. Dominick (1998), 320. On the environmental history of West Germany, see Sandra Chaney, *Nature of the Miracle Years: Conservation in West Germany, 1945–1975* (New York: Berghahn Books, 2008); Blackbourn (2006). See also Dominick (1992); Brüggemeier and Engels (2005).

41. On the environmental consequences of the global trade in coffee, tropical fruits, and other commodities, see Richard P. Tucker, *Insatiable Appetite: The United States and the Ecological Degradation of the Tropical World* (Lanham, Md.: Rowman and Littlefield, 2007); John Soluri, *Banana Cultures: Agriculture, Consumption, and Environmental Change in Honduras and the United States* (Austin: University of Texas Press, 2005); Shawn William Miller, *An Environmental History of Latin America* (New York: Cambridge University Press, 2007).

42. On communist regimes, resource use, and Malthusianism, see Blackbourn (2006); DeBardeleben (1985). See also John Robert McNeill and Corinna R. Unger, eds., *Environmental Histories of the Cold War* (Washington, D.C.: German Historical Institute, 2010); Stephen Brain, *Song of the Forest: Russian Forestry and Stalinist Environmentalism, 1905–1953* (Pittsburgh: University of Pittsburgh Press, 2011); Paul R. Josephson, *Resources under Regimes: Technology, Environment, and the State* (Cambridge, Mass.: Harvard University Press, 2004); Judith Shapiro, *Mao's War against Nature: Politics and the Environment in Revolutionary China* (Cambridge: Cambridge University Press, 2001).

43. Karl Marx, *Capital*, vol. 3 (London: Lawrence and Wishart,1959), 101, quoted in Reiner Grundmann, *Marxism and Ecology* (Oxford: Clarendon, 1991), 76.

44. Karl Marx, *Capital*, vol. 1 (New York: Vintage, 1976), 860. Works on Marx and ecology include John Bellamy Foster, *Marx's Ecology: Materialism and Nature* (New York: Monthly Review Press, 2000); John Bellamy Foster, "Marx's Theory of Metabolic Rift: Classical Foundations for Environmental Sociology," *American Journal of Sociology* 105, no. 2 (September 1999): 366–405; Daniel Berthold-Bond, "Hegel and Marx on Nature and Ecology," *Journal of Philosophical Research* 22 (1997): 145–79; Ted Benton, *The Greening of Marxism* (New York: Guilford, 1996).

45. Such sentiments were expressed in a piece of Soviet propaganda celebrating

Stalin's transformation of nature. See Viktor Baranovichi Kovda, *Great Construction Works of Communism* (Moscow: Foreign Languages Publishing House, 1953).

46. Karl Marx, *Communist Manifesto* (Boston: Bedford/St. Martin's, 1999), 69.

47. James C. Scott, *Seeing Like a State: How Certain Schemes to Improve the Human Condition Have Failed* (New Haven: Yale University Press, 1998). See also Diana Mincyte, "Everyday Environmentalism: The Practice, Politics, and Nature of Subsidiary Farming in Stalin's Lithuania," *Slavic Review* 68, no. 1 (Spring 2009): 31–49.

48. General works on German environmental history before 1945 include Blackbourn (2006); Joachim Radkau and Frank Uekötter, eds., *Naturschutz und Nationalsozialismus* (Frankfurt am Main: Campus Verlag, 2003); John A. Williams, *Turning to Nature in Germany: Hiking, Nudism, and Conservation, 1900–1940* (Stanford: Stanford University Press, 2007); Thomas Lekan and Thomas Zeller, eds., *Germany's Nature: Cultural Landscapes and Environmental History* (New Brunswick, N.J.: Rutgers University Press, 2005); Franz-Josef Brüggemeier, Mark Cioc, and Thomas Zeller, eds., *How Green Were the Nazis? Nature, Environment, and Nation in the Third Reich* (Athens: Ohio University Press, 2005); Christof Mauch, ed., *Nature in German History* (New York: Berghahn Books, 2004); Mark Cioc, *The Rhine: An Eco-Biography, 1815–2000* (Seattle: University of Washington Press, 2002); Frank Uekötter, *The Green and the Brown: A History of Conservation in Nazi Germany* (Cambridge: Cambridge University Press, 2006); Lekan (2003); William H. Rollins, *A Greener Vision of Home: Cultural Politics and Environmental Reform in the German Heimatschutz Movement, 1904–1918* (Ann Arbor: University of Michigan Press, 1997).

49. Marcus Hall, *Earth Repair: A Transatlantic History of Environmental Restoration* (Charlottesville: University of Virginia Press, 2005).

50. Richard Hölzl, "Historicizing Sustainability: German Scientific Forestry in the Eighteenth and Nineteenth Centuries," *Science As Culture* 19, no. 4 (2010): 431–60; Joachim Radkau, "Wood and Forestry in German History: In Quest of an Environmental Approach," *Environment and History* 2 (1996): 63–76; Joachim Radkau, *Nature and Power: A Global History of the Environment* (Washington, D.C.: German Historical Institute, 2008).

51. See Blackbourn (2006); William B. Husband, "'Correcting Nature's Mistakes': Transforming the Environment and Soviet Children's Literature, 1928–1941," *Environmental History* 11, no. 2 (April 2006): 300–318.

52. William Cronon, "The Trouble with Wilderness, or Getting Back to the Wrong Nature," in *Uncommon Ground: Rethinking the Human Place in Nature*, ed. William Cronon (New York: W. W. Norton, 1996), 69–90; Roderick Nash, *Wilderness and the American Mind* (New Haven: Yale University Press, 2001).

53. On the American and global histories of conservation, a good introduction is provided by Paul Sutter, "Reflections: What Can U.S. Environmental Historians Learn from Non-U.S. Environmental Historiography?" *Environmental History* 8, no. 1 (January 2003): 109–29. See also Thaddeus Sunseri, "Reinterpreting a Colonial Rebellion: Forestry and Social Control in German East Africa, 1874–1915," *Environmental History* 8, no. 3 (July 2003): 430–51; Richard Drayton, *Nature's Government: Science, Imperial Britain, and the "Improvement" of the World* (New Haven: Yale University Press, 2000); Richard Grove, *Green Imperialism: Colonial Expansion, Tropical Island Edens, and the Origins of Environmentalism, 1600–1860* (Cambridge: Cambridge Uni-

versity Press, 1995); Louis Warren, *The Hunter's Game: Poachers and Conservationists in Twentieth-Century America* (New Haven: Yale University Press, 1997); Karl Jacoby, *Crimes against Nature: Squatters, Poachers, Thieves, and the Hidden History of American Conservation* (Berkeley: University of California Press, 2001); Jake Kosek, *Understories: The Political Life of Forests in Northern New Mexico* (Durham: Duke University Press, 2006); Stephen Fox, *The American Conservation Movement: John Muir and His Legacy* (1981; reprint, Madison: University of Wisconsin Press, 1985); Samuel P. Hays, *Conservation and the Gospel of Efficiency: The Progressive Conservation Movement, 1890–1920* (Cambridge, Mass.: Harvard University Press, 1959).

54. Dominick comments on the poor geographical luck of East Germany. Its coal was of worse quality than West Germany's. Its waterways were less able to flush wastes, and its topography did not provide many ideal hydroelectric opportunities (Dominick [1998], 324).

55. See Dominick (1992); Chaney (2008). See also Brüggemeier and Engels (2005); Jens Ivo Engels, *Naturpolitik in der Bundesrepublik: Ideenwelt und politische Verhaltensstile in Naturschutz und Umweltbewegung 1950–1980* (Paderborn: Schöningh, 2006).

56. Jarausch and Geyer (2003).

57. The relationship between theories of a postmaterialist society and environmentalism is discussed in Dominick (1992) and Chaney (2008).

58. Chaney (2008), 248.

CHAPTER I

Conquering the Countryside:
Athletic Tourism in the Early GDR

Immediately after the conclusion of World War II, the victors redrew the map of Germany, handing over much of eastern Prussia to Poland and dividing the remaining territory among the Allied powers. In the Soviet Occupation Zone, the Red Army helped establish the dominance of the German Communist Party, which soon pushed through a merger with the Social Democrats to form the Socialist Unity Party, or Sozialistische Einheitspartei Deutschlands (SED). Under Walter Ulbricht, the SED established the occupied zone as the German Democratic Republic in 1949. According to principles of democratic centralism, the SED shaped social and economic policy from above, even though a parliament, or *Volkskammer*, continued to meet. All other political parties (from the Christian Democratic Union to the Liberal Democratic Party) had to join the National Front, a parliamentary coalition controlled by the SED, which dominated the list of candidates put forward for election. In 1952, the SED further centralized governance by replacing the traditional federal states, or *Länder*, with new administrative districts, or *Bezirke*, whose borders corresponded very little with historical, political, or cultural precedents.

As symbolized by these new districts, the new East German state made it a priority to conquer the countryside and reshape it economically, politically, and symbolically. The SED never enjoyed the popular legitimacy of the Nazi dictatorship, and it especially questioned the loyalties of the rural areas where Marxist political parties rarely had fared well. Both conservatives and Nazis had celebrated the "organic" relationship between the German race and native landscapes—thus marking the countryside as a space of national rejuvenation. The Third Reich's Strength through Joy organization had offered inexpensive hiking excursions and other vacations, to the delight of many German workers. For German communists, therefore, rural spaces threatened to undermine the new regime's power and remind its subjects of political alternatives.

The most visible intervention of the SED in the countryside was agricultural. According to the Soviets, socialist societies were now free to "correct nature's mistakes" and rationally use the soil in ways capitalists could not imagine.[1] To outcompete West Germany economically, the SED also insisted on lower food prices. The keys to lower food prices and agricultural productivity were mechanization and chemicalization, and economic planners accordingly celebrated tractors, artificial fertilizers, and chemical pesticides as means to transform nature into a more productive machine. To facilitate technological and social change, the SED collectivized small farms (after it initially divided large estates into small farms and distributed them to poorer farmers and German refugees from Eastern Europe). Agricultural experts also drained wetlands, straightened waterways, and removed hedges and woodlots that interfered with economies of scale or the operation of heavy machinery. Ironically, more land had to be put into production because mismanaged collective farms led to low soil fertility and soil erosion on older plots. In the following decades, lakes suffered from hypertrophication because of fertilizer runoff, pesticides contaminated groundwater, and water tables began to collapse due to irrigation and land reclamation.[2] Through this collectivization and industrialization, the SED imagined stitching city and countryside together into a modern, technological utopia where culturally and politically "backwards" peasants became modern proletarian laborers.[3]

The SED state also fought to overcome the regionalism that defined its new territory. Intense pride in regional identity, or Heimat, characterized German-speaking lands for centuries. At the end of the nineteenth century, Heimat associations provided an infrastructure for the celebration of local culture, history, and nature. Heimat fueled, in turn, a notion of a German national homeland defined by its collage of unique regions. In particular, Heimat could become a refuge from SED centralization in the early years of the GDR, as intellectuals and nature enthusiasts immersed themselves in the enjoyment of regional folklore, hiking trails, and history. As Jan Palmowski has shown, cultural authorities attempted to create new loyalties to a Socialist Heimat. To do this, the Kulturbund centralized all Heimat-related cultural activities (ranging from local history to amateur natural sciences) and promoted the countryside as a unified space, or socialist homeland, meant to contribute to a new East German national identity.[4]

While Palmowski has written about the Kulturbund and regional loyalties, this chapter will explore the ways that sports and leisure authorities in East Germany sought to merge bodies and landscapes into a new productive machine. Landscapes can be transformed through mechanical agriculture or through cultural production, but their meaning and significance can also be experienced and transformed through bodily practice.[5] Before 1945, different German states and social groups made competing bodily claims over rural spaces. Regional Heimat clubs appropriated hills and valleys and marked them as their own with trails, singing, cabins, and built monuments. Middle-class Heimat clubs destroyed the trail markers left behind by working-class hiking clubs, and communist hard-liners unfurled red flags to claim a space as their own.[6] In the Austro-Hungarian Empire, German nationalists promoted hiking excursions as opportunities to assert hegemony over non-German regions of the multiethnic empire.[7] East German authorities hoped that hikers and other vacationers would experience the Socialist Heimat as something tangible that would, at the same time, transform their bodies and minds at a molecular level. Soviet and Soviet-inspired leisure experts had long insisted on "productive leisure" that helped build socialist personalities and prepare citizens for labor and military service. Just as nature needed conquering, bodies needed to be controlled and redirected toward more productive ends. Leisure experts would discipline bodies and minds made "unnatural" by urban settings and capitalist depravity. In this way, conquering the countryside and conquering bodies went hand in hand. Both were necessary for moral improvement and for economic productivity.[8]

While later chapters in this book will explore how vacationers and conservationists shared certain values and assumptions with the SED regime, this chapter's history of athletic tourism stresses the SED's attack on local traditions, as well as the immense imbalances of power that defined East German society. Athletic tourism became an essential tool for the total mobilization of society for ideological goals.[9] In these early years, the SED worked hard to eliminate competition for the loyalties of East Germans, and it centralized leisure as dramatically as it did the government and the economy. For many Marxists, nature enthusiasm was nothing more than middle-class romanticism and an irresponsible (and often reactionary) escape from political and economic realities. For this reason, the SED vilified tourist organizations such as the Alpine Society or the Saxon Mountain Climbers League. That many conservationists and nature enthusiasts had supported National Socialism in the 1930s was, of course, still fresh in the minds of East Germany's new leaders. Leisure authorities thus aggressively rooted out possible class enemies among outdoor recreationists and attempted to transform hiking and tourism into a sport, in order to assert social control. At this early stage, as this chapter explores, many East German hiking and climbing enthusiasts fled westward or retreated into traditional and local tourist practices, to hide as best as possible from attempts to politicize their free-time pursuits.

In rare cases in the 1940s and 1950s, however, some nature tourists and leisure planners tentatively engaged the regime and defended their "nonathletic" leisure practices as politically legitimate. They presented an alternative understanding of outdoor recreation that they believed to be compatible with the building of a socialist utopia. In part, they could sometimes engage the regime because socialist outdoor recreation had roots in the German past and was not simply a Soviet imposition or a creation of a totalitarian regime. This chapter thus begins by recounting the history and fate of Germany's Friends of Nature, a socialist leisure organization founded in the nineteenth century. As veterans of this organization had long insisted, Marxism and nonathletic nature enthusiasm were not incompatible, though communist radicals and moderate Social Democrats already battled in the Weimar years over the meaning of leisure and nature. For the moderates, nature was a space of freedom and rejuvenation from capitalist exploitation. Radical nature enthusiasts further on the left, however, stressed militarism, athletics, and "productive" tourism, with leisure as an opportunity to train for class warfare. After 1945, as this chapter will demonstrate, the radicals won out and came to dominate early East German nature tourism. Yet they promoted athletic tourism at a remarkably inopportune moment—exactly when Cold War regimes (including the Soviet Union) increasingly promised vacationers material pleasures. Now facing a Cold War for the hearts and stomachs of Germans, the SED promised that socialist modernism would create a socialist utopia of limitless economic growth and high living standards. Critics linked their alternative leisure to the regime's promises of high quality of life. They suggested, in fact, that socialist modernity's promises of limitless abundance and better living conditions demanded leisurely, nonathletic encounters with nature.

Collectivizing Nature Experiences, 1895–1958

A wide range of middle-class Wilhelmine and Weimar German nature enthusiasts had fretted over the consequences of industrialization and urbanization since the late nineteenth century. Most understood their countrymen to have a special connection to the land, with local and national identities closely tied to forest and pastoral landscapes. As political socialism grew in importance, many middle-class Germans also believed that landscape degeneration contributed to a social unraveling, as urban workers cut off from nature's beauty became enthralled with radical political ideologies. To promote healthy hiking excursions, regional homeland associations published hiking guides, built trail shelters, and organized hikes to celebrate local culture and nature.[10] Youth hiking organizations before World War I, such as the Wandervogel, employed nature excursions as part of their rebellion against Wilhelmine materialism and morality. These rebels saw nature as a "realm of emotional, moral and social freedom beyond reach of adult institutions."[11] Middle-class hiking and nudist clubs emphasized the importance of rural adventures for the restoration of bodies damaged by modern technology and urban overstimulation. Turning to nature was the key to taming deviant sexuality, alcoholism, and social radicalism, as the countryside provided a respite where urban minds and souls could relax and rejuvenate.[12] Other youth groups integrated hiking into a project of citizen building; in this, the youth hostel movement played an important role. From the Wandervogel to the Hitler Youth, German hiking clubs did not just celebrate nature; they also managed human nature.[13]

Social Democrats enjoyed and promoted the benefits of nature excursions no less than did their middle-class liberal and conservative counterparts. Party members in Germany (as in France and other neighboring countries) often blamed the moral weakness of workers on slum conditions bred by a capitalist political economy.[14] While not alone in their social hygienist fears, European socialists especially focused on the physical and psychological damage inflicted on the working class by industrial working conditions. Many life reformers promoting nudism or vegetarianism made socialist arguments for nature outings to rehabilate workers damaged by factory work and cramped living quarters.[15] Germany's Friends of Nature became one of the most prominent socialist organizations for nature enjoyment. Austrian Social Democrats founded the Friends of Nature, or Touristenverein Die Naturfreunde, in 1895. Weimar Germany's Friends of Nature had a membership of 116,000 by 1923 and owned 230 cabins or trail shelters by 1933. Members mostly included skilled male factory workers and artisans rather than unskilled workers, but the organization also attracted a significant number of teachers, shopkeepers, and farmers from the lower middle class. The Friends of Nature shared with the Social Democrats of the 1920s a moderate reformist character that appealed more to the lower middle class than did the radical militarism of the German Communist Party.[16]

As historian John Alexander Williams has demonstrated, the Friends of Nature mixed Marxist ideology with a reverance for nature's wonders. Williams argues, moreover, that it would be wrong to believe that an aesthetic appreciation of nature "depoliticized" the organization into a mere copycat of bourgeois hiking or conservation clubs. Members denounced private owner-ship of forests and mountains and understood nature as a utopian realm of es-cape from industrial exploitation. They also saw nature as a source of health and even as having intrinsic beauty. This attitude distinguished members from the many Marxists who intended to conquer and transform nature for the ben-efit of the working class. The Friends of Nature even became involved in nature conservation efforts in the 1920s, but unlike many middle-class conservation groups, the Friends of Nature placed class conflict at the center of their endeav-ors; social hiking, for example, became an important means to explore rural (and sometimes urban) landscapes with an eye toward local labor history and capitalist exploitation.[17]

Weimar communists within the Friends of Nature did not trust their col-leagues of a moderate socialist bent. Foreshadowing similar developments in the GDR, the communists dismissed emotional attachment to nature as "empty and sentimental *Naturschwärmerei*, or gushing about nature."[18] Escape to na-ture, they believed, was an abandonment of political struggle and often a tool used by middle-class reformers to prevent social revolution. Communist mem-bers of the Friends of Nature escalated their critique after the rise of Josef Stalin in the Soviet Union when some broke away to join the Communist sport-ing federation, the Fighting League for Red Sport Unity, or Kampfgemein-schaft für rote Sporteinheit. Inside the Friends of Nature, an oppositional group emerged to publish a journal, *Der proletarische Wanderer*. The communists increasingly sponsored separate youth groups to practice productive "proletar-ian tourism" as taught in the Soviet Union and to prepare for military struggle with the fascists. In response, the moderate leadership of the Friends of Nature expelled local hiking groups and individuals who embraced this more radical path.[19]

After 1933, the National Socialists also emphasized the importance of hiking for social cohesion and physical health, but they uniquely stressed the importance of a racial community that overcame class warfare blamed on Marxists and Jews. The Hitler Youth organization valued athletic competition and overnight backpacking trips as a means of preparing young boys for future labor and military service. Elsewhere, the German Labor Front's Strength through Joy program organized hiking excursions in addition to cruise vaca-tions and workplace beautification programs. For Strength through Joy and the Hitler Youth, hikes provided an opportunity to prepare workers mentally and physically for political sacrifice and struggle. Moreover, healthy workers better ensured the continued reproduction of Aryan genetic purity. Leisure and tourism centralized within Nazi organizations also allowed for the disciplining and control of social behavior, as leaders hoped to eradicate what they understood as morally and socially poisonous cultural pursuits, particularly anything associated with urban commercial culture and mass consumerism. At the same time, Strength through Joy also promised new access to tourist pleasures. While the Friends of Nature had insisted that private ownership of forest and mountain landscapes prevented workers from enjoying healthy nature excursions, Strength through Joy sought political loyalty from workers and began to offer vacation entitlements without any accompanying criticism of property relations. Subsidized vacations offered many working-class Germans new opportunities to travel, but as Shelly Baranowski has argued, class differences never truly disappeared.[20]

Strength through Joy's attempt to appease workers' leisure desires was only one part of a broader attack on independent socialist leisure organizations. The Third Reich dissolved the Friends of Nature and expropriated all their cabins, with many repurposed as hostels for Hitler Youth. As former members came under close surveillance, the organization's national leaders even clumsily tried to save the organization by pledging loyalty to the National Socialists. Friends of Nature leaders Xavier Steinberger and Leonhard Burger went as far as denying their attachment to Marxist ideals. The Friends of Nature, they insisted, had merely promoted a love of nature and homeland and differed little from Strength through Joy in its promise to bring nature's pleasures to all Germans. In this vein, they presented their "civil war" with communist agitators as proof of their ideological compatibility.[21]

In hopes of eradicating nonproductive tourist pleasures and crushing fascism, postwar Soviet and communist authorities shut down traditional tourism organizations in a series of ordinances far harsher than similar policies in Western zones of occupation. In all the zones, authorities banned Nazi organizations. The second law of Allied Occupation called for the closing and liquidation of Nazi organizations, including the Reichsbund für Leibesübungen, the athletic organization for mountain climbers. In December 1945, Allied Occupation Directive 23 called for the demilitarization of sport. Subsequently, the occupation administration of Dresden outlawed all traditional athletic clubs, mountain associations, and independent youth hostels, including but not limited to the Friends of Nature, the German Alpine Society, and the Saxon Mountain Climbers League. In 1947, the Allies allowed for the creation or reestablishment of "nonpolitical" organizations, but while the Western powers began to allow national independent associations to rebuild, the Soviets continued to allow sport and leisure only on a small, communal scale. The regime revealed its intent to collectivize leisure with Soviet Occupation Directive 82 of April 1948, which transferred the German Youth Hostel Association's properties to the Free German Youth (Freie Deutsche Jugend, or FDJ), an organization established by the SED in March 1946 to organize the free time of the young.[22]

The socialist Friends of Nature did not fare any better than other organizations for nature appreciation. In the eyes of the new postwar SED regime, the attempted self-synchronization of Friends of Nature leaders during the Nazi era made socialist nature enthusiasts as suspect as all the middle-class hiking organizations. Given a certain level of sympathy for the regime, however, veterans of the Friends of Nature felt that they might actually find a home, possibly as an adult auxiliary of the Free German Youth. Some individuals were being pragmatic; Soviet occupation appeared to be inevitable. Others, troubled by revelations about Nazi crimes, welcomed the SED's regime as the more radical and, thus, legitimate antifascist state in postwar, German-speaking Europe. The German Communist Party had openly resisted the Nazi regime and seemed to offer the best opportunity for a thorough rejuvenation of society.[23] In its early years, the FDJ (similar to the Soviet Komsomol) even worked to attract new members with hikes, dances, and other purely social events.[24] For instance, early in 1948, the FDJ proposed the creation of *Ferien und Wanderwerk* (offices for recreation and hiking) and initially welcomed members of the Friends of Nature.[25] By 1949, however, the FDJ pushed the former Friends of Nature out. In explaining their action, youth organizers wrote, "In many cases there is the danger that the majority of the members in Friends of Nature groups . . . might even be enemies of the FDJ."[26]

After the Free German Youth pushed them out in 1949, some Friends of Nature turned to Sektion Touristik, a division within the Deutsche Sportbewegung, or German Sport Movement.[27] The turn to a sports organization was not entirely surprising given that some left-wing Friends of Nature in Weimar Germany had joined the communist athletes in the Fighting League for Red Sport Unity. The GDR's Sportbewegung, which oversaw sport clubs throughout the GDR, meant to politicize sport and eliminate private, nonsanctioned social practices that might lead East Germans to cultivate alternative identities and question the SED's legitimacy. While each sport affiliated with the Sportbewegung had executive leadership in Berlin (as was the case with the Sektion Touristik), local sports clubs organized daily athletic activity. Factories and other employers created sport clubs, known as *Betriebsportgemeinschaften*. In other words, each factory or major enterprise, or *Betrieb*, had a sport club divided into different sports (or sections), such as soccer, table tennis, or tourism. Each section of a *Betriebsportgemeinschaft* was responsible both to the local factory's needs and to the GDR-wide organizers of their particular sport—a potential source of conflict if organizers of a local *Betreibsportgemeinschaft* imagined sport or tourism differently from their colleagues in Berlin.[28] In 1958, Sektion Touristik became the German Association for Hiking and Mountain Climbing (Deutscher Wanderer- und Bergsteigerverband, or DWBV), an affiliate of the German Gymnastics and Sport League (Deutscher Turn und Sportbund, or DTSB).[29] By 1976, the organization had 36,680 members in 569 local sections.[30]

Former Friends of Nature also had the option of joining the Kulturbund's Nature and Heimat Friends after 1950, with its more than fifty thousand members.[31] As Jan Palmowski has shown, the Kulturbund promoted the notion of a Socialist Heimat—a homeland that was untouched by American popular culture and where the advancements of socialist economic change could be seen and felt first hand. Much like the communist factions within the Weimar Friends of Nature, the organizers of the Nature and Heimat Friends feared that a love for nature encouraged an escape from social realities into mysticism and idealism.[32] As Jan Palmowski has demonstrated, guidebooks produced by the Kulturbund reoriented tourist itineraries away from local homelands and romantic escapism. Much like the social hiking promoted by the Friends of Nature, these guidebooks noted evidence of class conflict in the countryside. They also instructed tourists to witness evidence of socialist rebirth in the countryside—whether sites of antifascist resistance, examples of socialist economic ambition, or new housing developments.[33] As late as the 1970s, television programs such as *Auf Schusters Rappen* presented hiking in the countryside as a way to discover the diversity of the new socialist homeland.[34]

Athletic Tourism and the Bodily Experience of Socialism

While the regime's leisure authorities eliminated independent tourism and sports organizations that might discourage loyalty, it also went out of its way to make officially sanctioned tourism more "productive," especially by transforming hiking into competitive sport. For leisure authorities, athletic hikers learned to become loyal socialist personalities and also gained the health and physical fitness needed to become the untiring heroes of East Germany's hoped-for economic miracle. Productive tourism also helped East Germans experience the countryside as socialist. Sport, indeed, was meant to integrate tourism, tourists, and the countryside into a larger political and economic project.

Socialist authorities did not take sports and tourism lightly. According to some historians of Eastern Europe, competitive sports served totalitarianism well, as they helped to discipline and regulate the population.[35] Authorities expected athletic competition to suppress individualism, maximize bodily production, and cultivate loyalty among participants. As Kai Reinhart notes, the introduction of rock climbing as a sport served as an assault on a culture with its own distinct norms and values that the regime understood as incompatible with socialist modernism.[36] Throughout the Soviet bloc, leisure planners insisted that tourism, sport, and leisure become more productive. The goal of tourism, they argued, was no longer to escape the dismal living conditions of a capitalist system. Under socialism, tourism "was meant to involve work, the enhancement of one's intellectual and physical capital, not leisure."[37] Transforming tourism into sport served as East Germany's path toward a new productive leisure regime and toward eliminating the dangers of escapism.

We should not oversimplify sport's role in solidifying totalitarian rule, however. As Molly Wilkinson Johnson has demonstrated, sport also allowed for East Germans to engage with the regime and even shape it somewhat to their desires. Leisure authorities did not just impose competitive sport but sought to draw citizens into a broad public culture of socialism through festive and enjoyable sporting events.[38] Competitive events often proved popular and thus useful for attracting East Germans to mass organizations. They were so popular that earlier Marxist-Leninist skepticism about competition dissipated. During the 1920s, debates raged in the Soviet Union between defenders of competitive sport and "hygienists" who hoped to replace competitive sport's focus on individual glory. In theory, noncompetitive exercises retained all the moral and physical benefits of sport while jettisoning individualism. Beginning in 1925, however, Soviet reformers faded into the background, and sports authorities shifted attention to training professional athletes for international competition. In East Germany, a somewhat similar dispute took place. Authorities in athletic institutions debated whether they should mobilize the public for broad participation in physical activity or invest resources into training world-class athletes. Manfred Ewald, who came to dominate the DTSB from 1959 to 1989, ultimately backed competitive sport, but advocates of *mass sport* continued to organize mass forest runs, "socialist games," and collective gymnastics in the early years of the GDR. As it turned out, though, most sports enthusiasts preferred the excitement and challenges of competitions. Competitive events became key arenas in which citizens could act out their individual desires under state surveillance.[39] Competition, for example, might have appealed to some former Friends of Nature, especially those on the left wing of the organization who had practiced hiking and rock climbing within Weimar sports organizations and eventually joined clubs such as SG Dynamo Dresden.[40]

No matter the appeal of competition to some participants, the DWBV clearly promoted athletic competition to eliminate traditional tourist practices and political enemies. Its overwrought fears of traditional tourism reflected a genuine disdain for romantic escapism rooted in 1920s disputes within the Friends of Nature. In January 1952, the German Athletic Committee called for the uniform ranking of all sport performances in order to facilitate competition and to groom talented athletes for international competition. In response, the DWBV created a classification system oriented around a series of climbing trails of various difficulty cataloged in regional climbing guides. By scaling a sufficient number of peaks of a certain difficulty, a climber earned climbing badges and eventually became a "Master of Sport."[41] In 1953, the head of the DWBV's Training Commission worried, "As always the spirit of 'idealism' rules." The trainer added, "Through the introduction of classification, we break ties with the out-of-date, calcified 'idealistic' views and stress the athletic character of mountain climbing."[42] Competition, the DWBV president claimed, taught East Germans all the personality traits of the modern socialist citizen: "courage, endurance, commitment, a strong will, a collective spirit, and a great love for one's homeland."[43] In one comment to this effect, the DWBV functionary wrote,

> The enforcement of sport classification . . . was first and foremost an ideological affair, in which it was valid to smash conservative prejudices and to engage in debate with the still widespread Alpine-Society-Ideology. Again and again, counterarguments surfaced, [claiming that] mountain climbing is no competition . . . [and] that through classification the ethic of mountain climbing and the alpine experience is lost.[44]

Through training and by adhering to the new classification system, a formerly ideologically suspect climber transformed not only his muscles but also his mind.

Within the DWBV, authorities certainly used sport as a blunt tool against tradition, but they also emphasized sport to gain funding within the German Gymnastics and Sports League. The tourist organization soon discovered that the East German sports organization to which it belonged cared little for traditional hiking and mountain climbing.[45] As late as 1951, sports authorities had not even named a president for Sektion Touristik.[46] That same year, tourists grumbled that they lacked equipment and lodging and could afford few trips abroad to important climbing regions.[47] When one Dresden hiker went to Berlin in November 1951, he complained that fourteen other sports disciplines had training manuals published by the *Sportverlag Berlin*. Eighteen others had a club journal, but Sektion Touristik had none of these things.[48] As late as 1960, a frustrated DWBV functionary wrote, "It must be noted that the German Gymnastic and Sports League's executive committee does not give the problem of developing tourism . . . the [deserved] attention."[49]

To better emphasize sport, Sektion Touristik authorities in Berlin celebrated the *Orientierungslauf*, or orienteering race (a sport popular in several European countries), as a means of transforming superficial, rebellious youth into fit, economically productive socialist citizens. In an orienteering race, contestants used a topographical map and a compass to seek out several hidden markers on a forest course, with participants combining orienteering skills, endurance, and speed to achieve victory. While some competitions featured hiking contestants, most events showcased runners.[50] At the head of this effort was Dr. Edelfried Buggel, a key figure in East German sport, who hoped to convince vacationers to spend their leisure time in healthy athletic events rather than waste the day tanning, grilling, or drinking. An avid fan of orienteering, Buggel helped found the International Orienteering Federation in 1961 and acquired the title of vice president of the organization through 1971.[51] Under Buggel's influence, the DWBV filled its annual calendar with orienteering competitions.[52]

Orienteering helped organizers better link tourism and nature to antifascist culture and traditions, as is evident in the role that orienteering played at the memorial ceremonies staged at the Buchenwald concentration camp. The DWBV held East Germany's largest annual orienteering race at Buchenwald, where participants ran a course that took them through the camp and its surrounding forests on the anniversary of the camp's communist uprising. According to the GDR's antifascist myth, the communist prisoners of Buchenwald distinguished themselves from other prisoners as they rose up against their captors rather than suffer as passive victims. At the orienteering competition, athletes sought to emulate Buchenwald's communist inmates, who were portrayed as courageous, optimistic, determined, and dedicated to the socialist struggle. The orienteering race at Buchenwald was not the only opportunity to celebrate antifascism. Throughout the year, in fact, hiking guides led participants to sites of antifascist resistance, such as Burg Hohenstein, where the Nazis had imprisoned many antifascist climbers. DWBV leadership also christened a significant climbing route the Willi Hauptmann Memorial Path, in memory of an antifascist climber, and lionized Kurt Schlosser and Wilhelm

Dieckmann, both rock climbing enthusiasts murdered by the Nazis after smuggling literature across the border with Czechoslovakia.[53] At Buchenwald and elsewhere, athletic achievement, productivity, and political awareness thus became inseparable.[54]

The DWBV made their athletic priorities especially clear as they gave ever-dwindling attention to leisurely hiking. Throughout the late 1950s, hiking enthusiasts in its Hiking Commission complained about the organization's weak investment in noncompetitive hiking.[55] When hiking did enter into the agenda, the DWBV channeled individual, sporadic hiking desires into organized collective enterprises, often of a competitive nature.[56] The "100 Kilometers for Peace" initiative provided a venue for hikers to collect points toward a special tourist badge, for instance.[57] In accordance with the DWBV strategy, simple competitive events (such as scavenger hunts, orienteering competitions, photo contests, and plant identification contests) complimented traditional hiking events at Pentecost and the summer solstice and during GDR Youth Week.[58]

To ensure a properly scripted bodily experience of the countryside, leisure authorities also worked to transform tourist infrastructure. Youth hostels worked especially well for making the SED visible in the countryside. The FDJ named hostels after famous antifascists or other leading "socialist personalities." For example, the largest youth hostel in East Germany took the name of Ernst Thälmann, the most prominent communist victim of Nazi concentration camps, and the second largest hostel adopted the name of Adolf Hennecke, a coal miner who exceeded work quotas and was celebrated by the SED in the tradition of the Stakhanovites in the Soviet Union.[59] Similarly, hiking paths led tourists to sites of memory commemorating antifascist resistance and other historic achievements of the labor movement. The Kulturbund and the Committee for Tourism and Hiking proposed a series of educational trails organized in a unified system of paths that would allow hikers systematically to explore and learn about the new socialist state.[60] A 1959 ordinance for marking hiking paths and a 1961 guide to the four thousand kilometers of GDR hiking trails suggested that by hiking through it properly, East Germans would learn to experience the new state as a real and permanent physical entity.[61] Ideally, hiking groups on these hiking trails sang socialist hiking songs composed by the FDJ or DWBV or inherited from the Friends of Nature, thus furthering the bodily experience of socialism for anyone who could hear them.[62]

Promotion of a *Massenwaldlauf*, or mass forest run, superbly illustrated DWBV belief that scripted bodily experience had positive political consequences.[63] One *Massenwaldlauf* leaflet portrayed a runner literally coughing up cigarettes a mere meter from the race's finish—as if a body pushed to extremes amid nature's goodness could no longer tolerate toxic substances. In the foreground, a young man with a trendy haircut and baggy chinos collapsed from exhaustion, and a young woman in fashionable attire gasped for breath. In contrast, fit, properly attired athletes ran confidently in the background.[64] The race promoters suggested that by eliminating unhealthy consumerism and forging fitter bodies, athletic tourism better contributed to an increasingly productive economy.

Athletic tourism in the GDR thus became part of a general program for overcoming nature's limits (and the GDR's geographical limitations) to produce a utopia of limitless abundance. Political oppression was central to this program, but it was not the only reason for celebrating sport. In many ways, sport reflected the regime's faith in science and planning to take unruly and unproductive nature (both landscapes and bodies) and discipline it into a more effective machine—better able to defeat the capitalist West. Not only could agricultural landscapes be made more productive through mechanization and chemicalization, but the bodies of East Germans could be improved. By developing athletic training programs, reorienting hiking trails, and transforming tourist infrastructure, leisure authorities imagined a well-oiled machine working in unison for utopian change. Much as the SED promoted synthetic plastics as an opportunity to produce material abundance despite a scarcity of natural resources, athletics offered a partial solution to the demographic crises associated with the war and the migration of disgruntled workers to West Germany. Athletic tourism promised to create abundance by making scarce and unfit workers more efficient and productive.

Limits of Dictatorship: Alternative Nature Experiences

As the Kulturbund promoted a Socialist Heimat and the DWBV celebrated athletic tourism, many East Germans simply ignored them. Individuals continued to travel on their own, and small groups of disgruntled tourists and nature enthusiasts gathered in small clubs illegally. Indeed, as Jan Palmowski has argued, many East Germans continued to understand tourism as part of their local culture and essentially ignored mass organizations. Opposition, however, was not always couched in Heimat localism. While many Germans clung to traditional views of nature, some sought a compromise between nature enthusiasm and socialism, if for no other reason than to find official support and funding for their outdoor pleasures. In the example explored below, former Social Democrats offered an alternative intepretation of tourism's role in socialism. They pointed to the SED's promises of material abundance and high living standards as justification for their nonathletic and recuperative nature outings.

The limits to the Kulturbund's vision for a socialist homeland became clear very early. As Jan Palmowski argues, the notion of an East German national identity had difficulty overcoming East German desires to experience and celebrate tradional local Heimats. The Kulturbund gave little real support to Heimat enthusiasts, not giving enough monetary support to publications by the Nature and Heimat Friends and resisting the merging of the Nature and Heimat Friends with the DWBV. As Palmowski writes, cultural "functionaries in Berlin had no interest in creating a strong, united voice for the practical concerns of Heimat enthusiasts."[65] Local Kulturbund leaders also found their clubs and festivals often ignored by locals.[66] The attempted centralization of hiking trails met a similar fate. Local town leaders and Heimat clubs had traditionally maintained most trails, so the Kulturbund found it difficult to recruit locals to take part in maintaining statewide paths that did not immediately serve local leisure interests.[67] In the Harz Mountains, for instance, local Kulturbund leaders could not convince villages to mark hiking trails for outsiders or connect local paths to statewide trail networks. Halle's Kulturbund leadership noted, "Completely different markings had been made in each locality." They complained, "There still remains a tendency among a few local leaders to put up trail markings that direct [hikers] to an especially prominent excursion destination and then most often directly back to the trailhead."[68] It appeared that locals had little interest in transforming their region into an educational space for the bodily experience of socialism.

Within the DWBV, local opposition to the new emphasis on athletic competition was quite common. In the annual reports prepared for the DWBV at the end of 1959, several district leaders wrote strikingly frank rebuttals of organization policy. Competitive athletics especially alienated older members, Magdeburg representatives insisted.[69] Members from Halle complained, "We are [members of] a hiking and mountain climbing organization, not an athletic association."[70] In Dresden, climbers rebelled by attempting to carve out some independence from Berlin authorities. One of the leading tourist and Heimat organizations in Dresden had long been the Saxon Mountain Climbers League (Sächsische Bergsteigerbund, or SBB). After 1945, many dissident former SBB members joined the Betriebssportgemeinschaft Empor-Löbtau (BSG Empor-Löbtau), where nonathletic traditions of nature enjoyment flourished.[71] In 1950, the BSG Empor-Löbtau had 256 members in its section for *Wandern und Bergsteigen,* and by 1958, it had 638 members. The BSG Empor-Löbtau even began to publish its own journal in 1952 (the DWBV published an official journal called *Freundschaft* at the time). Mountain climbers within the BSG Empor-Löbtau divided themselves into climbing teams, which served as clubs within the club and operated relatively independently (organizing their own excursions, for example). Altogether, sixty small climbing teams joined the BSG Empor-Löbtau, where they continued to practice climbing and hiking much as they had before 1945.[72] According to one former member, sports authorities tolerated the climbing teams because they could not get rid of them without extreme, imprudent measures.[73] In the summit registers of Saxon Switzerland, club members often spoke out against the SED state and celebrated their local Heimat as a realm of freedom from tyranny.[74] Disgruntled climbers in 1960 even wrote a letter of complaint to Walter Ulbricht arguing that the DWBV's single-minded crusade for competitive climbing generated dogmatism, careerism, and simpleminded physical efficiency while traditional climbing taught character and morals.[75]

SED loyalists and veterans of Weimar communism within the DWBV saw the BSG Empor-Löbtau as a serious threat to their legitimacy within the DTSB. They attacked, in particular, the BSG Empor-Löbtau's resistance to athletic competition. In February 1953, Hans Pankotsch (editor of the journal *Freundschaft*) claimed that members of the BSG Empor-Löbtau secluded themselves from the DWBV, avoiding leadership responsibilities or cooperation with other tourists in Dresden.[76] In a report to the SED in Dresden, DWBV leaders complained when leaders of the BSG Empor-Löbtau insisted that "the true rock climber rejects all competition."[77] The president of the DWBV elsewhere identified the BSG Empor-Löbtau as a refuge "for the bourgeoisie and their out-of-date ideology."[78] To discredit Fritz Petzold, a prominent mountain climber and leader of the tourist section of the BSG Empor-Löbtau, the SED accused him of distributing propaganda provided by the middle-class West German Alpine Society.[79] An article in *Sportecho*, East Germany's premier sports magazine, even linked the BSG Empor-Löbtau to Martin Wächtler (the chair of the Saxon Mountain Climbers' League from 1933 to 1945, who, sports authorities noted, trained Nazi mountaineers and was later prominent in West Germany's Alpine Society).[80]

Despite accusations from sports authorities, the BSG Empor-Löbtau did not reject socialist modernism altogether, and several sources hint that these opponents of athletics looked back to the nature enthusiasm of Weimar Social Democrats and Friends of Nature for alternatives to DWBV doctrines. Dresden functionaries hinted at the role of older Friends of Nature in the DWBV when they reported on grumbling among their members about "the 'wild running' on display at the International Orienteering Race" and blamed "the old members of the *Naturfreunde*" for encouraging such dissent.[81] Fritz Petzold was an SED member, had been a Social Democrat before 1933, and had been affiliated with working-class sport after World War I. In the 1920s, he joined the SBB rather than the climbing affiliate (Vereinigten Kletterabteilungen) of the Friends of Nature, perhaps because of a more radical communist orientation of the Friends of Nature climbers in Dresden. In defending his protection of the climbing teams within the BSG Empor-Löbtau, he argued, "One cannot, especially with the younger climbers, make them into Socialists overnight . . . It would be a thoroughly worthwhile task to explain to these climbers—perhaps in a large gathering of club representatives—the meaning, the purpose, and the tasks of our new, emerging socialist state."[82] For Petzold, progress toward a better socialist future was gradual and best accomplished through the creation of a comfortable, joyous, and relaxing life where all members of society could fulfill their potential in work and leisure. The BSG Empor-Löbtau also echoed the moderate wing of the Friends of Nature in their bimonthly journal's promise of "*Lachen, Lust und Frohsinn*" (laughter, joy, and cheerfulness). In the opening statement of the *Werbeschrift* in 1952, the editors wrote, "Away from the worries of everyday life, a person from the metropolis should relax, recover, and gather new strength for the struggle for existence, for the construction of the homeland."[83] As workers toiled to build a prosperous future, ramblings in the woods would now be a right, not a privilege, in a worker's state.

Leisure enthusiasts outside the DWBV also criticized the regime's focus on political indoctrination and athletic competition. Union representatives in Thuringia, for example, argued that mine workers had been promised a better standard of living in the new workers' state.[84] In the Erzgebirge, numerous residents complained about a hostel that closed its doors to hungry and thirsty tourists. The Kulturbund, in another example, questioned how youth policies that benefited only FDJ members served the majority of workers and their leisure needs.[85] In this and other incidents, the trade union pressed to wrest control over tourist facilities from the FDJ and the sports league.[86] In general, as Christopher Görlich has shown, the local representatives of the FDGB Feriendienst established themselves as representatives of the workers and the people against the SED and a central FDGB leadership seemingly oblivious to the real living conditions of its workers.[87]

In these early years, to be certain, the scales tipped to athletic tourism and the fight to eliminate traditional tourist practices. In the 1940s and early 1950s, the SED wanted to stitch together the countryside, the land, and its people into a productive, well-oiled machine. Through scientific management and central planning, limited resources could be overcome. For this to work, people had to be mobilized and transformed as well. Through competitive sport, leisure planners hoped to overcome unproductive romantic longing to make tourism productive. In other words, they sought to make East Germans fitter and more determined workers who could wring abundance out of a less-than-promising situation. It would be an oversimplification, however, to depict the BSG Empor-Löbtau as only the resistance of a local Heimat culture to totalitarian centralization and scientific management. A few individuals, at the very least, sought a middle ground and envisioned a prosperous future with a socialist leisure culture that made room for relaxed nature enjoyment. Economic growth and working-class revolution, they suggested, promised material and leisure benefits for the working class and thus must make room for the leisurely enjoyment of natural and historical spaces. While rare initially, this alternative reading of socialist modernism and material abundance later appeared more frequently in critiques of SED economic and land use policy, as the next chapter will demonstrate.

NOTES

1. Husband (2006). See also Blackbourn (2006).
2. See Nelson (2005);George Last, *After the "Socialist Spring": Collectivisation and Economic Transformation in the GDR* (New York: Berghahn Books, 2009); Gerhard Krenz, *Notizen zur Landwirtschaftsentwicklung in den Jahren 1945–1990: Erinnerungen und Bekenntnisse eines Zeitzeugen aus dem Bezirk Neubrandenburg* (Schwerin: Ministerium für Landwirtschaft und Naturschutz des Landes Mecklenburg-Vorpommern, 1996); Hermann Behrens, "Naturschutz und Landeskultur in der Sowjetischen Besatzungszone und in der DDR. Ein historischer Überblick," in *Die Veränderung der Kulturlandschaft: Nutzungen, Sichtweisen, Planungen*, ed. Günter Bayerl and Torsten Meyer (Münster: Waxmann, 2003), 213–71; Klaus Stern, *Wirkung der grossflächigen Landbewirtschaftung in der DDR auf Flora, Fauna und Boden*, Osteuropastudien der Hochschulen des Landes Hessen 174 (Berlin: Duncker und Humblot, 1990).
3. Gregory R. Witkowski, "On the Campaign Trail: State Planning and Eigen-Sinn in a Communist Campaign to Transform the East German Countryside," *Central European History* 37, no. 3 (2004): 400–422; Patrice Poutrus, *Die Erfindung des Goldbroilers: Über den Zusammenhang zwischen Herrschaftssicherung und Konsumentwicklung in der DDR* (Cologne: Böhlau, 2002).
4. See Palmowski (2009).
5. The links between bodies and imagined collectives was first explored by George Mosse, *Nationalism and Sexuality: Respectability and Abnormal Sexuality in Modern Europe* (New York: Howard Fertig, 1985), 16. As Mosse indicates, nationalism was concerned not just with promoting beautiful images of the nation but also with the con-

stant rejuvenation of nationalized bodies. In a similar manner, Ghassan Hage argues, "The national imaginary operates like a Lacanian fantasy. In being such an always-yet-to-be-finalised structure that invites the nationalist to do more work on it, it provides an imagined space where the attainment of a fully satisfying goal (in our case, a nation) is perceived as 'not too far away.' In so doing, it provides the imaginary grounds on which individuals are symbolically constructed as purposeful (because hopeful) and meaningful nation builders . . . This is highly significant, for it means that, in the process of nation building, the national subject is not only building a nation but also constantly building itself" (Ghassan Hage, "The Spatial Imaginary of National Practices: Dwelling-Domesticating/Being-Exterminating," *Environment and Planning D: Society and Space* 14 (1996): 478). See also Scott Moranda, "Maps, Markers, and Bodies: Hikers Constructing the Nation in German Forests," *The Nationalism Project*, December 1, 2000, http://www.nationalismproject.org/articles/Moranda/moranda.htm.

6. Jakob Schmitz, "Naturfreunde und Wegebezeichnung," *Rheinisches Land: Nachrichten des Gaues Rheinland in Touristin-Verein `Die Naturfreunde* 7 (1926): 152.

7. Pieter Judson, "Every German Visitor Has a *Völkisch* Obligation He Must Fulfill": Nationalist Tourism in the Austrian Empire, 1880–1918," in *Histories of Leisure*, ed. Rudy Koshar (Oxford: Berg, 2002), 147–68.

8. On Soviet tourism, see Gorsuch and Koenker (2006); Koenker (2003); Anne E. Gorsuch, *All This Is Your World: Soviet Tourism at Home and Abroad after Stalin* (Oxford: Oxford University Press, 2011). On Soviet sport and festivals, see Karen Petrone, *Life Has Become More Joyous, Comrades: Celebrations in the Time of Stalin* (Bloomington: Indiana University Press, 2000); James Riordan, *Sport in Soviet Society: Development of Sport and Physical Education in Russia and the USSR* (Cambridge: Cambridge University Press, 1977); Rodert Edelman: *Serious Fun: A History of Spectator Sports in the USSR* (New York: Oxford University Press, 1993).

9. On totalitarianism and Cold War sport, see David L. Andrews and Stephen Wagg, eds., *East Plays West: Sport and the Cold War* (London: Routledge, 2007). For a history of sport in the GDR informed by totalitarianism theory, see Michael Krüger and Kai Reinhart, "Funktionen des Sports im modernen Staat und in der modernen Diktatur," *Historical Social Research* 32, no. 1 (2007): 43–77.

10. On homeland associations and tourism, see Thomas Lekan, "A 'Noble Prospect': Tourism, Heimat, and Conservation on the Rhine, 1880–1914," *Journal of Modern History* 81, no. 4 (December 2009): 824–58; Celia Applegate, *A Nation of Provincials: The German Idea of Heimat* (Berkeley: University of California Press, 1990); Alon Confino, *The Nation as a Local Metaphor: Württemberg, Imperial Germany, and National Memory, 1871–1918* (Chapel Hill: University of North Carolina Press, 1997); Rudy Koshar, *German Travel Cultures* (Oxford: Berg, 2000); Rudy Koshar, ed., *Histories of Leisure* (Oxford: Berg, 2002).

11. Williams (2007), 109. This chapter's summary of the Friends of Nature's history owes a great debt to Williams' excellent history of the organization.

12. On middle-class hiking organizations and their relationship with the FDJ, see Helga Gotschlich, Katharina Lange and Edeltraud Schulze, eds., *Aber nicht im Gleichschritt: Zur Entstehung der FDJ*, ed. Gotschlich, et al. (Berlin: Metropol, 1997). For further reading on youth movements in a similar vein, see Elizabeth Heineman, "Gender Identity in the Wandervögel Movement," *German Studies Review* 12, no. 2 (May

1989): 249–70; Rudolf Kneip, *Wandervögel ohne Legende: Die Geschichte eines pädagogischen Phänomens* (Heidenheim: Südmarkverlag Fritsch, 1984); Walter Laqueur, *Young Germany: A History of the German Youth Movement* (New Brunswick: Transaction Books, 1984); Peter Stachura, *German Youth Movement, 1900–1945: An Interpretative and Documentary History* (New York: St. Martin's, 1981).

13. Williams (2007), 110. See also, John Alexander Williams, *Steeling the Young Body: Official Attempts to Control Youth Hiking in Germany, 1913–1938* (Edmonton: University of Alberta, 1997).

14. Laura Lee Downs, *Childhood in the Promised Land: Working-Class Movements and the Colonies de Vacances in France, 1880–1960* (Durham: Duke University Press, 2002), 12.

15. Williams (2007), 257–59. On social hygiene and socialism in Germany, see note 31 in the present book's introduction.

16. Williams (2007), 67–104. See also Dagmar Günther, *Wandern und Sozialismus: Zur Geschichte des Touristenvereins "Die Naturfreunde" im Kaiserreich und in der Weimarer Republik* (Hamburg: Verlag Dr. Kovacĕ, 2003).

17. Williams (2007), 17, 67, 72.

18. Williams (2007), 82.

19. Williams (2007), 92–93. For more on the conflict between Social Democrats and communists, see Heinrich Steinbrinker, "Der Geist der Gemeinschaft: Wechselwirkungen zwischen Arbeiterjugendbewegung und `bürgerlicher' Jugendbewegung bis 1933," in *Jahrbuch des Archivs der Deutschen Jugendbewegung 1978–1981* (Burg Ludwigstein, 1981), 7–23; Eva Wächter, "'An der lauten Stadt vorüberziehen!' Naturfreundejugend 1918–1933, zwischen Jugendbewegung und Jugendpflege," in *Wir sind die grüne Garde: Geschichte der Naturfreundejugend*, ed. Heinz Hoffman and Jochen Zimmer (Essen: Klartext Verlag, 1986), 13–62. See also Joachim Wolschke-Bulmahn, *Auf der Suche nach Arkadien: Zu Landschaftisidealen und Formen der Naturaneignung in der Jugendbewegung und ihrer Bedeutung für die Landespflege* (Munich: Minerva, 1990).

20. On National Socialist tourism, see Baranowski (2004). See also Kristin Semmens, *Seeing Hitler's Germany: Tourism in the Third Reich* (Houndmills: Palgrave Macmillan, 2005); Hasso Spode, "Fordism, Mass Tourism, and the Third Reich: The 'Strength through Joy' Seaside Resort as an Index Fossil," *Journal of Social History* 38, no. 1 (2004): 127–55.

21. Williams (2007), 94–104.

22. Zentralrat der FDJ, "Jugendheim GmbH," November 22, 1947, Stiftung Archiv der Parteien und Massenorganisationen der DDR im Bundesarchiv (hereinafter SAPMO-BArch): DY24 3626. On the early history of hiking in the GDR, see Joachim Schindler, *Zur Entwicklung von Wandern und Bergsteigen in der Sächsischen Schweiz sowie zur Arbeit touristischer Organisationen Dresdens von 1945 bis 1953* (Dresden: Joachim Schindler, 1999); Günter Wonneberger, "Sowjetische Sportpolitik für die SBZ und DDR," *Grüner Weg 31a: Zeitschrift des Studienarchivs Arbeiterkultur und Ökologie* 10 (January 1996): 57.

23. On this attraction to the GDR, see Ingeburg Wonneberger, "Breitensport: Studie zum Breitensport/Massensport in der Sowjetischen Besatzungszone Deutschlands und

der DDR (1945–1960)," in *Der Sport in der SBZ und frühen DDR*, ed. Wolfgang Buss and Christian Becker (Schorndorf: Hofmann, 2001), 401.

24. For more on the FDJ's attempts to provide appealing leisure activities to young East Germans, see Ulrich Mählert, *Blaue Hemden, Rote Fahnen: Die Geschichte der Freien Deutschen Jugend* (Opladen: Leske und Budrich, 1996); Helga Gotschlich, ed., *"Links und links und Schritt gehalten . . .": Die FDJ; Konzepte—Abläufe—Grenzen* (Berlin: Metropol, 1994); Helga Gotschlich et al., eds. (1997); Mark Fenemore, "The Limits of Repression and Reform: Youth Policy in the Early 1960s," in *The Workers' and Peasants' State: Communism and Society in East Germany under Ulbricht, 1945–1971*, ed. Patrick Major and Jonathan Osmond (Manchester: Manchester University Press, 2002), 171–89; Leonore Ansorg, *Kinder im Klassenkampf: Die Geschichte der Pionierorganisation von 1948 bis Ende der fünfziger Jahre* (Berlin: Akademie Verlag, 1997). On Soviet youth policy, see Anne E. Gorsuch, *Youth in Revolutionary Russia: Enthusiasts, Bohemians, Delinquents* (Bloomington: Indiana University Press, 2000), 42.

25. "Richtlinien für das Erholungs und Wanderwerk in der sowjetischen Besatzungszone," February 25, 1948, SAPMO-BArch: DY30 IV 2/16/1; Jugendheim GmbH, Letter to the Secretariat of the FDJ, "Betrifft: Naturfreunde," December 23, 1948, SAPMO-BArch: DY24 3626; Schindler (1999), 49; "Protokoll der Sitzung der provisorischen Landes und Zonenleitung der Natur und Heimatfreunde," July 6, 1948, in Schindler (1999), 40.

26. Zentralrat der FDJ, "Vorlage: Das Ferien und Wanderwerk der FDJ," April 12, 1949, 8a, SAPMO-BArch: DY24 3627.

27. Schindler (1999), 41.

28. Molly Wilkinson Johnson, *Training Socialist Citizens: Sports and the State in East Germany* (Leiden: Brill, 2008). Other work on East German sport includes Mike Dennis and Jonathan Grix, *Sport Under Communism: Behind the East German "Miracle"* (Houndmills: Palgrave Macmillan, 2012); Patrick Litz, *Der Beitrag des Sports zur Entfaltung der sozialistischen Persönlichkeit in der DDR* (Berlin: Weissensee Verlag, 2007).

29. "Arbeitsentschliessung des 1. Verbandstages des DWBV im DTSB am 14 und 15 Juni 1958 in Dresden," June 14, 1958, 1, eco-Archiv: Verbandstag I. In 1970, the DWBV changed its name to the German Association for Hiking, Mountain Climbing, and Orienteering (Deutscher Verband für Wandern, Bergsteigen und Orientierungslauf, DWBO). To avoid confusion, I use DWBV throughout.

30. "Organisationsstatistik des DTSB: Wandern/Bergsteigen/OL," December 31, 1977, eco-Archiv: DTSB-Deutscher Verband für Wandern, Bergsteigen und Orientierungslauf (hereinafter DWBO) Abteilung II: Sport.

31. Erich Hobusch, "Naturfreunde auf dem Weg zum Kulturbund, 1945–1953," *Grüner Weg 31a: Zeitschrift des Studienarchivs Arbeiterkultur und Ökologie* 10 (January 1996): 68. Membership numbers come from Palmowski (2009), 15. For more on Friends of Nature in the GDR, see Wolfgang Bagger, "Vom Weiterleben der Naturfreundeidee—Das Beispiel Bockwitz," *Grüner Weg 31a: Zeitschrift des Studienarchivs Arbeiterkultur und Ökologie* 10 (January 1996): 47–52; Jürgen Lorenz, "Warum gab es in der DDR keine Naturfreunde?" *Arbeiterkultur und Ökologie: Rundbrief* 2(1992): 30–31.

32. Palmowski (2009), 34.

33. Palmowski (2009), 99–101.

34. Palmowski (2009), 124.

35. Reinhart and Krüger (2007), 52.

36. Reinhart and Krüger (2007), 60.

37. Gorsuch and Koenker, 3.

38. See Johnson (2008). See Erik Jensen for more on meritocracy in modern sport. Erik Norman Jensen, *Body by Weimar: Athletes, Gender, and German Modernity.* (Oxford: Oxford University Press, 2010).

39. Johnson (2008), 102; Wonneberger (2001), 414. On the Soviet Union and performative culture, see Jeffrey Brooks, *Thank You, Comrade Stalin!: Soviet Public Culture from Revolution to Cold War* (Princeton: Princeton University Press, 2000).

40. Reinhart and Krüger (2007), 61

41. "Richtlinie für die Anfängerschulung im Bergsteigen," September 13, 1958, SAPMO-BArch: DY12 4291.

42. Robert Otto Franz, "Sportklassifizierung im Bergsteigen," *Freundschaft* 1 (1953): 7–8.

43. Heinz Schlosser, "Ist Touristik Leistungssport?" *Unterwegs* 8 (1959): 1.

44. "Einige Bemerkungen zur Entwicklung und zum Stand der Alpinistik in der DDR," January 10, 1961, 4, SAPMO-BArch, DY12 4408.

45. Schindler (1999), 42 and appendix 8: Letter from Landesvorstandes Sachsen der SED to Hans Frank, September 22, 1948.

46. Schindler (1996): 105; (1999), 60.

47. Schindler (1999), 60.

48. Schindler (1999), 61–62.

49. DWBV, "Thesen zur Sekretariatsvorlage über die Aufgaben und Entwicklung der Touristik, des Wanderns, Bergsteigens und Orientierungssportes in der DDR," November 11, 1960, 2, SAPMO-BArch: DY12 4408.

50. Orienteering in Scandinavia and Germany was not new. The first competitions in Scandinavia took place in 1897. See "Die touristischen Wettkämpfe und ihre Stellung im Sportgeschehen Europas," *Skisport und Touristik* 8 (1960): 14; Sigismund Schmidt, BSG Motor-West Erfurt, "Beitrag zur Geschichte des OL," *Wandern und Bergsteigen* 2 (1971), 2.

51. Edelfried Buggel, *Die Touristik im Massensport*, Kleine Bücherei für den Übungsleiter und Sportlehrer 2 (Berlin: Sportverlag, 1957; reprint, 1961), 53.

52. "Wettkampfterminkalender 1963," October 17, 1962, SAPMO-BArch: DY12 4408.

53. Fritz Leder, "Kurt Schlosser—ein truer Sohn der deutschen Arbeiterklasse," *Der Tourist* 8 (1964): 3–5; Max Zimmering, "Wilhelm Dieckmann," *Skisport und Touristik* 1 (1959), 10; Eva-Ursula Petereit, "Hohnstein," *Wandern und Bergsteigen* 9 (1960), 1–2; "Willi Hauptmann Gedächtnisweg," August 26, 1957, SAPMO-BArch: DY12 4291.

54. For more on Buchenwald and its role in East German memory politics, see Rudy Koshar, *From Monuments to Traces: Artifacts of German Memory, 1870–1990* (Berkeley: University of California Press, 2000); James Young, *The Texture of Memory* (New

Haven: Yale University Press, 1993); Manfred Overesch, *Buchenwald und die DDR, oder die Suche nach Selbstlegitimation* (Göttingen: Vandenhoeck und Ruprecht, 1995); Sarah B. Farmer, "Symbols That Face Two Ways: Commemorating the Victims of Nazism and Stalinism at Buchenwald and Sachsenhausen," *Representations* 49 (Winter 1995): 97–119; Detlef Hoffmann, ed., *Das Gedächtnis der Dinge: KZ-Relikte und KZ-Denkmaler, 1945–1995* (Frankfurt am Main: Campus Verlag, 1998); Volkhard Knigge, "Die Gedenkstätte Buchenwald: Vom provisorischen Grabdenkmal zum Nationaldenkmal," in *Die Nacht hat zwölf Stunden, dann kommt schon der Tag: Antifaschismus, Geschichte und Neubewertung*, ed. Claudia Keller and literaturWERKstatt Berlin (Berlin: Aufbau, 1996), 309–31; Volkhard Knigge, "Vom Reden und Schweigen der Steine: Zu Denkmalen auf dem Gelände ehemaliger nationalsozialistischer Konzentrations- und Vernichtungslager," in *Fünfzig Jahre danach: Zur Nachgeschichte des Nationalsozialismus*, ed. Sigrid Weigel and Birgit Erdle (Zürich: vdf Hochschulverlag AG an der ETH Zürich, 1996), 193–234.

55. DWBV, "Protokoll der Präsidumstagung," November 1, 1958, 6, SAPMO-BArch: DY12 4287; DWBV, "Rechenschaftsbericht des Präsidiums des DWBV zum II Verbandstag 1961 in Halle," March 20, 1961, 8, eco-Archiv: Verbandstag II.

56. DWBV, "Die Schönheiten der Heimat erwandern!," *Der Tourist* 3 (1961), 13.

57. Komitee für Touristik und Wandern (hereinafter KTW), "Hundert Freidenskilometer," *Unterwegs* 6 (1960): 4.

58. DWBV, "Perspektivplan für die Entwicklung des Deutschen Wanderer und Bergsteigerverbandes bis 1965," March 14, 1961, 3, SAPMO-BArch: DY12 4408.

59. Letter from Rat der Kriese (hereinafter RdK) Marienberg, Abteilung (hereinafter Abt.) Jugendfragen, Körperkultur und Sport to Abt. Volksbildung, RdK Marienberg, "Betr: Bericht über die Tätigkeit der Jugendherberge im Sommer 1963," January 16, 1963, Kreisarchiv Marienberg-Zschopau (hereinafter KarchMZ): E1648.

60. KTW, "Sekretariatsvorlage über die Wegemarkierung in der DDR," 1958, SAPMO-BArch: DY12 4286.

61. "Entwurf einer Anordnung über die Markierung der Wanderwege in der DDR," 1959, SAPMO-BArch: DY27 2810. See also Horst Berger, *4000 km Hauptwanderwege DDR* (Leipzig: VEB Bibliographisches Institut, 1960).

62. KTW, "Beschlussprotokoll der 1. Beratung der Arbeitsgruppe Wanderlieder," February 19, 1959, SAPMO-BArch: DY12 4286.

63. Arbeitsgruppe Sport, Central Committee of the Socialist Unity Party (hereinafter ZK der SED), "Einschätzung zur Lage auf dem Gebiete des Sportes in Vorbereitung des V Parteitages," May 21, 1958, 1, SAPMO-BArch: DY30 IV 2/18/3. According to the SED, five hundred thousand citizens participated in forest runs in the spring of 1958. Johnson (2008) discusses in detail the true figures of participation, which may have been much lower.

64. *Heraus zum Frühjahrs-Massen-Waldlauf*, 4, Bundesarchiv in Berlin-Lichterfelde (hereinafter BArch): DR5 72.

65. Palmowski (2009), 46.

66. Palmowski (2009), 74–80, 105–7.

67. Letter from Kulturbund, Zentralkommission Natur und Heimatfreunde, Dr. Liesel Noack to Members, February 14 1957, SAPMO-BArch: DY27 2810.

68. Memo from Kulturbund, Kreissekretariat Quedlinburg (Bezirk Halle) to Zentralkommission Natur und Heimatfreunde, Dr. Liesel Noack, January 11, 1958, SAPMO-BArch: DY27 2809.

69. Bezirksfachausschuss Magdeburg, "Jahresanalyse 1959," November 23, 1959, 3–4, SAPMO-BArch: DY12 4290.

70. Bezirk Halle, "Jahresanalyse 1959," November 8, 1959, 4, SAPMO-BArch: DY12 4290.

71. Schindler (1999), 48.

72. Reinhart and Krüger (2007), 61; Schindler (1999), 24–25.

73. Reinhart and Krüger (2007), 63.

74. Reinhart and Krüger (2007), 66.

75. Reinhart and Krüger (2007), 61.

76. Hans Pankotsch, "Antwort an BSG Empor Dresden-Löbtau," *Freundschaft* 2 (1953), 27. For a DWBV statement on private tourist clubs, see DWBV, "Massnahmen zur weiteren Verbesserung der touristischen Arbeit im DTSB und Festlegung der Perspektiven des DWBV bis 1965 und der dazu notwendigen Massnahmen," December 5, 1960, SAPMO-BArch: DY12 4408.

77. Karl-Heinz Guttmann, Vorsitzender Touristik Dresden, "Niederschrift über die Situation der Sektion Touristik im Kreis Dresden-Stadt," March 20, 1958, 4, SAPMO-BArch: DY12 4289.

78. Heinz Schlosser, "Massnahmen für weiteren Entwicklung der Wander und Bergsteigerbewegung und ihrer organisatorischen Festigung in der DDR," November 1957, 9, eco-Archiv: Verbandstag I.

79. Ibid., 10.

80. "Schluss mit der Gemütlichkeit," *Sportecho*, June 23, 1958.

81. Bezirk Dresden, "Jahresanalyse 1959," October 18, 1959, SAPMO-BArch: DY12 4290.

82. Quote from untitled document of November 23, 1946, in Joachim Schindler's private collection.

83. "Liebe Bergfreunde! Liebe Wanderfreunde!" *Werbeschrift*, January 1953, 1.

84. Letter from IG Bergbau Suhl Gera to RdB Suhl, 1956, BArch: DR2 2814.

85. RdK Marienberg, Abt. Planung und Bilanzierung, "Gutachten über die Möglichkeiten der Verwirklichung von Wählerauftragen an der Volkswahl am 20.10.1963," September 13, 1963, KarchMZ: E1648. For another example, see Letter to Zentrale Kommission from Kreiswegemeister, Erzgebirge West, Arbeitsgemeinschaft Natur und Heimatfreunde, Kreis Klingenthal, Bezirk Karl Marx Stadt, October 22, 1958, SAPMO-BArch: DY27 2809. See also "Behindertes Wandern im Westerzgebirge," *Natur und Heimat* 1 (1959), clipping found in SAPMO-BArch: DY27 2809.

86. See also SAPMO-BArch: DY34 1/266/4235, DY34 29/1592/6003, and DY34 1/264/4234.

87. Görlich (2012), 78.

CHAPTER 2

Rejuvenating Socialist Workers: Conservation and Landscape Care in the 1950s

In 1954, a West Berlin newspaper reported that East German authorities had proposed a national park in the beloved forests of "Saxon Switzerland" to the south of Dresden. The proposal, in the journalist's opinion, revealed the growing penetration of a centralizing regime into every nook and cranny of everyday life. In a sense, the reporter was correct; as the previous chapter revealed, sports authorities did hope to transform and control the leisure practices of rock climbers and hikers in Saxon Switzerland. Dresden's day-trippers, he wrote, "Seem intent on weekends to enjoy some small amount of freedom from the regime's harsh regimentation." He concluded, "No wonder the functionaries are concerned."[1]

This particular piece of Cold War propaganda got quite a bit wrong, however. The newspaper's attack on the SED obscured the highly controversial nature of the national park proposal, which authorities ultimately scuttled as a threat to economic growth. A national park did not fit very well into the plans of a regime that embraced a Soviet-style growth of heavy industry. Propaganda campaigns in the 1950s celebrated steel factories and coal mines while glorifying austerity and individual sacrifice for the collective good, and the regime, in part to pay reparations to the Soviet Union, also rapidly expanded mining and timber harvesting with little consideration of long-term environmental consequences.[2] In part due to these policies, authorities struggled with a growing exodus to West Germany of skilled workers and professionals tired of austerity and scarcity. In 1953, construction workers even instigated a strike in East Berlin that sparked a widespread revolt eventually put down by Soviet tanks and the East German police. One response to the 1953 uprising was the growth of the secret police, or Stasi, into a formidable surveillance force, but the regime actually tacked rather nervously between concessions to workers and purges of reformers. After 1953, the regime implemented a "New Course" that paid more attention to workers' benefits and even briefly adapted cultural policy to better reflect popular desires, especially among the young. The regime thus very publicly promised a higher quality of life and even tentatively promoted consumerism alongside heavy industry. Josef Stalin's death in 1953 and successor Nikita Khrushchev's hope that the GDR would serve as a model of socialist modernity only encouraged the new thinking about consumer goods. Before 1958, however, the SED and its economic planners remained very uncomfortable with consumer desires and feared the influence of the consumer culture emerging in West Germany. At that point, the regime preferred to respond to popular unrest through lower food and housing prices that demanded ever greater transformations of the natural environment to benefit industrial agriculture and forestry, thus making a national park nearly impossible even if the SED had no other reason to oppose it.[3]

Still, the reporter was not completely off base about the park proponents. He correctly identified the park as a control mechanism, but he oversimplified the origins and intent of those controls. Park proponents failed to convince the SED of the park's necessity, but they too had a desire for control—to protect nature against abuse by businesses and vacationers, to mold citizens into productive citizens uncorrupted by Western consumer decadence, and to rationally transform the land for optimal economic efficiency. Like their counterparts at the heights of political power, landscape architects saw, in the words of James C. Scott, "like a state." Scott argues that modern states, whether socialist or capitalist, subscribe to a high-modernist ideology that demands the mastery and simplification of nature to expand production and satisfy the needs of citizens.[4] Outright opponents of socialism or authoritarianism rarely appeared in bureaucratic debates; such antagonists retreated into silence or moved to the West. The protagonists of this chapter saw like a state and thus accepted the legitimacy of the new regime insofar as it offered greater opportunity than the capitalist West for constructing a "healthier" society.

It would be easy, given the GDR's environmental record, to write the history of conservation and landscape planning with an eye toward totalitarianism theory, but this chapter will insist instead that the statist embrace of authoritarian planning fit into a history of German conservation that did not begin or end with Nazism or Stalinism. Following totalitarianism theory, historians stress either the Stalinist tone of landscape planning or the overlap (in personnel and attitudes) between Nazi and East German landscape architects. As described by historians David Blackbourn and Andreas Dix, landscape planners dreamed of gigantic schemes to transform nature that mimicked Soviet policies. Dix also stresses the Nazi past of many architects who merely continued to design landscapes that a few years earlier had been associated with a "blood and soil" ideology, and he rightly points out their affection for planning regimes (whether Nazi or communist) that would overcome the chaos of liberal capitalism.[5] Yet East Germany's place within the longer history of German environmentalism should not be underestimated or oversimplified. Some East German landscape architects had been members of the Nazi Party and did work on Nazi mega-projects, and their faith in the state's ability to rationally manage and restore landscapes did transfer well from one authoritarian state with utopian fantasies to another. Nonetheless, landscape planners did not just throw themselves into the arms of dictatorship as silent collaborators, as much as they continued a long tradition of statism, recapitulated in the first section of this chapter.[6]

Upon closer investigation, it is clear that these conservationists cannot be labeled simply as collaborators in Stalinist terror, as victims, or as heroic resistance fighters. As in chapter 1's story of athletic tourism, the regime repressed nature lovers, and the conservationists discussed in this chapter also fought painful battles to remain relevant in a growth-oriented Ministry for Agriculture. Their lives, however, became intertwined with the state in complicated ways. In their struggle with economic interests, they often went out of the way to position themselves on the side of the SED. Conservationists even complained that the regime needed to become more centralized and interventionist, at least in the arenas of economic planning and land use. Sometimes they vilified their colleagues in order to establish their own credentials to the SED. While some of these individuals later positioned themselves as conscientious opponents of dictatorship, they usually defined themselves in the 1940s and 1950s in relation to the project of socialist modernism. They imagined themselves as agents of antiliberal change or reformers ensuring the survival of a "good" socialism in the face of shortsighted policy decisions.

In addition, almost all the protagonists of this chapter, even when fighting among themselves, reached a consensus with the regime on certain givens. In particular, they believed that authoritarian conservation, if properly implemented, could ensure limitless abundance without sacrificing social order or landscape integrity. To push their common agenda, almost all conservationists agreed that tourism, or *Erholung*, justified landscape care. On the one hand, their focus on tourism and recreation built on longer middle-class or Nazi traditions of promoting productive leisure in Germany. It also fit into a Marxist understanding of tourism as work that improved citizens mentally and physically. On the other hand, *Erholung* helped landscape architects and other conservationists identify themselves as indispensable to economic reconstruction.

They emphasized that social progress and worker productivity required recreation in healthy landscapes. In other words, *Erholung* provided conservationists a vocabulary with which to challenge policy and still endorse the socialist economic project. I also argue that it helped scientists ally with doctors, leisure experts, and architects to form a "conservation bloc" across ministerial boundaries and state committees. This conservation bloc insisted on an alternate vision of socialist modernism that paid attention to landscape care. It is this complicated history of negotiation and consensus building that the story of Saxon national park proposals actually revealed, as the last section of this chapter demonstrates.

Early GDR Conservation and Historical Continuity

At first glance, one might believe that 1945 represented a "zero hour" for traditional preservation organizations in East Germany, but certain traditions of German conservation did survive in the GDR. My assertion of continuity here is novel in and of itself. The collaboration of prominent landscape planners and nature preservationists with the Nazi regime tainted traditional nature preservation in the eye's of East Germany's antifascist regime. As described in the previous chapter, leisure organizations that promoted nature protection and nature tourism had been disbanded shortly after World War II. Typically, the coexistence of Stalinism and nature protection has been doubted by historians, often quite rightly. As Frank Uekötter has noted, conservation in the Soviet Union was limited at best; he pointedly refers to David Blackbourn's comment that "[a] conference on conservation and Stalinism would certainly be much shorter than [one on Nazism and conservation]."[7] Uekötter notes, however, that some landscape planners did work in East Germany and that these men could find certain similarities between the Third Reich and the GDR, particularly in their common disdain for a "free wheeling liberalist economy."[8] Another similarity goes unmentioned by Uekötter. As in the Third Reich, conservationists in the GDR insisted that landscape planning must not harm (and, in fact, should assist) the economy. This compromise with economic and technological growth actually has roots deeper than 1933.

Even in the early days of German nature protection, preservationists often chose to compromise with modern industry rather than retreat into outright antimodernism. Early preservationist Hugo Conwentz, for example, called in 1912 for a compromise with economic interests.[9] As told by many historians, organized German nature preservation, or *Naturschutz*, made its first appearance in 1897 with Ernst Rudorff, who went on to found the Deutscher Bund Heimatschutz in 1904. The German word *Naturschutz* suggests outright protection rather than "managed use," even though Germany certainly never sought to preserve wilderness areas as did the United States. The goal was to preserve small nature sanctuaries and cultural landscapes unsullied by modern materialism. *Heimatschutz*, or homeland protection, pushed to protect regional homelands (both cultural and natural landscapes) from homogenization and commercialism as well. For this largely conservative and middle-class movement, modern urban culture and industrialization bred social and political instability. Preservationists thus sought not only to protect pastoral landscapes but also to educate the masses away from materialism and political radicalism and toward an appreciation of nature. While earlier histories of this movement stressed its aversion to modernity, historians have more recently shown how preservationists aspired to an alternative or greener modernity. As William H. Rollins has written, homeland preservationists hoped for an organic modernity in which economic progress remained in harmony with rural nature.[10]

In the crisis-ridden years of Weimar Germany, preservationists placed a growing emphasis on rational state planning to balance economic growth and landscape health. According to Thomas Lekan, postwar instability and a need for economic recovery led to calls for "accommodating economic conditions rather than confronting them, rationalizing the landscape instead of romanticizing its beauties, promoting the therapeutic benefits [for workers] rather than seeking sentimental attachment."[11] The best example of this new pragmatism came in the form of landscape care, or *Landschaftspflege*. Homeland preservationists had always worked closely with the state as they did in Prussia, but proponents of landscape care after World War I imagined a more expansive role for technocrats working with the state to manage capitalism and citizens. Landscape care would follow a new path to harmonizing industry and nature; instead of protecting nature from humans, architects would design the landscape so that industry blended with nature rather than haphazardly consuming it. They also hoped to triumph over the narrow self-interest of private property owners by finding "objective criteria for distributing land and avoiding social conflict."[12] This "new objectivity" even pushed Weimar preservationists to recast their paternalism toward the working classes in terms of the technical language of therapy. They now sought to improve the physiological and psychological health of workers by improving their built environment and adding green spaces to industrial districts, much as Marxist social hygienists did (though Marxists still envisioned a future revolution against private property).[13]

Germans were not alone in their embrace of a new technocratic language of therapy and health. Around the world, notions of therapeutic nature and healthy landscape "organisms" captivated conservationists in the late nineteenth and early twentieth century. Many nineteenth-century Americans imagined an intimate relationship between the individual body and local environments—identifying certain landscapes or uses of the land as more healthful than others. As Conevery Valencius explains, nineteenth-century American medical experts subscribed to a Hippocratic worldview, which emphasized biological equilibrium between the individual body, the land, and society. In other words, people and landscapes composed a total organism whose overall health depended on the behavior of its inhabitants.[14] The American conservationist Aldo Leopold, for example, described degraded environments as organisms that "suddenly developed pathological symptoms, i.e., self-accelerating rather than self-compensating departures from normal functioning."[15] This Hippocratic worldview lost ground in the twentieth century with the rise of modernism and its faith in science and central planning. Germ theory, in particular, increasingly downplayed the interaction between the body and its local environment. In the Nazi period, many (but not all) medical professionals built on germ theory to embrace the idea that certain groups or races were deemed more likely to carry disease; health had much less to do with a healthy interaction with local environments and more to do with eliminating certain populations and alien invaders.[16] As we will see, a Hippocratic worldview resurfaced in the GDR in the work of the conservation bloc.

By the early 1930s, middle-class conservationist hopes for a therapeutic regime led to growing frustration with Weimar Germany's political chaos, and many nature enthusiasts sought out antidemocratic alternatives, including Nazism. The statist tendencies of German conservation allowed for cooperation with the regime, especially after the passage of the 1935 Reich Conservation Law, which became one of the first and most comprehensive nature protection laws in Europe at the time. Through the law, technical experts hoped to overrule egotistical or individualistic desires to promote the well-being of the land and society. Conservation interests especially appreciated that the law applied equally to all of Germany, not just to one federal state as had previous pieces of preservation legislation. As enemies of liberal capitalism, they loved that the law allowed for the state to designate private property for protection without compensation to property owners and required developers to consult landscape advocates before beginning any significant alteration of natural landscapes. Moreover, the law insisted on protecting whole landscapes, not just tiny nature preserves—just as proponents of supralocal planning had been demanding already during the Weimar Republic. In its enforcement, authorities often ignored landscape preservationists and privileged economic needs, but conservationists took solace in the fact that the letter of the law was on their side. Some local preservationists even moved faster than central authorities and threatened property owners with the law's private property clause to gain conservation concessions.[17]

Even though they shared Adolf Hitler's disdain for liberal capitalism, conservationists had a complicated relationship with the Third Reich. Few conservationists aggressively promoted racial theories or joined the Nazi Party before 1933.[18] Regional preservationists after 1933 also were well aware of how Nazi military preparation trumped conservation goals and how their regional outlook clashed with the centralization of the Nazi state. For example, local homeland preservationists complained of the Autobahn's disregard for cultural landmarks in the Rhineland, and advocates of *Dauerwald* sustainable forestry soon realized that Nazi nods to their reforms meant nothing, as forest production ramped up to supply the war effort.[19]

While some local homeland preservationists expressed skepticism, key national preservation leaders joined landscape planners such as Alwin Seifert and Heinrich Wiepking-Jürgensmann to promote centralization and comprehensiveness. These Third Reich conservationists embraced a compromise between conservation and economic growth, believing that prosperity and abundance could be reconciled with nature protection. Much like the proponents of landscape care in Weimar Germany, they believed that rational experts could unleash the economic potential of the land while also preserving green spaces for popular enjoyment. In landscape plans for the Autobahn and the conquered lands in former Poland, modernization became intertwined with a racial war, as planners increasingly saw non-German populations as the primary threat to an orderly and productive landscape. In other words, they adapted their modernism (sometimes enthusiastically and sometimes pragmatically) to the Nazi vision of limitless abundance acquired through racial struggle and imperial conquest. Even as the task of complete planning became increasingly violent (in the East), officials representing the Reich Conservation Agency, serving in Heinrich Himmler's Reich Commissariat for the Strengthening of German Nationality, or working as one of Seifert's Autobahn landscape advocates, remained enamored with their new power and freedom to plan on a "grand scale."[20]

In East Germany, these dreams for a therapeutic regime survived in an altered form, as prominent landscape planners continued to believe that a compromise between nature protection and economic growth could be reached. However, the path to abundance no longer traveled through conquered Eastern

European lands subjugated to a German Empire. Trained in garden architecture and landscape planning, they knew and understood well the lessons of Weimar landscape care. The language used by East German landscape planners also, of course, resembled, at some levels, Nazi "blood and soil" discourse, in which Germans and the land constituted one organism, thriving when uninfected by foreign peoples and ideas. Under Nazism, after all, leading landscape advocates had interpreted ecological theory to imagine Aryan landscapes as harmonious climax communities composed of plants, animals, and humans thriving in delicate balance with each other.[21] Most striking, however, are the continuities that bridge the entire period from 1918 to 1960. Landscape planners working in the Weimar, Nazi, or SED regimes all hoped for an end to unplanned exploitation of natural resources and imagined modernist regimes securing limitless abundance through science and planning.

Regardless of their political affiliations, East German landscape planners still struggled to find new institutional homes. Their task was made more difficult by communist suspicions about romantic, middle-class nature enthusiasm even though, on paper, the GDR had nature protection laws and institutions. In 1954, conservationists received support from Karl Kneschke, a prominent Kulturbund (Culture League) functionary, member of East Germany's largely meaningless parliament, and nature protection advocate. With his support, the parliament passed a nature protection law that copied the National Socialist's groundbreaking 1935 Nature Protection Law almost exactly. Although some conservationists had pushed for a central nature protection agency since 1951, the law did not specify who administered nature protection (a problem that bedeviled many Third Reich conservationists as well).[22] Kneschke himself hoped that the law would soon be amended to give experts in landscape care a greater say over economic planning.[23] Rather than establish a powerful, central conservation agency, authorities instead created the Central Administration for Nature Protection inside the Ministry for Agriculture and Forestry, which was dominated by advocates of industrial agriculture and high-yield forestry. The Kulturbund's Natur und Heimatfreunde provided an organizational home for old Heimat friends and conservationists, but this leisure organization had little influence over the official policy on land use. Ignored by economic planners in the Ministry for Agriculture, landscape planners managed to carve out space for themselves in academic institutes. For example, architects in the Bauakademie, an East German institute for architecture and land-use planning, often criticized shortsighted economic planning. In the German Academy of the Agricultural Sciences (Deutsche Akademie der Landwirtschaftswissenschaften, or DAL), scientists researched landscape health and proposed policy initiatives within the Sektion Landeskultur und Natur-schutz (Department for Conservation and Nature Protection) and the interdis-ciplinary Ständige Kommission für Landschaftspflege und Naturschutz (SKLN, or Standing Committee for Landscape Care and Nature Protection). In the DAL, Dr. Hans Stubbe, president of the academy and ally of conservation interests, created the affiliated Institut für Landesforschung und Naturschutz (ILN, or Institute for Regional Research and Nature Protection). Stubbe's pres-tige and friends in high places insured the short-term survival of nature protec-tion within this academic setting, although academics rarely had an opportu-nity to influence planning decisions.[24]

Two men in particular pushed the Bauakademie toward conservation in the 1950s, and their experiences revealed the initial possibilities and limits of conservation in the German Democratic Republic. These men were Reinhold Lingner and Frank Erich Carl. As proponents of landscape care often did, Lingner got his start in garden architecture. At the age of twenty-five, Lingner became the lead architect in the project to commemorate the fallen German soldiers of World War I and coordinated the design of war cemeteries in Bel-gium. Described by some scholars as a committed socialist, he married a Ger-man communist and, as a result, lost his job when the Nazis purged commu-nists from civil service positions. Following a short exile in Western Europe, Lingner returned to Germany in 1936 in search of work. Unable to work offi-cially for the Third Reich because of his political affiliations, he found short-term positions assisting landscape advocates working on the Autobahn. With their support, he founded a private firm in 1942 and worked in occupied Poland designing green spaces for small cities. As the head of landscape planning in the East German Bauakademie after the war, Lingner specialized in designing recreation spaces. He submitted designs, for example, for parks, athletic stadi-ums, and the Pioneer Republic Wilhelm Pieck, a summer camp for Young Pio-neers (the East German equivalent of the Cub Scouts). Fellow architect Frank Erich Carl joined his good friend Lingner on these projects in East Germany. Carl had trained in Berlin with Lingner to be a garden architect during the 1920s before joining his friend to design German military cemeteries in Bel-gium from 1931 until 1940. During the war, he served in the Wehrmacht and was taken prisoner.[25]

Despite their different class and political backgrounds, East Germany's remaining conservationists all placed great faith in modernist planning and statism to balance nature and economic growth in such a way that material abundance could be reconciled with healthy landscapes. The most prominent figures of early East German conservation did have connections to either the

Social Democrats or the Communists. According to Axel Zutz, Lingner placed "social well-being" at the center of his work and joined the SED in 1946.[26] Georg Bela Pniower, a Humboldt University garden architect who had been persecuted by the Nazis for his Jewish heritage, also shared a Marxist worldview. Many other apolitical and non-Marxist academics and local preservationists continued, nonetheless, to work in East Germany, either as local preservation advocates or within universities or government ministries. Many never joined the SED.[27] They all, however, had their doubts about liberal capitalism and recognized the moral bankruptcy of fascism. They all looked with suspicion on modern mass culture and the everyday leisure practices of the masses. Notably, they all also shared in frustration. Even those who did come from working-class backgrounds or joined the SED had little success in promoting more assertive landscape care.

Rather than occupy themselves with small design projects, Lingner and Carl quickly embarked on the ambitious Landscape Diagnosis initiative. Begun in 1948, this project intended to diagnose the causes of erosion, vegetation change, and pollution and received official approval from the Ministry for Planning in 1950.[28] They imagined the diagnosis and its accompanying maps helping local economic planners overcome the poor planning of the liberal capitalist past. After first mapping a century of landscape changes in the Niederlausitz strip-mining district, Lingner and Carl turned their attention to the rest of the republic, with the assistance of over ninety employees—many of whom were former landscape advocates in Nazi Germany.[29] Bicycling across the countryside, these architects and conservationists produced detailed topographical maps of historical environmental change, ecological communities, patterns of air and water pollution, and proposed landscape improvements, such as reforestation or contour planting. Participants also researched the effects of those changes on the local water cycle and soil conditions. To describe their goals, these landscape architects used the medicinal and technocratic language of Weimar landscape planners. They sought out "symptoms of a serious sickness" and identified "alarm bells" indicating worse problems to come, such as floods in Oderbruch in 1946/47, the epidemic of bark beetles in Thuringia in 1947–49, the flooding in 1950 at Bruchstedt, and recurring flooding disasters in the Elbe watershed.[30]

The medicinal language of the Landscape Diagnosis reflected larger trends in the work of architects and conservationists in the early GDR and also around the world at the time. Many landscape architects, biologists, doctors, and sports experts promoted the state's role in developing "healthy" environments in order to improve worker health and productivity. East German social hygienist Hans Grimm, for example, wrote, "The medical scholarship of the classical Greeks already praised the health-influencing factors of water, air, and local living conditions. The life of every individual creature is in diverse ways connected to the 'natural' processes in their broadest sense, even if this is not always evident to residents of a metropolitan, technological environment."[31] He concluded, "Since the socialist state sees the care for people as a top priority, the concern for prophylactic medicine is highly recommended. There are many close connections between preventive medical care and the tasks of nature and landscape protection."[32] Hermann Meusel, the director of the ILN, also embraced the notion of a landscape organism (or climax community)—in which the fate or health of individual species had as much or more to do with interconnections with their surroundings (microclimates, water tables, and soil conditions) as with their genetic composition. As a leading biogeographer, Meusel specialized in the geographical distribution of plant species determined by analysis of plant morphology, geology, and climate; in this field, specialists often thought about landscapes as organic wholes.[33] As noted earlier, American conservationists also imagined landscapes as whole organisms that could become sick or recover health. In fact, Lingner understood his work as part of a global initiative. He pointedly compared the Landscape Diagnosis to schemes such as the Tennessee Valley Authority.[34] In addition to the TVA, Lingner familiarized himself with Hugh Bennett's *Soil Conservation* (1939) and Magnus Teller and Elston Waring's *Roots in the Earth* (1943).[35] Of course, his work also fit into broader Soviet bloc trends as well, such as Stalin's ambitious plans to reroute entire river systems in order to provide irrigation for landscapes suffering from desertification.[36]

Erholung and the Conservation Bloc

Despite their affinities for social engineering and authoritarian planning, architects and doctors often found themselves disappointed with the new regime, which, given its economic priorities, quickly censored the work of the Landscape Diagnosis. After a background check on participating architects and conservationists, the Ministry for Planning ordered architects to discontinue work in August 1950. Although only 75 percent of the work had been completed, authorities immediately removed the completed maps and texts from public access. The ministry then dissolved all work contracts for the project, without any explanation given to Lingner or Carl, who began a letter-writing campaign to uncover a cause.[37] The Interior Ministry, it turns out, initiated the attack on the diagnosis. Intelligence officers did not approve of participating scientists with Nazi pasts and feared that the maps could be used by the enemy for military and strategic purposes. One officer noted that one map revealed a shortage of clean water for priority industries in Bitterfeld; someone, he feared, might use such information for sabatoge.[38] A number of other factors may have been responsible. Looking back, Lingner blamed the project's demise on "egotistical interests and careerism," "bureaucrats," and possibly "economic sabotage."[39] Planning officials at the Ministry for Construction, a ministry keen on unhindered industrial growth, had initiated much of the criticism of the diagnosis. According to one historian, "The documentation of environmental damage raised doubt ultimately about the path of industrial development in the GDR and, in doing so, questioned the decisions" of the SED.[40] By 1952, a scaled-down version of Lingner's project reemerged within the Bauakadamie, with select results published after 1957. Most of the files, however, remained off limits to the public.[41]

Within the Ministry for Agriculture, conservationists also found few opportunities to alter that ministry's push to expand industrial agriculture. Hermann Meusel (with the ILN) and Hans Stubbe (the president of the DAL) repeatedly complained to the ministry that nature protection laws collapsed in the face of economic priorities.[42] A report from the DAL forwarded to the Agricultural Division within the Central Committee of the SED grumbled that the "pursuit of nature protection work often ran headlong into great difficulties because of the marked economic orientation of the administrative apparatus" that repressed everything that could be easily dismissed as "pure cultural goals."[43] The Sektion Landeskultur und Naturschutz in the DAL, in particular, insisted to the Ministry for Agriculture and Forestry that land-use planning could not be squeezed into a minor department focused primarily on melioration, which was the conversion of so-called wasteland (*Ödland*) into productive cropland.[44] The Five-Year Plan's promotion of wasteland cultivation, in particular, posed the danger that "spaces would be cultivated that in other respects are very important for our landscape."[45]

Conservationists generally faced constant harassment from their superiors if they questioned proposed increases in production levels.[46] The Ministry for Agriculture, for example, often reprimanded Hermann Meusel. Under Meusel, the ILN insisted that collective agriculture's general plans for mechanization and chemical use needed to be refined to account for local biological communities—at least sparing some wetlands, hedges, and woodlands in the agricultural landscape.[47] In response, ministry officials suggested that nature preservationists such as Meusel were politically suspect and potentially disloyal.

Only eleven of the two hundred county nature protection officers, the ministry reported, were members of the SED. The ministry complained, "These people passionately present their pleas for the conservation of often singular landscapes without connecting these arguments to a fundamental rejection of capitalistic economic models." The ministry then tarnished the ILN and its allies as "romantics and aesthetes" and as "petit bourgeois," a label often given to victims of purges and show trials throughout the Eastern bloc in the 1950s.[48]

Meusel and Lingner did not just face criticism from the SED. Some of their own colleagues also raised doubts about their work, and those critics sometimes aided attempts to discredit Meusel and Lingner within the Ministry for Agriculture. Georg Bela Pniower at Humboldt University called for an entirely new and progressive landscape care. He specifically rejected Lingner's continued focus on native vegetation and his medicinal descriptions of landscapes as organisms.[49] Dr. Kurt Wiedemann, the chief of regional planning in Dresden, also rejected this medicinal language. He criticized "the 'pessimistic attitude' that portrays people as a parasite on the earth."[50] Pniower reminded the regime that landscape architects had gained considerable prestige during the Nazi period and had embraced the opportunity to plan the Autobahn and the conquered Eastern territories to cure "sick" landscapes. He thus condemned "the application of a medical term such as *diagnosis* in the study of a geographical milieu," writing, "This term can give the impression that the landscape . . . is an 'organism' that can get sick. This is not the case."[51] Such language, Pniower elsewhere suggested, could only mean that conservationists had not overcome their racist past. Pniower despaired that the new Nature Protection Law of 1954 replicated the Nazi predecessor except for a few superficial changes.[52] Moreover, he blamed the "absolutist" Meusel for the minimal reforms of the law. In his critique of the new law, he insisted, "It must be made clear in the Preamble that we do not pursue nature and landscape protection in the traditional sense but instead introduce a progressive landscape care."[53] The relationship between Meusel and Pniower became so sour, in fact, that they refused to appear at the same functions.[54] Pniower at least partially benefited from critiques of Lingner; intelligence officers revealed that they canceled the Landscape Diagnosis in part because Pniower had begun a competing project at Humboldt University to improve the eroded landscape of the Huy Hakel region on the edge of the Harz Mountains.[55] In his own project, Pniower even celebrated industrialized collective agriculture for overcoming the ignorance of the poor capitalist farmer and eliminating erosion and flooding.[56]

Meusel also faced criticism from Kurt Kretschmann. While a prisoner of war during World War II, Kretschmann joined the Communist Party, and after the war, he established an environmental education center, campaigned to protect East Germany's dwindling beaver population, and created the signage (the so-called nature protection owl) that today marks many nature preserves throughout Germany. He held positions as a local nature protection official in Brandenburg, as well as within the Kulturbund and the DAL's *Sektion Landeskultur and Naturschutz*. In the wake of his death in 2007, Kretschmann has been honored by several German nature protection groups. Most obituaries celebrate his valiant efforts to protect Brandenburg's endangered species and landscapes, often emphasizing his heroic efforts in the face of political oppression and ruthless economic exploitation. One fellow East German preservationist later portrayed Kretschmann as a heroic advocate of a national park whose idea to include a park provision in the Nature Protection Law of 1954 was overturned by scientists (including Meusel) who saw the park proposal as too ambitious.[57]

While Kretschmann did struggle against the Ministry for Agriculture's economic priorities, he was not simply a victim; as Pniower had, Kretschmann also sought to discredit his colleagues to help his own cause. In a letter to the Ministry for Agriculture and Forestry's deputies in Brandenburg, Kretschmann complained, "I do not get the impression that anyone is willing to support nature protection . . . with [more than] pleasing speeches."[58] After the ministry later accused Kretschmann of out-of-date romanticism and petit bourgeois views, Kretschmann (perhaps understandably) tried to divert attention to others.[59] He revealingly wrote, "The clear majority of the leading activists in nature protection are uninterested in political matters . . . Many see nature protection as a fully apolitical concern, as [an arena] where the spirit of yesterday can be kept alive." While praising Meusel's important contributions, Kretschmann nonetheless insisted, "Meusel is not in the position to give nature protection the necessary political direction." Elsewhere Kretschmann noted, "The seven colleagues in the ILN who are party members have not worn their party insignia for years and do not appear political."[60] The reasons for Kretschmann's attempt to discredit Meusel are not entirely clear. Perhaps Kretschmann was merely fighting a turf battle for scarce funds. Perhaps he feared for his political legitimacy so much that he felt the need to attack others. Perhaps he believed that the SED would only embrace nature protection under the leadership of a dedicated pacifist and communist such as himself. No matter the motivations, Kretschmann's criticisms seemingly had a real influence on the SED's treatment of the ILN. Soon after Kretschmann's scathing letters in January 1958, the Central Committee of the SED wrote a letter to the Ministry for Agriculture, in which Franz Mellentin informed the ministry of the suspect political beliefs described by Kretschmann.[61] Two weeks after Mellentin wrote to the ministry, the ministry complained about the "ILN, where Meusel is absolutely apolitical."[62]

Despite the acrimony, all of these men embraced the concept of *Landeskultur*, which tied nature conservation to economic prosperity. They now spoke less about nature protection, or *Naturschutz* (deemed a concept too narrow, conservative, and politically compromised), and more about resource conservation, or what they called *Landeskultur*, which was defined as "a system of social imperatives for the preservation and planned improvement of the natural bases for life and productivity" that would also "insure an optimal and sustainable use of the land in ways compatible with local ecological and aesthetic characteristics."[63] While Pniower claimed the moral high ground, he joined Lingner and others in accepting and even celebrating the continued use of natural resources to fuel economic growth and turned to a new vocabulary to talk about nature. This *Landeskultur* consensus built on longer traditions of landscape care but also responded to political and economic realities. To not emphasize "improvement" and "growth" was to risk immediate condemnation from the Ministry for Agriculture.

In response to repeated political attacks of the 1950s, conservationists also hoped that the planning of recreation or rejuvenation areas, or *Erholungsplanung*, would help them gain influence. Conservationists and landscape architects partly focused on *Erholung* because they worried about the negative impacts of vacationers on precious natural landscapes.[64] Their concerns, of course, built on a long-standing German conservationist critique of urban tourists destroying the very beauties they sought to experience.[65] Conservationists, however, also turned to *Erholung* for tactical reasons under a "dictatorship of the proletariat." Dr. Hans Lehmann of the Bauakademie wrote in 1957, "A healthy landscape is a prerequisite for everything related to the reproduction of worker productivity, as, for example, with the tasks related to the *Erholung* [rejuvenation] of the working population."[66] In another case, President Stubbe of the Academy for Agricultural Science expressed his hopes that an emphasis on the public health benefits of outdoor recreation might push their respective ministries into action. In this conversation with Stubbe, a conservationist noted "how powerfully nature protection ideas are connected to practical necessity and to sober economic and medical considerations and how false it is to dismiss nature protection as the result of old fashioned nature feelings."[67] At this time, Lingner's collaborator, Frank Erich Carl, also began a new project planning recreation landscapes for the architectural academy. In his 1960 publication *Erholungswesen und Landschaft*, Carl insisted that even as engineers transformed East German landscapes and made them economically productive, they must remain "first-rate for popular *Erholung*" and "offer a person invigorating [*kräftespendende*] nature experiences, regardless of the extensive changes to the primordial landscape."[68] Carl used many of the same mapping techniques and landscape analyses that he and Lingner had begun with the Landscape Diagnosis to help plan recreation districts and their protection.[69] If tourism aided worker productivity and political mobilization, as Walter Ulbricht had insisted, then so did conservation. Carl turned to a medical expert, Prof. Dr. Hans Grimm, for support. Grimm wrote, "If it is true that health and productivity is secured and strengthened in landscapes suitable for *Erholung*, then these *Erholung* landscapes are as economically worthy as the richest mineral treasures."[70] These arguments, it should be noted, never questioned economic development and growth-oriented planning directly. In fact, they maintained that the economy could grow without limits if only properly managed.

Carl's collaboration with Grimm also revealed how a conservation bloc centered on *Erholung* emerged within planning agencies; instead of an isolated or a silent minority, conservation interests collaborated to create headaches for higher authorities. Carl engaged with *Erholung* working groups created by the central State Planning Commission, the trade union's Feriendienst (Vacation Services), and the ILN. In these working groups, representatives of dozens of institutions talked to each other and pressed a common agenda, hoping to influence not just their own disciplines but the entire planning structure. In 1957, the ILN worked with the Bauakademie and the Nature and Heimat Friends to develop a system of landscape preserves, or *Landschaftschutzgebieten*. These preserves were larger than nature preserves, allowed continued economic development within limits, and were intended as recreation spaces.[71] In 1957 and 1958, in another example, Meusel and Grimm organized two conferences of conservationists, tourism planners, biologists, and medical experts to discuss the relationship between landscape protection and public hygiene. At the Hygiene Day in Leipzig in July 1957, Meusel and medical allies criticized the effect of pollution on *Erholung* destinations important for public health. In a resolution forwarded to Minister President Otto Grotewohl, participants wrote, "Presenters and discussion participants agreed wholeheartedly that it was urgently important to preserve the existing *Erholung* landscapes in the interests of public health and, moreover, to secure further *Erholung* spaces." *Erholung*, they continued, benefited the economy.[72] The Hygiene Day participants also wrote a brochure to educate the public about the relationship of nature protection to public health. Later, at a May 14, 1958 joint conference of the DAL and the Academy of Science, participants praised the Landscape Diagnosis, called for more landscape preserves, and suggested using funds dedicated to industrial planning to help pay for landscape planning that benefited worker productivity. They proposed creating a Ministry for Health and Nature Protection to manage rural landscapes key to public health and recreation. Their attempt to create an alliance was never clearer than when participants discussed Ministry for Agriculture efforts to censor their brochure; they encouraged Grimm and other doctors to convince the ministry of the important connections of landscape preservation to health and economic productivity.[73]

Erholung and National Park Saxon Switzerland

The political debate over a proposed national park near Dresden reveals how this *Erholung* consensus became increasingly important over time. Local nature enthusiasts took the lead in promoting the park and drew on traditional homeland preservation rhetoric to make their case, but park proponents increasingly emphasized the importance of *Erholung* to counter the economic arguments against the park. Key promoters of the park included nature preservationists, landscape architects, biologists, and rock climbers.

From the outset, a proposal for a national park in the GDR faced formidable challenges. East Germany had an ambiguous relationship with national heritage. The new state's boundaries had no historical precedence, and the West German government refused to recognize the legitimacy of the new state—claiming that all East Germans belonged to a German nation represented internationally by the liberal capitalist West. East Germans emigrating to the West easily acquired West German citizenship, and the Federal Republic's constitution officially declared unification as a central goal. Moreover, communist leadership equated traditional German nationalism with fascism and labeled nature preservation as escapist romanticism. At best, the SED claimed to represent progressive German national traditions. A no less important factor was that national parks had little precedence in German history. A movement for establishing such parks had roots in the nineteenth century, but preservationists put more energy into establishing regional nature parks, because few areas within Germany seemed to fit the definition of a national park as established in the United States—that is, a large unpopulated area.[74]

Despite these obstacles, the national park proposal emerged in 1953. In cooperation with participants in the Landscape Diagnosis, landscape architects in Dresden from 1950 to 1954 had mapped sites eligible for nature protection and thus had begun thinking about how to best protect Saxon Switzerland.[75]

Erwin Winkler, chief of Dresden's Institute for Nature Protection and Monument Care, expressed hope in 1953 that the upcoming drafting of a nature protection law would pave the way for a national park.[76] In 1954, however, the ILN only proposed a tiny nature preserve along the Elbe River.[77] Prominent supporters of a national park, which would ensure higher standards of protection than typical landscape preserves, included Kurt Kretschmann and Reimar Gilsenbach, who constantly reminded authorities that other socialist countries already had national parks.[78]

The modest proposal became the focus of a passionate campaign led by locals steeped in the traditions of homeland preservation. Supporters included scientists from the technical university in Dresden, the State Museum for Geology in Dresden, and the local zoological institute.[79] Dr. Kurt Wiedemann, the head of Dresden's offices of reconstruction, received twenty-three letters from assorted local interests in support of the park, and the local press also gave their support.[80] Reflecting a push from below, the Dresden affiliates of the Kulturbund hinted at local frustrations with central authorities when they wrote to the DAL (the institutional home of the ILN) to ask for greater support for the national park.[81] Further reflecting local enthusiasm, hikers and mountaineers who were organized in Dresden's BSG Empor-Löbtau repeatedly promoted the park proposal, which would allow them nearly unlimited access to local cliff faces.[82] The club's *Yearbook for Tourism* prominently featured articles on nature protection and published Wiedemann's formal park proposal.[83]

A narrative of local Heimat enthusiasm crushed by centralized authority shaped later reflections on the SED's rejection of the national park. Kurt Kretschmann suggested that Meusel and the ILN actually hindered the park's success by failing to support local park proponents at crucial moments in 1954 and 1955.[84] Elsewhere, East German environmentalist Reimar Gilsenbach argued that Kretschmann led the national park effort while high-ranking nature preservationists (i.e., Meusel) cared too little to engage the SED and Walter Ulbricht on the issue.[85] Meusel, however, seemingly recognized that local enthusiasm when he insisted that local preservationists take a leading role in the planning, management, and naming of the park. He rejected, for example, Kretschmann's calculated suggestion to name the future park after Wilhelm Pieck, the president of the GDR.[86] Given the disputes between Meusel and Kretschmann, it is difficult to know how accurate Kretschmann's judgment of Meusel's role was. If nothing else, Gilsenbach and Kretschmann exaggerated the power that Meusel had to push through the national park proposal, given that Meusel himself endured attacks from the Ministry for Agriculture.

Regardless, the park campaign gained increasing recognition over the next year. On March 24, 1954, East German landscape architects, tourists, artists, geographers, and foresters gathered expectantly in Dresden to discuss plans for the national park and prepare a proposal for the government.[87] There, ILN representatives proposed to outlaw all industrial facilities, advertising, and bungalow structures within the planned boundaries. Even timber production would be limited. Within the boundaries, park administrators (designated by local officials) also would have the right to set aside *restricted areas*, off limits even to tourists.[88] Wiedemann insisted that the cut rate in the entire park not exceed growth rates and that harvests only be allowed in restricted areas when needed to fight fire or disease.[89] In a subsequent May 22 meeting in Bad Schandau, park supporters chose local landscape architect Otto Schweitzer to prepare a detailed plan of the parkland.[90] Park proponents desired an administration independent of the Ministry for Agriculture, to ensure "as great a protection of natural scenery as possible."[91]

Even if locals took the initial lead, the plans for the national park increasingly reflected the interests of planners inspired by the potential of central, scientific planning.[92] Wiedemann expressed a desire for comprehensive planning in the spirit of Lingner and Carl's Landscape Diagnosis (a comprehensive planning that, it should be noted, Meusel also advocated within the Ministry for Agriculture). Wiedemann believed that those "Nature Protection Laws are not good enough for the needs of our time and do much more for the [mere] preservation of what remains than for planning and designing [better landscapes]."[93] Both Wiedemann and Otto Schweitzer, the architect from Dresden's Institute for Regional Planning, contrasted their plans' landscape care and complex, holistic planning with the narrow interests of foresters.[94] To this end, Schweitzer prepared detailed studies of local climate, geology, and biology to establish the local forests' native species composition.[95]

Foresters recognized a clear threat to their harvest plans and intervened against park plans as early as April 1954. In their critique, they presented themselves as admirably progressive, while attacking park advocates as reactionary and unscientific hacks who threatened to undermine the building of socialism. One official insisted, "Our forest is an economic forest, which above all else serves the interests of the economy and only in a secondary fashion serves cultural needs."[96] Blame for any "forest devastation" rested entirely on the shoulders of the Nazis and their capitalist predecessors.[97] At the same time, foresters dismissed landscape care as irrational and ignorant of biological science. "[One only relies on the] absurd, amateurish opinion of leading figures in landscape design, landscape protection, and landscape architecture," one forester concluded, "if one promotes the adjustment of timber cutting for the retention of distinct landscape characteristics."[98] More concretely, the Ministry for Agriculture reprimanded the ILN for failing to notify foresters of their plans for a national park.[99] If the ILN failed to support the park in full, these interventions from the ministry were the reason.

In response, park supporters defended themselves by touting their progressive credentials and broadening the definition of economic planning to account for the contributions of *Erholung* to worker productivity. Otto Schweitzer praised the region as the premier *Erholung* landscape in the GDR.[100] Winkler prefaced proposals for the park by observing, "[W]orking people of the GDR want to find joy and *Erholung* in Saxon Switzerland and return to their workplaces healthy and satisfied with their adventures."[101] In his article for the BSG Empor-Löbtau's *Yearbook for Tourism*, Wiedemann repeatedly described the future national park as an *Erholung* landscape in the need of management.[102] Aesthetics, Wiedemann astutely argued, influenced economic performance by inspiring workers to greater productivity. Attractive forests allowed for a "brisk reproduction of our [state's] required manpower." He insisted, "The *Erholung* reserves that are contained in our beautiful landscape have an economic potential that cannot be underestimated."[103] Erwin Hartsch of the Geographical Institute at Karl Marx University in Leipzig agreed when he observed that beautiful landscapes could strengthen, conserve, and rejuvenate the productivity of workers.[104]

In the end, East Berlin scuttled the park proposal. By April 1955, the Kulturbund sounded quite pessimistic about the park's future and recommended that Dresden officials only designate a smaller landscape preserve.[105] The Nature Protection Law of 1954 allowed, in one key provision, for landscape preserves especially meant as recreation districts, where planners theoretically balanced recreation, farming, forestry, and industry.[106] In September 1956, Dresden officially established a landscape preserve, but this did not satisfy those who wanted a national park.[107] As Wiedemann described events later, economic goals prevented architects from establishing the more robust regulations associated with a national park.[108] Arguments for *Erholung*'s contribution to economic productivity failed to find any traction at a time of intense reconstruction. Nonetheless, proponents still relied on *Erholung* as a justification for reform in their continued, if less vigorous, campaign to convince authorities of the park's necessity.[109]

Of course, such attempts at compromise with economic planners were not unique to the GDR in this time period. A similar evolution took place in West Germany, as conservation interests also encountered an economic environment hostile to their concerns. According to historian Sandra Chaney, conservationists in the Federal Republic of Germany struggled in a political climate where political leaders promised a society of abundance and feverishly rebuilt to accommodate an increased population. West German conservationists also increasingly worked with regional planners to tie *Erholung* to landscape-scale planning.[110] Nonetheless, the discussion of recreation and landscape care evolved very differently in West Germany. Conservationists there operated in a state that actively reversed centralization and devolved many planning decisions to federal states. In addition, West Germany's democracy allowed for a greater range of conservation approaches than were available in the East while GDR economic planners easily censored unwanted critics, as this chapter revealed. In contrast to West Germany, *Erholung* became the only politically acceptable foundation in East Germany for promoting conservation to authorities.

Despite one West German journalist's efforts to argue otherwise, the proposed national park in Saxony was much more than a symbol of the SED's totalitarian ambitions. Instead, the debate over the park revealed a reformist rhetoric that combined an authoritarian desire for social and economic control with doubts about the SED's ability to plan land use for long-term sustainability. Reformers intended to use the resources of the central state to plan society holistically—insuring productive behavior and improved public health. They imagined a utopia with optimistic, socially well-adjusted citizens with excellent minds and bodies nurtured by protected landscapes. Even the bitter feuds between Meusel, Lingner, Pniower, and Kretschmann reveal as much about the willingness of individuals to cast their fate with the SED as they tell us about repression of nature protection (which they do). Historian Nikola Knoth concludes that the regime, after some initial acceptance of conservation, mostly ignored proposals to reform landscape planning.[111] While she is correct, I emphasize here that these reformers were more than just a historical footnote. While the national park proposal failed, the history of East German conservation did not end in silence even before it had a chance to begin. Battered by "witch hunts" initiated by agricultural planners, landscape architects took the SED's tentative public statements about *Erholung* and leisure, embellished them, and, in turn, pressed the regime to make them essential doctrine. An *Erholung* argument could pose a threat to entrenched powers, especially as broad coalitions emerged around *Erholung* and landscape protection. Foresters, made nervous about being left out of discussions for so long, appeared genuinely worried that the park movement had an opportunity to influence land-use policy. Drawing on social hygiene and eugenics in creative ways, the nature enthusiasts established a reformist, if not antiestablishment, consensus often adopted in the following thirty years by doctors, biologists, architects, and even vacationers to criticize the status quo in leisure and environmental policy. The grumbling about East Germany's environment in the 1960s and 1970s discussed in later chapters thus took its cues and its vocabulary from a discourse established in the 1950s.

NOTES

1. Christoph Beekh, "Auf der Bastei steht man Schlange: Sächsische Schweiz soll 'Nationalpark' werden," *Die neue Zeitung*, July 11, 1954.
2. See Nelson (2005).
3. On SED policies on production and consumption, see Landsman (2005). On the Stasi, see Gary Bruce, *The Firm: The Inside Story of the Stasi* (Oxford: Oxford University Press, 2010). On reactions to West German consumer culture, see Poiger (2000); Mark Fenemore, *Sex, Thugs, and Rock 'n' Roll: Teenage Rebels in Cold-War East Germany* (New York: Berghahn Books, 2007).
4. Scott (1998).
5. See Blackbourn (2006); Andreas Dix, "Nach dem Ende der 'Tausend Jahre': Landschaftsplanung in der Sowjetischen Besatzungszone und frühen DDR," in Radkau and Uekötter (2003), 354.
6. See Axel Zutz, "Die Landschaftsdiagnose der DDR: Reinhold Lingner und Frank Erich Carl," *Garten und Landschaft* 3 (March 2003): 34–38. In a critique of Dix, Zutz writes, "'No differences in the planned measures,' argued Dr. Andreas Dix decisively." Zutz added that Dix "analogously described the investigations into landscape rehabilitation and development . . . , as well as the Landscape Diagnosis initiated by Lingner with his friend and colleague (and former prisoner-of-war) Frank Erich Carl, as the eventual realization of a centralized state's power fantasies. Such an attribution of National Socialist planning tendencies not only ignores the indignities, persecution, and career bans suffered by Lingner and Pniower under the Third Reich. They are also similar in tone to the 1951 assessment recorded in a note by a member of the Central Commission for State Control of the DDR." Finally, Zutz asks "What was the Landscape Diagnosis? Who organized it and what were its goals? Was the Landscape Diagnosis in fact a project that shared planning ideals with the National Socialists?" Zutz here somewhat misrepresents Dix's argument, as Dix did not argue that East German and Nazi planning had the exact same goals, but that they shared a desire for authoritarian centralized control and envisioned a total reworking of the landscape. Nonetheless, Zutz rightly questions any lumping together of the two dictatorships and usefully highlights the complexities at play here, as planning under the two regimes evolved in very different circumstances.
7. Uekötter (2006), 8. The following overview of conservation, especially under Nazism, owes a debt to Lekan (2004), J. Williams (2007), and Charles Closmann, "Legalizing a Volksgemeinschaft: Nazi Germany's Reich Nature Protection Law of 1935," in Brüggemeier, Cioc, and Zeller (2005), 18–42, as well as to the numerous other essays in Brüggemeier, Cioc, and Zeller (2005) and Radkau and Uekötter (2003).

8. Uekötter (2006), 196–97.

9. J. Williams (2007), 227.

10. Rollins (1997). See also J. Williams (2007), 223.

11. Lekan (2004), 101.

12. Lekan (2004), 123; on landscape care, see 99–152.

13. Lekan (2004), 130–42. On social hygiene and eugenics in Germany, see note 31 in the introduction.

14. Conevery Bolton Valencius, *The Health of the Country: How American Settlers Understood Themselves and Their Land* (New York: Basic Books, 2002); Gregg Mitman, *Breathing Space: How Allergies Shape Our Lives and Landscapes* (New Haven: Yale University Press, 2007); Gregg Mitman, "In Search of Health: Landscape and Disease in American Environmental History," *Environmental History* 10, no. 2 (April 2005): 184–210.

15. Mitman (2005), 187.

16. Weindling (1989); Linda Lorraine Nash, *Inescapable Ecologies: A History of Environment, Disease, and Knowledge* (Berkeley: University of California Press, 2006); Chad Ross, *Naked Germany: Health, Race, and the Nation* (Oxford: Berg, 2005), 81–82; Michael Hau, *The Cult of Health and Beauty in Germany: A Social History, 1890–1930* (Chicago: University of Chicago Press, 2003).

17. On the Reich Conservation Law of 1935, see J. Williams (2007); Lekan (2004); Closmann (2006). On local enforcement of conservation law; see Uekötter (2006), especially 143–45.

18. Uekötter (2006), 15.

19. Lekan (2004), 204–51; Thomas Lekan, "Regionalism and the Politics of Landscape Preservation in the Third Reich," *Environmental History* 4, no. 3 (July 1999): 384–404. On *Dauerwald*, see Uekötter (2006), 70–72.

20. Uekötter (2006), 141–57. See also Thomas Zeller (2000); Gröning and Wolschke-Bulmahn (1986); Gröning (1996).

21. See Lekan (2004); Zeller (2000); Gröning and Wolschke-Bulmahn (1986); Gröning (1996).

22. "Erfurt," November 13, 1951, BArch: DKI 3752. On the 1954 law, see Karl Kneschke, "Begründung des Gesetzes zur Erhaltung und Pflege der heimatlichen Natur," *Natur und Heimat* 3 (1954): 300; Hermann Behrens, "Die ersten Jahre—Naturschutz und Landschaftspflege in der SBZ/DDR von 1945 bis Anfang der 60er Jahre," in Auster (2001), 15–86.

23. Letter from Reimar Gilsenbach to Schulmeister, October 31, 1962, SAPMO-BArch: DY27 308.

24. On the ILN and the DAL, see Hermann Behrens, "Das Institut für Landesforschung und Naturschutz (ILN) und die Biologischen Stationen," and Ludwig Bauer, "Zur Arbeit der Sektion Landeskultur und Naturschutz der Akademie der Landwirtschaftswissenschaften," in Behrens and Hoffmann (2007), 68–72, 63–67.

25. See Dix (2003). See also Zutz, *Garten und Landschaft* (2003); Frank Erich Carl, "In Memoriam Reinhold Lingner," *Deutsche Gartenarchitektur* 9, no. 2 (1968): 35–38; Kerstin Nowak, "Errinerung an Reinhold Lingner: Pionier der Landschaftsdiagnose," *Garten und Landschaft: Zeitschrift für Landschaftsarchitektur* 9 (1991): 7–8; Peter Fibich and Joachim Wolschke-Bulmann, "Planungsideen des Wiederaufbaus: Der Tier-

gartenstreit zwischen Reinhold Lingner und Walter Rossow," *Garten und Landschaft* 3 (2003): 26–30; Olaf Hiller, ed., *Die Landschaftsdiagnose der DDR: Zeitgeschichte und Wirkung eines Forschungsprojekts aus der Gründungsphase der DDR* (Berlin: Technische Universität Berlin, 2002). For a short biographical sketch of Carl and Lingner, see "Biographen," *Garten und Landschaft* 3 (2003): 30. For a longer biography, see Johann Greiner, "Frank Erich Carl—Mitautor der Landschaftsdiagnose der DDR," in Hiller (2002), 131–36.

26. Zutz's observation here comes from the text just before note 25 of his longer version of his article "Die Landschaftsdiagnose der DDR" (2003 online) posted on the website for *Garten und Landschaft,* accessed August 31, 2004, http://www.garten-landschaft.de. As of 2013, the longer version can no longer be found on the website.

27. BArch: DK107 77/12; "Mitarbeiter der Arbeitsgruppe Naturschutz der DAL zu Berlin," February 4, 1957, BArch: DK107 25/13; "SKLN Mitglieder," August 8, 1966, BArch: DK107 64/85. Dr. Ludwig Bauer was the head of the ILN's research station in Jena and would later become director of the ILN. Prof. Dr. Jordan led the Dresden research station and played a key role in agitating for a national park in Saxon Switzerland. Others participating in the DAL included Kurt Kretschmann and Prof. Dr. Alexis Scamoni, a forester at Eberswalde. In the SKLN, participants included Werner Bauch, a landscape architect from Dresden; Prof. Dr. Hans Grimm, a social hygienist and director of the Institute for Anthropology at Humboldt University; Dr. Hugo Weinitschke from the ILN, leader of the Kulturbund's Natur und Heimatfreunde; Fritz Wernicke of the Staatliches Komitte für Forstwirtschaft beim Landwirtschaftsrat der DDR; and Prof. Dr. Ernst Neef, a geographer from the Dresden University of Technology. These men came from various political backgrounds, with some not members of any party. SED members included Meusel, Bauer, and Weinitschke.

28. Behrens (1997), 147. Olaf Hiller, "Daten und Fakten zum Ablauf, zur Unterbrechung und Wiederaufnahme des Forschungsauftrages Landschaftsdiagnose der fünf Länder der DDR," in Hiller (2002), 83–84.

29. Reinhold Lingner and Frank Erich Carl, *Landschaftsdiagnose der DDR* (Berlin: VEB Verlag Technik, 1957). Participating landscape architects included Werner Bauch in Saxony, Martin Ehlers for Mecklenburg, Hermann Göritz for Brandenburg, Otto Rindt for Sachsen-Anhalt, and Rudolf Ungewitter for Thuringia (later replaced by geographer Dr. Ruth Günter after Ungewitter fled to the West). Bauch, Göritz, Rindt, und Ungewitter were "landscape advocates" before 1945, and Bauch apparently participated in planning for the city of Auschwitz during the war. Bauch, Ungewitter, and Ehlers were members of the National Socialist German Workers Party (NSDAP), and Rindt was a member of the Sturmabteilung (SA). Göritz belonged to the German Communist Party (KPD) from 1931 to 1933 but dropped his membership and became a candidate for membership in the NSDAP.

30. For more on landscape planning in the GDR, see Zutz, *Garten und Landschaft* (2003); Knoth, "Eine 'grüne' SED?"(1993); Behrens (1997); Irmela Wübbe, "Landschaftsplanung in der DDR," and Hermann Behrens, "Landschaft und Planung in der SBZ/DDR bis 1961 unter besonderer Berücksichtigung der 'Landschaftsdiagnose der DDR,'" in Auster and Behrens (1999), 33–56, 57–86. In addition, Hermann Behrens, "Landeskultur als Naturgeschehen auf höherer Ebene: Georg Bela Pniower (1896–1960) und der Naturschutz," in Kreuter (2003), 227–44.

31. Grimm, "Natur und Landschaftsschutz dient der Volksgesundheit," *Naturschutz und Volksgesundheit*, 5, BArch: DK 107 77/30.

32. Ibid.

33. Meusel also was a member of the Kulturbund, as well as director of the Institute for Systematic Botany and Biogeography and the Botanical Garden at the Martin Luther University in Halle. See E. Jäger and E. G. Mahn, "Hermann Meusel—ein Nachruf," *Hercynia* 30 (1997): 153–54; K. H. Grosser, "Professor Hermann Meusel zum Gedenken," *Naturschutz und Landschaftspflege in Brandenburg* 3 (1997): 109; http://people.wku.edu/charles.smith/chronob/MEUS1909.htm (accessed June 1, 2010); Erich Hübl, "In memoriam Hermann Meusel," *Verhandlungen der Zoologisch-Botanischen Gesellschaft in Österreich* 135 (1998): 381–84.

34. See Zutz (2003 online), especially the text between notes 22 and 25. See also, Reinhold Lingner, *Landschaftsgestaltung* (Berlin: Kulturbund, 1952); Hermann Behrens, "Das gesellschaftliche Umfeld der Landschaftsdiagnose und ihre Bedeutung aus der Sicht angrenzender Fachgebiete," in Hiller (2002), 51–71.

35. See Zutz (2003 online), text between notes 17 and 20. For more on ideas about holistic ecosystems or landscape "organisms," see Donald Worster, *Nature's Economy: A History of Ecological Ideas* (Cambridge: Cambridge University Press, 1994).

36. Otto Möller, *Die Umgestaltung der Natur in der Sowjetunion* (Berlin: Verlag der Nation, 1952).

37. Hiller (2002), 84–85, 92.

38. Hiller (2002), 86–87.

39. Hiller (2002), 88. See Zutz (2003 online); the quote comes from the text just before note 28.

40. Zutz (2003 online); the quote comes from the text just before note 91. Zutz also discusses the Nazi past of architects and how that affected the project (text between notes 29 and 40).

41. Hiller (2002), 93.

42. Hermann Meusel,"Bericht des ILN über Schwierigkeiten bei der Pflege von Schutzgebieten," no date, and Letter from Stubbe (DAL) to Minister Grüneberg, ZK der SED, August 23, 1962, BArch: DK107 A154/101.

43. DAL, "Denkschrift der DAL zu Berlin über die Erhaltung der Naturschutzgebiete und die Verbesserung der Arbeit der Naturschutzverwaltung," March 1955, BArch: DK107 25/13. There is a similar later complaint in Letter from Hermann Meusel to Staatliches Komitee für Forstwirtschaft, Zentale Naturschutzverwaltung, December 30, 1966, BArch: DK107 A154/180.

44. Sektion Landeskultur und Naturschutz (DAL), "Kurzbericht über die 1 Sitzung 1956 der AG Naturschutz am 9.2.1956," February 28, 1956, BArch: DK107 A132/1; "Stenoaufzeichnungen zur Sitzung der AG Naturschutz (DAL) am 3. Mai 1956," May 3, 1956, and Natur und Heimatfreunde, DKB, "Resolution," June 5, 1956, BArch: DK107 25/13.

45. "Stenoaufzeichnungen zur Sitzung der AG Naturschutz (DAL) am 3. Mai 1956," May 3, 1956, BArch: DK107 25/13; Sektion Landeskultur und Naturschutz (DAL), "Kurzbericht über die Verbindung mit der AG Naturschutz der DAW am 3.5.1956," June 4, 1956, DK107 A132/1; Hermann Meusel, "Stenoaufzeichnungen über die Diskussion betr. Bezeichnung der Sektion, der Abt. von Herrn Henkel und der Abt. in der

Bezirks und Kreisebne auf der Sektionssitzung am 22.11.1956," December 3, 1956, BArch: DK107 25/4.

46. The ministry published its own growth-oriented guidelines for nature protection, to the dissatisfaction of the ILN. For various drafts of these guidelines, see BArch: DK1 1039 and DK1 3754, as well as Ministry for Agriculture and Forestry, "Bemerkungen des Genossen Erich Mückenberger zur Konzeption über den Naturschutz," September 9, 1958, BArch: DK1 10288. Complaints about these guidelines can found in Letter from Dr. Schwarz to Schult, ZK der SED, Abt. Landwirtschaft, August 25, 1958, BArch: DK107 77/30.

47. Generally, the ILN organized its research regionally. See, for example, ILN Dresden, "Protokoll einer Besichtigungsfahrt mehrerer Erzgebirgsmoore zwecks Überprüfung auf deren wissenschaftlichen Wert bzw. Festellung der weiteren Schutzwürdigkeit," June 29, 1955, BArch: DK1 10290; Letter from Hermann Meusel to Präsidium der DAL, March 18, 1954, BArch: DK107 77/12.

48. Ministry for Agriculture and Forestry, "Anlage 1, Richtlinien des Naturschutzes," September 28, 1958, 1–4, BArch: DK1 1039.

49. Behrens, "Landeskultur als Naturgeschehen auf höherer Ebene" (2003). See also Behrens, "Naturschutz und Landeskultur in der Sowjetischen Besatzungszone und in der DDR. Ein historischer Überblick," in Bayerl and Meyer (2003), 221–22.

50. Zutz (2003 online); his discussion of Wiedemann is at note 72. See also Zutz (2002), 113.

51. Pniower, quoted in Axel Zutz, "'Kranke' und 'gesunde' Landschaft—Anmerkungen zur Kritik des Landschaftsbegriffs bei der Landschaftsdiagnose," in Hiller (2002), 112. See also Fibich and Wolschke-Bulmahn (2003), 26–30.

52. Georg Pniower, "Bemerkungen zur Problematik der Landeskultur," March 1956, 27, BArch: DK107 25/13. For background on Pniower, see Behrens, "Landeskultur als Naturgeschehen auf höherer Ebene" (2003), as well as Klaus-Dietrich Gandert, "Georg Bela Pniower—sein Leben und Wirken für die Garten- und Landeskultur," in Auster and Behrens (1999), 221–35.

53. Georg Pniower, "Abschrift: Verlesung von Herrn Bickerich auf der zentralen Tagung des Naturschutzes am 13.9.1953," September 13, 1953, BArch: DK107 77/12.

54. Behrens, "Landeskultur als Naturgeschehen auf höherer Ebene" (2003), 244.

55. Hiller (2002), 87.

56. Georg Pniower, "Bemerkungen zur Problematik der Landeskultur," March 1956, 8, BArch: DK107 25/13.

57. Reimar Gilsenbach, "Die größte DDR der Welt—ein Staat ohne Nationalparke: Des Merkens Würdiges aus meiner grünen Donquichotterie," in Auster (2001), 533–46. This view also appears in Markus Rösler, "Nationalparkinitiativen in der DDR bis zur Wende 1989," in Auster and Behrens (1999), 549.

58. For example, Kretschmann, "Bericht über die Lage des Naturschutzes innerhalb der Landschaftsgestaltung," December 11, 1951, BArch: DK1 3752; Letter from Kretschmann to Herrn Bergner, September 6, 1958, BArch: DK1 10288.

59. Ministerium für Land- und Forstwirtschaft (hereinafter MLF), "Die Aufgaben des Naturschutzes beim Aufbau des Sozialismus," July 10, 1958, BArch: DK1 3754.

60. See Letter from Kretschmann to the ZK der SED, Abt. Landwirtschaft, December 1, 1957, BArch: DK1 1039. See also Kretschmann, "Entwurf für den in MLF vorge-

sehenen Beirat für Naturschutz, Betr: Grundlagen für die politische und organisatorische Zielsetzung im Naturschutz der DDR," December 1958, BArch: DKı 3754. Kretschmann proposed the creation of his own nature protection association, where 60 percent of its executives would be party members. See Letter from Kretschmann to Seidel, MLF, Abt. Pflanzliche Produktion, May 22, 1958, BArch: DK 1 10288.

61. Letter from Franz Mellentin, ZK der SED to Hans Reichelt, MLF, July 1, 1958, BArch: DKı 1039.

62. MLF, "Kurzprotokoll über die Parteileitungssitzung am 22.1.1958 der HA III (Pfl Prod)," January 22, 1958, BArch: DKı 10288.

63. "Versuche einer Definition 'Sozialistisches Landeskultur' sowie 'Natürlicher Lebensraum,'" Prognossegruppe "Abprodukte und sozialistische Landeskultur," March 4, 1968, BArch: DC20 19122.

64. Carl (1960); Auster (1996), 43–45.

65. See Lekan (2004).

66. Lingner and Carl (1957), 144.

67. "Protokoll über die gemeinsame Sitzung der Sektion Landeskultur und Naturschutz der DAL, der Sektion Biologie und der Sektion Hygiene der DAW am 14.5.1958," BArch: DK 107 A132/1.

68. Frank Erich Carl, *Erholungswesen und Landschaft: Ein Beitrag zur Planung der Ferienerholung in der DDR* (Berlin: Sektion Städtebau und Architektur, Schriftenreihe Gebiets-, Stadt- und Dorfplanung, 1960); "Referat des Landschaftsarchitekten F. E. Carl, DBA, gelegentlich einer von der Staatliche Plankommission in Gemeinschaft mit dem FDGB und der Deutschen Bauakademie einberufenen Arbeittagung zur Erörterung von Problemen der Landschaftsplanung in Beziehung zum Erholungswesen," January 30, 1959, 9–12, SAPMO-BArch: DY34 3301. See also Johann Greiner, "Planung von Erholungsgebieten im Institut für Städtebau der Bauakademie," in Hiller (2002), 243–46.

69. Zutz (2003 online); his discussion of *Erholung* is at note 59.

70. Carl (1960), 41. The quote comes from H. Grimm, "Volksgesundheit in ihrer Abhängigkeit von Natur und Landschaftsschutz," *Sonderdruck aus der Zeitschrift für die gesamte Hygiene und ihre Grenzgebiete* 4, no. 3/4 (1959): 134.

71. On the creation of these landscape preserves, see BArch: DK107 77/12. See also Auster (1999), 445–47.

72. "Resolution der Hygiene Tag," Juli 1957, BArch: DK 107 77/30.

73. Prof. Dr. Hans Grimm, "Referat auf Naturschutzwoche," 14 May 1958, and "Stenoaufzeichnungen der gemeinsamen Sitzung der Sektion Landeskultur und Naturschutz der DAL, Sektion Biologie und Sektion Hygiene der DAW unter dem Thema 'Naturschutz und Volksgesundheit' am 14.5.1958," May 16, 1958, BArch: DK 107 77/30. See also "Protokoll über die gemeinsame Sitzung der Sektion Landeskultur und Naturschutz der DAL, der Sektion Biologie und der Sektion Hygiene der DAW am 14.5.1958," June 5, 1958, BArch: DK 107 A132/1.

74. Sandra Chaney, "Protecting Nature in a Divided Nation: Conservation in the Two Germanys, 1945–1972," in *Germany's Nature: Cultural Landscapes and Environmental History*, ed. Thomas Lekan and Thomas Zeller (New Brunswick, N.J.: Rutgers University Press, 2005), 220–43. For more on the role of national parks in German history, see Lekan (2003).

75. Otto Schweitzer, "Über Landschaftsplanungen in der Sächsische Schweiz," in *Berichte des Arbeitskreises zur Erforschung der Sächsische Schweiz in der Geographischen Gesellschaft der DDR (Sektion Dresden)* (Pirna: Rat der Kreis Pirna, 1963), 120.

76. Naturschutzbeauftragter Winkler, "Bericht über die Naturschutzarbeit im Bezirk Dresden," November 11, 1953, and "Bericht über die Naturschutz Tagung im Bezirk Dresden am 29.10.53," November 1, 1953, BArch: DK107 39/23.

77. Letter from Kretschmann to the Kulturbund, Frau Dr. Noack, January 5, 1954, BArch: DK107 77/12.

78. Gilsenbach (2001), 533–46.

79. Letter from Kulturbund, Bezirksleitung Dresden, Thümmler, to the DAL, March 26, 1955, BArch: DK107 77/47.

80. Gerhard Aust, "Gründung einer Naturkundlichen Arbeitsgemeinschaft," in *Jahrbuch für Touristik 1954* (Dresden: BSG Empor-Löbtau, 1954), 95; Kurt Wiedemann, "Die 'Sächsische Schweiz' als Künftiger Nationalpark der Deutschen," *Jahrbuch für Touristik 1955/1956* (Dresden: BSG Empor-Löbtau, 1956), 11.

81. Letter from Kulturbund, Bezirksleitung Dresden, Thümmler, the DAL, March 26, 1955, BArch: DK107 77/47.

82. Anlage 3, Entwurf, "Verordnung über die Errichtung des Nationalparkes 'Sächsische Schweiz'" 1955, BArch: DK107 77/47.

83. In addition to Wiedemann in the *Jahrbuch für Touristik 1955/1956*, see Gerhard Aust, "Informationsfahrt für Naturkunde und Jugendherbergswesen am 4. April 1954," in *Jahrbuch für Touristik 1954*, 94–95; Dieter Klotzsch, "Aus der Tätigkeit des 'Arbeitskreises zur Erforschung der Sächsische Schweiz," *Wandern und Bergsteigen* 7 (1966), 3; Erich Drechsel, "Darum Naturschutz," in *Jahrbuch für Touristik 1954*, 33–35.

84. Gilsenbach (2001), 534.

85. Gilsenbach (2001), 536.

86. Letter from Kretschmann to Dr. Meusel, ILN, April 2, 1954, and Letter from Meusel to Kreschmann, April 13, 1954, BArch: DK107 77/47.

87. Letter from ILN Halle to the head of the Staatlichen Forstwirtschaftsbetriebe im Bezirk Dresden, March 20, 1954, Sächsisches Hauptstaatsarchiv Dresden (hereinafter SäStArchD): Rat der Bezirkung (hereinafter RdB) 4811; Gilsenbach (2001), 536.

88. "Entwurf: Verordnung über die Errichtung des Nationalparks 'Sächsisches Schweiz,' 1954, SäStArchD: RdB 4811.

89. Wiedemann (1956), 28. See also "Bericht über die Naturschutztagung zur Einrichtung des Nationalparkes Sächsisches Schweiz am 3/24/1954 in Dresden Botanisches Institut," April 9, 1954, SäStArchD: RdB 4811.

90. Otto Schweitzer, "Aufgabenstellung," *Landschaftsraum Nationalpark Sächsisches Schweiz*, December 1954, 3, SäStArchD: Büro für Territorialplanung (hereinafter BfT) 20.

91. "Anlage 2: Durchführungsbestimmungen zur Verordnung vom . . . 1955 über die Errichtung des Nationalparkes Sächsische Schweiz" and "Anlage 3, Entwurf, Verordnung über die Errichtung des Nationalparkes 'Sächsische Schweiz' Vom . . . 1955," March 26, 1955. See also Wiedemann, "Anlage 6: Betr: Nationalpark 'Sächsische Schweiz' (gekürzt)," and Erwin Hartsch, Geogr Institut, "Anlage 9," March 26, 1955. All are in BArch: DK107 77/47.

92. Schweitzer, "Bericht über die 2 Arbeitstagung für Naturschutz," January 20–21, 1954, BArch: DK107 39/23.

93. Wiedemann (1956), 11.

94. Otto Schweitzer, "Aufgabenstellung," in *Landschaftsraum Nationalpark Sächsiches Schweiz*, December 1954, 13, SäStArchD: BfT 20; "Stenoaufzeichnungen über die gemeinsame Tagung des Instituts für Landesforschung und Naturschutz Halle/Saale und des KB in Leipzig am 28/29 August 1956 unter dem Motto: Naturschutz in Industrielandschaften," September 6, 1956, BArch: DK107 25/13; "Bericht über die Naturschutztagung zur Einrichtung des Nationalparkes Sächsisches Schweiz am 3/24/1954 in Dresden Botanisches Institut," April 9, 1954, SäStArchD: RdB 4811.

95. Otto Schweitzer, "Flora und Fauna," and "Erläuterungen zum Plan Nr. 6107/7—Flächenstruktur," in *Landschaftsraum Nationalpark Sächsiches Schweiz*, December 1954, 19, 22, SäStArchD: BfT 20.

96. Letter from Verwaltungsleitung Staatliche Forswirtschaftsbetriebe (hereinafter VStFB), Bezirk Dresden, Planung III/54 to the Verwaltungsleitung der VStFB Bezirk Dresden, "Betr: Stellungnahme zur Frage S. Schweiz/Auseinandersetzung mit dem Koll. Miedtank, RdB Dresden, Ref. Landschaftsschutz," April 21, 1954, SäStArchD: RdB 4811.

97. Verwaltungsleiter, VStFB, "Kurzreferat 'forstliche Aufgaben' bei der Errichtung des Nationalparkes S. Schweiz," May 21, 1954, SäStArchD: RdB 4811.

98. Letter from VStFB, Bezirk Dresden, Planung III/54 to the Verwaltungsleitung der VStFB Bezirk Dresden, "Betr: Stellungnahme zur Frage S. Schweiz/Auseinandersetzung mit dem Koll. Miedtank, RdB Dresden, Ref. Landschaftsschutz," April 23, 1954, SäStArchD: RdB 4811.

99. Letter from MLF to the VStFB Dresden, "Betr: Nationalpark S. Schweiz," April 22, 1954, SäStArchD: RdB 4811.

100. Otto Schweitzer, "Vorwort," in *Landschaftsraum Nationalpark Sächsisches Schweiz*, December 1954, 2, SäStArchD: BfT 20.

101. Erwin Winkler, "Anlage 1: Begründung zum Entwurf einer Verordnung über die Errichtung des Nationalparks 'Sächsische Schweiz,'" March 26, 1966, BArch: DK107 77/47.

102. Wiedemann (1956), 11.

103. Wiedemann (1956), 28.

104. Erwin Hartsch, "Anlage 9," March 26, 1955, BArch: DK107 77/47.

105. "Beschlussprotokoll der Sitzung des Zentral Fachausschusses 'Natur und Landschaftsschutz' am 16.4.1955," April 16, 1955, SAPMO-BArch: DY27 3172.

106. Irmela Wübbe, *Landschaftsplanung in der DDR: Aufgabenfelder, Handlungsmöglichkeiten und Restriktionen in der DDR der sechziger und siebziger Jahre* (Bonn: Bund Deutscher Landschaftsarchitekten, 1995), 53.

107. Erwin Winkler, "Anlage 1: Begründung zum Entwurf einer Verordnung über die Errichtung des Nationalparks 'Sachsische Schweiz' (Elbsandsteingeb.)," March 26, 1966, BArch: DK107 77/47.

108. Wiedemann, "Die Erholungsgebietsplanung Sächsische Schweiz," March 15, 1960, SäStArchD: BfT 22.

109. Between 1957 and 1962, members of the Working Circle for Research on Saxon Switzerland met sixty-eight times. See Arbeitskreis zur Erforschung der S. Schweiz in

der Geographischen Gesellschaft, "Analyse der Tätigkeit des Arbeitskreises S. Schweiz, 1957–1962," SäStArchD: BfT 22; Hans Prescher, "Der Arbeitskreis zur Erforschung der S. Schweiz in der geographischen Gesellschaft der DDR Stadt Wehlen, seine Entstehung, seine Arbeiten und Ziele," in *Berichte des Arbeitskreises zur Erforschung der S. Schweiz in der Geographischen Gesellschaft der DDR (Sektion Dresden)* (Pirna: Rat des Kreises Pirna, 1963); Dieter Klotzsch, BSG Empor-Löbtau, "Aus der Tätigkeit des 'Arbeitskreises zur Erforschung der S. Schweiz,'" *Wandern und Bergsteigen* 7 (1966): 3. Architects also continued planning, as seen in Otto Schweitzer, "Pläne zum Landschaftsraum S. Schweiz," SäStArchD: BfT 21; Otto Schweitzer, "Gutachten über landschaftsgestalterische städte und dorfbauliche Massnahmen im geplanten Nationalpark Sächsische Schweiz," December 1956, SäStArchD: BfT 20.

110. See Jens Ivo Engels, "Hohe Zeit und dicker Strich: Vergangenheitsdeutung und -bewahrung im westdeutschen Naturschutz nach dem Zweiten Weltkrieg," and Stefan Körner, "Kontinuum und Bruch: Die Transformation des naturschützerischen Aufgabenverständnisses nach dem Zweiten Weltkrieg," in Radkau and Uekötter (2003), 363–404, 405–34; Engels (2006); Chaney (2008).

111. Knoth, "Eine 'grüne' SED?" (1993), 75.

CHAPTER 3

Making Rough Nature More Comfortable: Camping in East Germany

In the 1970s as the GDR reached the end of its third decade, a state publishing company printed a series of East German postcards that featured scenes from bungalow colonies and campgrounds. Images of lakeshores and rolling hill country included Trabant automobiles, motorcycles, and tents nestled in a meadow or hidden in a small grove of trees. In these postcard images, the countryside appeared to be a comforting, if slightly chaotic, world of consumer happiness and private leisure.[1] While these images remained silent about the frustrating realities of shortages in food and consumer goods, they portrayed an ideal leisure landscape as imagined by many East German vacationers and endorsed by the regime.

Authorities, however, had originally condemned and sometimes outlawed such scenes. The SED had hoped to centralize the countryside into a "readable" space where citizens could be coordinated and mobilized toward the building of socialism. East Germany, as both the SED and the "conservation bloc" originally agreed, needed to nurture a community of austerity, citizen obligations, and heroic struggle untainted by frivolous consumerism. As the first section of this chapter will show, many conservationists still hoped for the countryside to be a space apart where citizens would "rough it" or productively improve themselves. In the 1960s, the proliferation of campgrounds, recreation equipment, and crowded resorts threatened these visions of an orderly countryside. Congregations of tourists around portable radios, grills, and beer coolers challenged the conservation bloc's image of unspoiled landscapes where tourists hiked or studied nature, even as they hinted, in the eyes of the SED, at a "bourgeois" subculture paying little heed to the building of socialism. These postcard images thus raise important questions about when and how state imperatives shaped popular leisure.[2]

Many commentators on camping and outdoor recreation in the GDR have suggested that the campgrounds and cottages featured in those postcards represented spaces of political resistance or apolitical escapism. At minimum, some suggest, East Germans pursued individual desires and even subversive practices only partially touched by state domination.[3] Other observers have gone further. Judith Kruse, in an essay on East German camping culture, tells the story of one tight-knit community organized unofficially (and illegally) as the "Crazy Camping Crew (CCC)."[4] As Kruse describes them, members hoped to escape the "coercion of the collective" and carve out independent social and political space for at least one or two weeks every year.[5] Martin Bütow suggests that campers chose their vacation styles for political reasons. He remembers sharp political discussions around a campfire and writes, "Not that one encountered outspoken dissidents in East German campgrounds, but the choice of a more individualistic, free form of vacation often reflected a certain philosophical, intellectual background."[6] Other scholars emphasize the apolitical escapism of camping enthusiasts living in communist states. Campgrounds, bungalow colonies, and community gardens marked a *Nischengesellschaft*, or "niche society," where an old-fashioned, even "petit bourgeois" culture survived relatively untouched by "real existing socialism."[7] According to Günter Gaus, who first considered the meaning of a "niche society," the GDR achieved political stability because many citizens withdrew "into the private sphere" and preoccupied themselves with the fulfillment of personal desires.[8] In all of these observations, the state and society remained apart, with society scurrying out of the sight of the powerful regime or with authorities masterfully manipulating consumer desires to gain political legitimacy.

This chapter argues instead that the countryside must be reconsidered as a space intertwined with and transformed by postwar economic, political, and social changes, rather than as a space apart, an escape into the past, or the last refuge of an untrammeled Heimat. Outdoor enthusiasts were not necessarily outsiders clinging to a sepia-toned past. East German campgrounds should be understood as hybrid spaces—distinct but profoundly shaped by larger social and political transformations. When moving through the countryside, vacationers encountered a tourist infrastructure that was both intentional and unintentional—a product of official policy (official leisure organizations, consumer goods policies, state resorts, the encouragement of athletics, and productivity during vacations) as well as of technological and environmental change only partially controlled or understood by the regime (expansion of automobile ownership, new consumer goods, pollution, overcrowding, and social welfare benefits). The campground was as much a creation of the SED and its postwar political and economic system as Berlin's avenues, reconstructed Dresden, or a *Plattenbau* apartment (a prefabricated, often high-rise building).

Despite Marxism's aversion to consumerism as the pursuit of false needs, consumer goods played a key role in the history of the SED, its vision of socialist modernism, and its struggles for political legitimacy. From the founding of the GDR, the regime celebrated socialist modernism as an opportunity to create a workers' paradise through technology, science, and planning.[9] Economic policy still remained wedded to heavy industry and the production of investment goods, but the uprising of 1953 set off alarm bells among East German leaders as they realized that they had to better provide consumer goods in order to maintain political legitimacy. In 1958, the SED identified its "Main Economic Task" as surpassing West Germany in the consumption of both food and durable consumer goods such as televisions, washing machines, and automobiles. In that same year, Walter Ulbricht also announced his implementation of the Chemistry Program, in which plastics came to symbolize the regime's ability to produce abundance from scarcity. The modern design of furniture and kitchen appliances not only provided material benefits to workers but also helped to control and enlighten the masses by removing them from living environments cluttered with remnants of less progressive material cultures.[10] Even with the New Economic System after 1963, such a utopia fit into a vision of collective sacrifice and social revolution, but the rise of Erich Honecker to power in 1971 ushered in an era of consumer socialism, during which the regime promised that the shelves would finally be full of technological wonders for individual enjoyment. Now, however, consumer abundance and political legitimacy would not be achieved through individual sacrifice, cybernetics, or university research as much as through loans from Western banks, trade deficits with West Germany, and industrial espionage.[11]

By considering East German camping culture within the context of East German consumer politics, it becomes clear that the boundaries between "state" and "society" remained quite fluid and messy. While many histories of East Germany depict a "state" that intruded and a "society" that retreated into niches, this chapter demonstrates that "state" and "society" constantly interacted and often seemed to reach an agreement about the importance of comfort and relaxed sociability on a nature excursion. Rather than vacationers building campgrounds, holiday cottages, and hiking cabins despite the regime, the GDR's political and economic system increasingly encouraged their construction. The outfitting and enjoyment of a vacation destination required intense engagement with the government authorities at the local, district, and state level. On vacation, East Germans never stopped encountering the state, as Christopher Görlich has also argued about the trade union's Feriendienst. Vacationers negotiated with authorities, pushed for better management of landscapes, and engaged in letter-writing campaigns to improve amenities at campgrounds. Moreover, the SED and government planners stopped criticizing campers; in fact, they began to cater to popular nature enthusiasm in the 1960s. Industrial designers created plastic camping equipment, and government market researchers analyzed tourism. What was most remarkable about camping in East Germany was not a conflict between vacationers and the SED. Most parties involved in vacationing and its planning accepted the basic contours of the GDR (authoritarian rule, central planning, utopian visions for the future).

In addition, this chapter argues that camping enthusiasts (and the economic authorities who catered to them) imagined nature and the countryside in new ways. Both the SED and the conservation bloc initially understood the countryside as a realm of austerity, sacrifice, and productivity. With constant reminders of West German wealth from relatives and on television, however, camping enthusiasts chafed at the primitivism and austerity celebrated by nature conservationists, ideologues, eugenicists, and medical experts. When enjoying the socialist countryside, vacationers from East Germany's major cities thus reimagined recreation spaces in the rural countryside as cluttered domiciles with many of the comforts and amenities of home. By the 1970s, nature was considered less often a rustic space apart and more often another everyday space that should be managed by an authoritarian welfare state guided by visions of limitless abundance. According to the argument of historian Christopher Görlich, East German tourism planners had hoped that citizens would begin to imagine the GDR as a unified vacationland or as a socialist Heimat and thus help the regime to anchor their utopian project in the land itself. Planners failed, he adds, since most East Germans continued to understand the landscape within their local or traditional spatial imaginings.[12] This chapter considers, however, how the goals of vacationers, economic planners, and leisure experts converged to reimagine the countryside. In their lived experience, the countryside did become something new. Tourists visited spaces associated with local Heimat, but they also entered them and experienced them in new ways. SED initiatives and consumer expectations radiated out of East Germany's cities to transform the material culture and spatial orientation of the country's regional homelands.

Roughing It

Landscape planners who insisted that authorities better protect *Erholung* experiences for workers did not just want to give workers greater access to vacation pleasures. They expected a centralized state to dictate popular behavior and manage leisure practices. Similar to all "high modernists" described by James Scott, they hoped to bring about "huge, utopian changes in people's work habits, living patterns, moral conduct, and worldview."[13] For the modern, bureaucratic state (and especially the SED), consumerism and commercial comforts threatened the ability of experts to control and educate—instead allowing for individual freedom and possibly counterproductive leisure activities. For the conservation bloc, commercial culture degraded the natural landscapes that offered mental and physical rejuvenation and a return to normality. Both groups, therefore, envisioned enlightenment and rebirth through productive leisure in untainted rural spaces—nature parks, landscape preserves, athletic festivals, or summer camps secluded from urban commercial culture.

In particular, many experts hoped to ensure that campers actually interacted with nature and "roughed it" during their vacations—that is, that they left behind urban consumer society and enjoyed Spartan nature experiences. Tourist planners, for example, insisted that workers at campgrounds vacation simply and athletically, without the burden of consumer goods.[14] Landscape architects in Dresden planning offices asserted that campground designs should "preserve the nature experience and encourage athletics."[15] Their preferred "tent life" encouraged vacationers "to voluntarily reduce their life needs to the basic physical needs."[16] A sympathetic social hygienist hoped, in another example, to keep campgrounds as "Sites of Relaxation and Silence" because "civilization, as beneficial as it is, has distanced us from nature to a great degree."[17] Frank Erich Carl also condemned the superficial commercialism of landscapes dominated by tents, bungalows, and retail kiosks—a phenomenon that Carl referred to as the *Verwüstung*, or "devastation," of the recreation landscape.[18] Campers needed to learn to live simply or to "rough it"—to distance themselves from the luxuries and corruption of commercial culture.

Proponents of "roughing it" made a particular point of distinguishing between *Zelten* (traditional German, meaning "to camp") and *Camping* (an English word introduced to German in reference to auto camping). The critique of *Camping* fit well into the SED's disdain for consumerism as the satisfaction of false desires nurtured by exploitive capitalist advertisers.[19] Critics condemned *Camping* for being too dependent on expensive consumer goods and for encouraging "passive" amusements rather than active exercise.[20] Landscape architects in Dresden defined *Camping* as *Zelten* with comfort and associated it with bourgeois weekend cottages.[21] According to them, a Marxist theory of capitalism explained the corruption of *Zelten* and the origins of *Camping*. As tourism by tent grew, entrepreneurs built camping grounds to profit from services such as providing drinking water, showers, toilets, and electricity. Private campgrounds protected by security guards, in turn, encouraged vacationers to purchase even more consumer goods.[22] After visiting a Leipzig trade exhibit in 1962, a Dresden planner complained, "The tent, previously shelter for a night, became here a living room; living in nature became life 'near nature.'"[23] With camping trailers, "the home furnishings of urban life could be brought along," and the tent "became a living space [*Lebensraum*], with physical activity limited to the campground and its immediate vicinity."[24] He hoped for the return of campgrounds to their true purposes—providing a space for vacationers to live "in nature," not "near nature."[25]

Subversive Pleasures?

Despite the attempts of youth, sport, and cultural functionaries to promote austere leisure activities, East Germans continued to travel "privately" and insist on modern comforts. Only 2 percent of vacationers in 1965 consistently participated in organized athletic or educational activities; 14 percent joined occasionally. Older workers especially avoided competitions or organized excursions.[26] Eighty-five percent of all East German vacationers traveled inside of the GDR, and almost half of these vacationed privately without any connection to a state institution or organization such as the Feriendienst.[27] In 1966, a quarter of all private vacationers spent their holiday at a campground.[28] In 1975, 522 public campgrounds registered a total of 18,326,549 overnight visits from East German tourists (almost as many overnight visits as registered in trade union dormitories and resorts).[29] By avoiding organized tourism, were East German camping enthusiasts nonconformists rebelling against the regime and its ideology?

Rather than suffering as outsiders, many camping enthusiasts instead seemed to have flourished as well as could be hoped within the East German economy. While camping enthusiasts came from many different social backgrounds, camping was most common among "white-collar" workers with incomes that were average or slightly above average. Camping families in the GDR usually had a head of household who came from the ranks of "white-collar employees" (office workers, or *Angestellten*) rather than "workers" (*Arbeiter*). In one 1970 study of camping grounds, the Institute for Market Research found that the head of a camping family usually had a white-collar job (just over 57 percent), while "workers" only accounted for 30 percent of camping families.[30] Unfortunately, the GDR published few reliable statistics breaking down the entire population by occupation; according to a 1970 statistical handbook, 84.5 percent of East Germans were either workers or white-collar employees, but no distinction was made between the two categories.[31] In 1974, when the household income in the GDR averaged 1,253 marks, 63 percent of families with average or above-average household incomes owned camping equipment of some sort.[32] In comparison, only 36 percent of all East German households owned camping equipment.[33] The per diem cost of camping, according to the GDR's Institute for Market Research, appeared to be just below the average for a domestic vacation in 1973 and only three marks above average in 1980.[34]

While camping vacationers were not economic losers, did the desire for private camping vacations rich in consumer goods reflect the emergence of subversive political communities even among the economic winners? Certainly, leisure pursuits have been known to contribute to identity building.[35] Despite the strategic planning of a state, social theorist Michel DeCerteau tells us, social groups seize momentary opportunities to improvise communities that resist coordination by authorities.[36] Social groups, moreover, "define themselves through the assertion of a specific style" or "in terms of the things they possess."[37] Leisure pursuits can help groups express resistant or subversive political ideas. For instance, leisure walking in Great Britain became a form of social protest against private property and capitalistic social relations when ramblers intentionally traversed fences to reclaim traditional walking paths.[38] As Urry adds, recreational walking also became intertwined with various consumer goods that allowed an individual to transform herself into a "hybrid, the leisurely walker."[39] A hiker's boots, anoraks, and hats acted as codes signifying social status and even political orientation.[40] Could it be that campers in East Germany also resisted state Marxism-Leninism through their enthusiasm for camping and purchase of certain consumer goods?

One important consumer good associated with camping enthusiasm in East Germany was the automobile, but it is very difficult to make definitive conclusions linking camping, car ownership, and desires for political freedom. Similar to camping, car ownership often has been associated with individual freedom. In his book on car culture, cultural historian Wolfgang Sachs has described how cars helped their owners imagine "the possibility of escape . . . [and] the attraction of travel guided by nothing but individual pleasure and mood."[41] Though many East Germans did not own a car, most camping enthusiasts did.[42] According to the Institute for Market Research, only 14 percent of households owned a car in 1970. At the same time, however, nearly 65 percent of households at campgrounds arrived by automobile.[43] By 1978, camping had become almost the exclusive domain of the owners of motorized vehicles.

Nearly 90 percent of all camping vacationers arrived for their vacations by automobile, motorcycle, or scooter.[44] Keep in mind that East Germans in 1989 paid an average of 12,000 marks for a Trabant (average monthly personal income was 800 marks) and spent years on a waiting list to receive their purchase. To shorten the waiting period, cash-rich East Germans paid shocking amounts to "jump the queue" or to illegally purchase a used car on the black market. As a result, citizens with excellent political and social connections or with access to large amounts of cash had a huge advantage in the car market. After factoring in the costs of camping equipment, one must assume that camping enthusiasts often benefited from the SED system and sometimes were very well-placed insiders.[45] Some vacationers may have engaged in political grumbling while sitting around a campfire, but many others may have avoided political discussions altogether. Moreover, camping vacationers may have had personal desires that they understood as reconcilable with East Germany's political system, and they may have worked to fulfill them within the SED system, as we will see in the next section of this chapter.[46]

The Countryside as a Unified Material Space

While the conservation bloc continued to imagine the countryside as a pure, rough space unsullied by commercialism, the SED began to promote consumer comforts as part of a socialist utopia of limitless abundance. The campgrounds disdained by the conservation bloc were, I will show, as much a creation of the SED as they were a reflection of popular longing for freedom or consumer comfort. In fact, an alternative imagining of nature emerged in the late 1950s and blossomed in the 1960s—among vacationers but also among economic planners. To visit an East German campground was to enjoy the comforts and consumer goods of home. Moreover, destinations in regional homelands became integrated into a vacation network dominated by white-collar vacationers from East Germany's largest cities and increasingly managed by large, politically connected firms. These spaces did not altogether lose their significance as sites of regional pride, but they increasingly blurred together into an officially-sanctioned vacationing culture that looked remarkably similar, whether on the Baltic Sea or in the southern mountains.

Unlike the conservation bloc, the SED's economic planners increasingly made no effort to distinguish between "soft" civilization and "hard" ramblings. A *Wochenpost* article in 1956 hints at this emerging trend. According to the author, "Hiking and camping are not always affairs for the young or the childless. Decades ago the equipment became modern." In fact, the article continued, "1956 sees monotone greens or green browns being replaced by brilliant red, yellow, or blue colors."[47] Consumers could now camp comfortably. The article gushed, "Lady Nylon also goes on hiking excursions in 1956."[48] Plastics and artificial fibers, the article added, allowed for drier, less expensive, and more colorful sleeping bags with rust-free zippers. This celebration of "Lady Nylon" pointed toward the soon-to-be-introduced Chemistry Program of 1958. While many goods remained prohibitively expensive, a belief in "roughing it" now clashed with the regime's pronounced desire to use plastics to build a modern, innovative society unencumbered by resource scarcity and enriched by its technological superiority.[49] Popular magazines, for example, portrayed a wide array of plastic camping equipment enjoyed by happy vacationers.[50] The regime even went out of its way to promote camping and its associated paraphernalia as trendy and futuristic, while labeling *Zelten* and "roughing it" as old-fashioned.[51] Authorities did not just promote vacations rich in consumer goods, they responded to popular desires. By the 1970s, for example, the Institute for Market Research paid closer attention to consumer demand for camping equipment and suggested that the state invest more into production to respond to demand, which it did.[52]

The regime's discussions of camping vacations increasingly depicted a countryside filled with comfortable domestic spaces, where campsites differed little from living rooms or kitchens back in Berlin or Dresden. Mother Nature would always welcome you, *Wochenpost* suggested, if "you keep your campsite in order as many women keep their own household."[53] Plastic dishes and equipment—lightweight, stackable, durable—saved space and were also easier to transport to campsites. Plastic camping equipment, in this context, was highly symbolic; as they had done with kitchens and apartments, designers imagined that modern plastics "rationalized" and revolutionized outdoor recreation, previously associated with tradition, escapism, bourgeois privilege, and nationalism.[54] In *Campinghygiene und Erholung*, Dr. Eberhardt Lange—the chief hygienist for Rostock—recognized that modern camping enthusiasts cared deeply about comfort and consumer goods.[55] Referring to a camping trailer, he wrote, "In comparison to a tent, it is a more expensive purchase, [but] the protection against extreme weather is better [and] the comfort is greater."[56] Visitors to the countryside no longer had to rough it.[57] Elsewhere, one architect described new camping trailers as objects "more akin to weekend homes or bungalows. They are only different in the material composition."[58] Designers, for example, had named one structure weighing thirty-eight hundred kilograms the "Transportable Weekend Home." Most East Germans could not afford such trailers or even find them for purchase, but even simple tents became more elaborate. New designs—with names such as "Dreamland" and "Vacation Bliss"—had multiple "rooms" and overhanging roofs to create a porch-like space for dinners and card playing.[59]

In part, camping enthusiasts and economic planners redefined East German nature as a domestic space because the car itself had already facilitated "a domestic mode of dwelling"—"a home away from home moving flexibly and riskily through strange environments."[60] Motorists often sought out the "primitive" and "rough," but a strong counterdiscourse among camping enthusiasts celebrated material comfort made possible by their machines.[61] Vacationers now could transport as much equipment as their vehicle could carry. Economists at the Institute for Market Research wrote, "The ownership of an automobile makes it possible . . . to undertake relatively comfortable vacations and weekend trips through the acquisition of high-quality camping goods and to transport athletic and camping equipment previously too cumbersome and heavy to use."[62] With campers trailing behind them or camping equipment stored in the rear of the automobile, the campground became even more of a "home away from home." The car, ultimately, was a machine for getting closer to nature without sacrificing comfort.[63]

While few East Germans actually purchased luxurious camping trailers, families with automobiles did spend increasingly more money on camping equipment to domesticate their campsites.[64] In the 1970s, camping families tended to double the worth of their camping gear.[65] In response to consumer demand, market researchers proposed better designs for resorts and camping grounds so that "furnishing corresponds to the familiar standard of domestic surroundings." Vacationers, in their opinion, deserved more than space for a tent; they should have access to "heated, running water, as well as separate restrooms."[66] A researcher at the Institute for Market Research acknowledged in 1978 that some vacationers desired an old-fashioned camping experience "close to nature," but she clearly considered these vacationers less important than tourists that desired "comfortable auto camping grounds."[67] She wrote, "The majority of camping grounds should be outfitted with modern sanitary and utilities."[68] Before the Nazi period, tents signified militaristic values or served as ascetic shelter appropriate for an "organic" connection to nature, but by the end of World War II, they came to have very different meanings associated with ethnic violence, the miseries of war, and the desperation of refugees. By the 1970s, tents thus symbolized the past; if consumers still wanted them, market researchers suggested, they needed to become comfortable and "modern."[69]

East Germans also traveled through the countryside and inhabited its spaces differently than in the past as Cold War political boundaries shrunk time and space. In East Germany, travel restrictions prevented East Germans from traveling in the West. Some tourists visited Czechoslovakia and Hungary, but political restrictions and cost limited travel even there.[70] As a result, most East Germans traveled domestically—flocking to popular destinations like the Ore Mountains (Erzgebirge), the Thuringian Forest, and the Baltic Sea. Vacationers traveled almost exclusively within a small area bounded by the Baltic in the north, Czechoslovakia in the south, the Elbe River to the West, and the Oder River to the East.

In addition, the growth of automobile ownership in East Germany transformed how vacationers used and understood this countryside, creating a new "vacation realm" shared by vacationers from many different points of origin across the republic. In the story of the BSG Empor-Löbtau told in chapter 1, locals climbed and hiked with other locals according to regional tradition. Now, many more families spread out over a wider landscape, as almost every nook and cranny of the East German countryside opened up to tourists from many points of origin. As the automobile proliferates, John Urry argues, it "reorganizes how people negotiate the opportunities for, and constraints upon, work, family life, leisure and pleasure."[71] Wolfgang Sachs also asserts that the "auto . . . cast space and geography in a new light."[72] Prior to 1945, however, most Germans traveled by train, as the automobile remained a luxury owned by a small minority.[73] In an attempt to showcase Nazism's "socialism of the deed," Adolf Hitler had hoped to make the dream of automobility a reality for all Germans with the creation of the Autobahn and the Volkswagen, or "people's car." Hitler's Autobahn had many implications for the future of German natural spaces. Landscape architects employed by the Nazi state hoped to create an Autobahn more "nature-friendly" than the railroad and to forge a new organic modernity that would preserve the bonds between Germans and nature. As historian Thomas Zeller tells us, however, "The road building administration was inclined to understand landscape as a backdrop for the drivers' experience."[74] Actual interaction between nature and automobile driver remained rare before 1945, as planning essentially ignored everyday motorists, who actually did not exist in great numbers at the time. In postwar Germany, though, camping enthusiasts with private automobiles or motorcycles parked wherever they could—in forests or farm fields. Campgrounds in the GDR, in other words, were located not just in petit-bourgeois social niches or local homelands but within a new geography created by the car and travel restrictions. Urban residents traveling by train had long visited tourist destinations such as the Grunewald near Berlin or the Bastei in Saxon Switzerland, where they helped shape a landscape filled with crowds, noisy cafes, and souvenir stands.[75] In East Germany, aided by the automobile, a similarly cluttered, noisy nature experience now spread to places out of the reach of railroad lines.

The realities of economic failure and consumer scarcity actually encouraged urban East Germans to find new vacation destinations once only frequented by local villagers. Demand for campsites outstripped supply. As a result, many camping aficionados looked far and wide to find new unclaimed camping sites. Once claimed, camping vacationers rarely gave up their precious campsite; another one might not be found easily. The yearly return to a campground also allowed vacationers time to make improvements that the cash-strapped state rarely could afford on its own. Villages, for example, offered long-term reservations to campers from Berlin or Dresden who could help improve the camp infrastructure. In one such agreement, local authorities annually provided an electronics firm with ten campsites without charge as long as the firm installed lighting in the campground. In other cases, campers offered SED-endorsed "voluntary work actions" to contribute to the construction of a sewer system and restroom facilities by providing the village with money and labor.[76] In other words, a campground was not necessarily for locals but was instead largely for residents of East Germany's different cities that returned to their "home away from home," the building of which often involved their own labor.

Regional distinctions further gave way to GDR-wide vacationing monoculture as state-owned firms came to dominate most campgrounds. By the 1970s, more and more East Germans spent their vacations at camps and resorts leased and managed by their employers. In 1979, businesses and organizations reserved over 35 percent of all campground capacity (increasing to 50 percent by 1989).[77] Most campgrounds also saw a tremendous growth in bungalow construction, and employers controlled 65 percent of beds in these bungalows.[78] Private vacations fell to 40 percent of the total by 1975, at the same time that vacations taken at sites owned or leased by employers increased to almost 30 percent of all vacations.[79] These vacations at employer-owned campgrounds were still technically private, in the sense that families traveled on their own. But now they depended on approval from their employers to use these sites. In 1979, as many vacationers visited resorts owned or leased by employers as visited FDGB resorts or public campgrounds.[80] Many of these employer-owned resorts, known as *Betriebliche Erholungseinrichtung*, dedicated much of their land to bungalows and campsites, hosting nearly two-thirds of their guests in bungalows or campsites.[81]

Greifenbach Reservoir

The integration of local homelands into an SED-sanctioned vacation landscape can best be illustrated in a case study, such as the following history of Greifenbach Reservoir near Chemnitz (or Karl Marx City, as it was called then). Lying between the villages of Ehrenfriedersdorf, Geyer, and Thum, the twenty-three-hectare Greifenbach Reservoir was the single biggest campground in the Karl Marx City district by the 1980s.[82] Before 1945, local farmers and businessmen dominated these lakeshores, though some tourists did visit the region before World War II, especially as middle-class hikers explored the Greifensteine. For the most part, however, farmers used the wet meadows surrounding the lake for grazing cattle. A photograph from the 1940s revealed a landscape free of bungalows and campsites, with far fewer trees and more extensive wetlands than witnessed in 2006; most likely, cattle grazing prevented ecological succession from replacing the meadows with woodland.[83] In the early 1960s, vacationers began to appropriate private and public spaces for activities only partially condoned by the SED and local authorities. Nonetheless, nearly every tent and nearly every blade of grass on those lakeshores felt the power of the SED and its cultural and economic priorities. Even unofficial uses of nature owed their form to economic and social changes (such as the new celebration of consumer goods) introduced either intentionally or unintentionally by state planners. In the sense that Eli Rubin argues in his own work, Greifenbach was part of a mainstream culture or a whole way of life emerging in the GDR in the 1960s and 1970s—partially created by the SED, partially unintentional, partially created by everyday citizens, and very much resented by some locals.

The local forests surrounding Greifenbach already had experienced radical changes long before the arrival of motor tourists. The surrounding Ore Mountains, or Erzgebirge, boasted one of the densest settlement patterns in all of Europe and one of the most complex geological formations in the world, famous for rich mines of silver, nickel, zinc, and lead. Zinc had been extracted from the streambeds around Geyer since the thirteenth century. Later in the century, miners in Ehrenfriedersdorf flooded the moors at the head of the Greifen Brook and built an aqueduct to provide water for deeper, more intensive mining operations five kilometers away. The processing of ore recovered from those mines also demanded large quantities of firewood. Long before the twentieth century, therefore, monotonous plots of scientifically managed fir and artificial water systems had replaced historic mixed beech-spruce-fir forests to meet these extraordinary resource demands. During World War II, the Nazis used Russian and French prisoners of war to raise the Greifenbach dam to grow the lake to its present capacity.[84]

The SED's quest for industrial self-sufficiency introduced even more demands on the local landscape. With the partition of Germany, the Soviets took ownership of one the richest known deposits of uranium outside of the United States and Canada—all just west of Chemnitz. In the next decade, tens of thousands of workers employed by Wismut—the joint Soviet–East German mining operation—arrived in the region to extract uranium for the Soviet military. These mines left behind a toxic array of slag heaps and radioactive wastewater ponds.[85] Intensified mining operations also began to spur intense growth in cities such as Annaberg, Zwickau, and Schwarzenberg—often at the expense of resource needs in smaller communities. No uranium mining took place at Greifenbach, but the campground felt the effects of the regional economic expansion. As reports in the 1940s indicate, industrial growth in these major centers placed ever greater demands on local water supplies previously used by smaller towns. For example, Ehrenfriedersdorf engineers complained that Zwickau received too much attention from planners, even as the water scarcity in smaller Erzgebirge communities such as Auerbach and Ehrenfriedersdorf intensified. According to alarmed civic leaders, local industry and agriculture went days without any water in 1950.[86] In late 1962, the drilling of an exploratory shaft by Wismut further threatened Ehrenfriedersdorf's water supply, as nearby springs and wells began to rapidly drop.[87] State engineers began to plan for additional reservoir capacity (including an expansion of Greifenbach) as one response to this scarcity.[88]

Even the tourist landscape of the Greifenbach valley reflected SED demands. As the reactions of some local farmers will reveal, to camp at Greifenbach was to enter into a leisure culture intertwined with the SED political and economic system.[89] Youth and conservation authorities initially promoted hiking and camping at Greifenbach for members of the FDJ and for schoolchildren. At this early stage, local businessmen imagined themselves resisting the encroachment of youth leaders. One local nature protectionist, for example, battled with Geyer farmers who threatened to dismantle a youth campground on the shores of Greifenbach Reservoir.[90] In another instance, nature preservationists fought a local landowner to prevent him from fencing in his property and building a weekend cottage in a space meant for youth camping.[91] The local zinc mine imagined itself a representative of local interests and also resented the changes at Greifenbach. Referring to leisure and youth planners, it complained, "We no longer had any rights here."[92] In the minds of some locals, the very presence of the campground symbolized the terror and misery of the

SED regime, even if they overlooked the very unplanned and chaotic evolution of Greifenbach Reservoir in the 1960s (as will be shown shortly). After 1990, some Geyer historians continued to insist that the lakeshore had been stolen from their community. They argued, for example, that the lake had been transformed by "Marxists" at the moment that leisure planners began to call the reservoir by the name "Greifenbachstauweiher" instead of "Geyerischer Teich." One former farmer (and mayor of Geyer in 2001) wistfully remembered the days before the recreation planners "took" his land and converted it into a bungalow settlement and campground. He exclaimed, "What happened here was a disgrace [*Schweinerei*]!"[93]

These bitter memories expressed in local newspapers depended on a heated language that obscured as much as it illuminated, but they correctly recognized that East German authorities played some role in thoroughly transforming the local landscape. In the 1960s, the VEB Naherholung (People's Enterprise for Local Recreation) appropriated (without monetary compensation) meadows surrounding the reservoir; former landowners were officially "owners," under GDR property law, but they had no say on the use of the land.[94] The VEB Naherholung, for example, claimed ownership of a campground already built and operated by the Zschopau motorcycle factory, though it did allow the factory preferred use.[95] Even when a few property owners did resist, the campground's history hints at the levels of control achieved by leisure planners as much as it suggests the "limits of dictatorship." A property known as Seidel's Erben provides a good example; the "property-owning" Seidel family rented out campsites on their own, even as the VEB Naherholung sought to ensure after 1976 that camp permits went through their offices. District authorities criticized Seidel's Erben as a "private campground" characterized by "uncontrolled development," but the VEB Naherholung never eliminated the Seidel anomaly. It did, however, invest funds to improve cultural activities at Seidel's Erben.[96] The VEB Naherholung also integrated campers into official organizations, such as a *Campingbeirat* (camp council), which helped regulate construction, ensured quiet hours at night, and organized labor brigades for camp improvements.[97] To a certain degree, this council pushed authorities to respond to its wishes, but the council also helped authorities assert their own control.[98] The VEB Naherholung required the council to organize athletic and educational activities meant to channel campers into approved activities. "Camping leaders" with a seat on the *Campingbeirat* also had to meet certain political requirements.[99] For example, vacationers chosen for the *Beirat* had to have worked previously in volunteer work brigades (a requirement also expected of vacationers who hoped to retain long-term camping permits).[100]

Like many campgrounds across the GDR, Greifenbach also became one node in a larger East German vacationland. The VEB Naherholung, for example, approved bungalow construction that benefited workers from distant cities such as Dresden and Berlin, rather than local residents. The vacation home Helmut Just was once a large and popular tavern and guesthouse open to the public, but it only served employees of one enterprise after 1945.[101] The former Guesthouse Börnichen served employees of Dresden's VEB Industriewerk, which refused public entry. The vacation home Waldschliesschen in Ehrenfriedersdorf belonged to the Reichsbahndirektion Berlin-Tempelhof, and since 75 percent of vacationers there were actually West Berliners, locals could not legally use the facility.[102] In discussions with the VEB Naherholung, firms agreed in principle that unused capacity could be opened up to local vacationers.[103] In reality, many declared themselves unable to accommodate outside guests.[104] In fact, demand for campsites and bungalows for firms increased so insistently that many private vacationers lost their access to campgrounds.[105]

While the regime's youth and leisure authorities "owned" the Greifenbach landscape and made plans for productive leisure, their "ownership" constantly encountered challengers. In the early 1960s, leisure planners hoping to encourage productive recreation built two sandpits at Greifenbach for long-jump competitions. Just a few years later, however, camp authorities discovered that these pits had been destroyed and that children happily built sand castles in the ruins.[106] Similarly, youth drowned out official musical performances with their portable radios and laughter.[107] One family challenged official control of the lake by suggesting that the campground was really built by vacationers themselves. They explained, "As you know, we contributed twenty hours of our own labor in order to improve the parcel to a proper condition [for camping]. Moreover, we leveled off recently drained land and sowed grass on the lakeshore."[108] In more explicit cases, the forests of Greifenbach served as a refuge for unofficial and unapproved activities. A preacher from Oberwiesenthal organized an illegal Bible camp at Greifenbach and at other local campgrounds in 1962.[109] In the summers, as the local Committee for Tourism and Hiking described it, "a mass of youth from the ages of fourteen to twenty-eight pitched their tents" and did as they pleased.[110] In 1969, leisure planners for the lake complained of youth with "sensational clothing and . . . long hair."[111] In response, Zschopau's educators attempted to ban "conspicuously dressed youth" from the campground and posted stricter camp rules.[112]

A brief environmental history of the postwar lakeshore and its development suggests that authorities often had little direct control over the campground and its development. The lake had previously provided water to miners and villagers, who cared little about the lake's appearance; as a result, wetlands dominated the lakeshore. Due to local weather patterns that encouraged heavy snows in winter and heavy summer rains, moors and wetlands were common across much of the relatively flat plateau between Greifenstein and Geyer.[113] Despite these impediments, tourists continued to arrive, demanding that authorities improve the lakeshores.[114] The mayor assured readers of the local newspaper of the upcoming development of a sandy beach and a grassy meadow for sunbathing, and the city hired a professional dredger in 1961 to begin draining the land.[115] With limited funds, however, benefits for tourists came slowly. By 1963, approximately twenty thousand vacationers visited the lake every weekend, but the government had not yet cleared the land or built an infrastructure for such crowds.[116] As one vacationer described it, tourists needed rubber boots to manage the swampy conditions.[117] In 1967, Zschopau encouraged further landscaping to expand sunbathing and camping possibilities by asking the tin mining concern that controlled the dam to drain (*entschlammen*) land in the direction of the youth hostel.[118] As late as 1968, however, swampland remained on the west side of the lake, and a meadow for sunbathing and camping had not been constructed.[119] On the edges of the lake, tourists dumped garbage, illegally chopped wood for campfires, camped in ecologically sensitive sites, and operated loud motorized boats.[120] Health officials especially worried about pollution to drinking water from "wild" campsites without proper toilets or garbage disposal.[121] Even in 1982, drainage and improvements still had not been completed.[122]

Was this the people's landscape? Was there freedom to be found in this chaos? Was the SED regime a weak authority, unable to shape daily life? Were locals wrong to label Greifenbach Reservoir a totalitarian space? At first glance, this seems possible, but the story is more complicated. While Greifenbach does reveal the "limits of dictatorship," even the unplanned activities of vacationers reflected a confluence of interests between the regime and society rather than the persistence of normality or freedom in the face of terror. Even when disrupting official planning, tourists participated in a vacationing culture approved and influenced by SED planners. The regime may not have had complete control over the leisure pursuits of Greifenbach vacationers, but it did go out of its way to satisfy popular desires. In part, this was necessary to secure popular legitimacy, but it also reflected the regime's own desire to construct a utopia of limitless abundance.

An overemphasis on the ineffectiveness of leisure planners, for instance, would ignore how they went out of their way to present themselves as responsive to the consumer desires of vacationers. The *Freie Presse*, an Erzgebirge newspaper, reported extensively (and sometimes negatively) on the refreshments offered at concession kiosks at the campground. The provision of milk and meat was particularly problematic, with shortages common.[123] Other newspaper articles reported frankly on shortages of bockwurst, beer, or baked goods at camps as demand outstripped supply. When provisions improved or were abundant, though, the press made sure to note it.[124] Reporters notified readers of all improvements to provisions and highlighted campgrounds that received awards for "best campground" each year.[125] The *Freie Presse* once asked a vacationer at Greifenbach, "Are you happy with the shopping opportunities?" She responded, "Yes, the offerings are as comprehensive as at my local supermarket. In general we are happy here. The only thing is that that the beach could use a few cartloads of sand."[126]

Authorities concerned about popular opinion even began to think in terms of "customer service," something hardly ever associated with East German material culture. Internal reports analyzed the VEB Naherholung's "customer service" and commented on efforts to improve food provisions, the rental of camping and boating equipment, and sanitary conditions.[127] The *Freie Press* noted, "Hans Mann, the boss of VEB Naherholung at Greifenbach, considers close contact with vacationers to be expedient customer service [*Kundendienst*] . . . [He wishes] that each of the four thousand vacationers at the campground feel content."[128] This emphasis on customer service was not just an anomaly, as local editions of the *Freie Presse* throughout the Erzgebirge reported on concerns about *Kundendienst*, or "customer service." In one case, a newspaper published an article with the title, "Good Service Will Be Practiced at the Campground" (*Auf dem Campingplatz wird auf guten Service geachtet*). Here, notably, the press even used the English term *service*.[129] District officials also offered a prize to campgrounds that best stocked kiosks and provided entertainment for vacationers, as a means "to increase a sense of good care [*Umsorgtseins*] among our patrons."[130] By the 1970s, the VEB Naherholung at Greifenbach offered outlets for razors and clothes irons, rental kiosks for camping and ski equipment, repair shops, and more electrical connections.[131] At times, regional officials even gave priority to leisure and customer service over collective agriculture and heavy industry. In 1959, district officials in Karl Marx City planned to expand the reservoir to address water shortages in the district's major cities, but they decided to delay plans for reservoir expansion until 1975.[132] The archives remain silent on the exact reasons for delay, but they do hint that authorities took popular desires for leisure into consideration.[133] Against the objections of agricultural planners in Karl Marx City, the town of Geyer in 1971 also approved the transfer of agricultural land near the campground to the VEB Naherholung to provide space for more bungalows, recreational vehicles, and camping wagons in the park.[134]

In the end, the interactions between vacationers, the official press, and government authorities mark this space as one of common expectations (if not values), rather than as one of refuge and resistance. To a certain degree, Greifenbach proved to be a thoroughly SED space—closely monitored and drastically changed by postwar developments. Consumers and planners understood outdoor recreation and material comforts as expected entitlements within the GDR. The complaints of Geyer farmers and local preservationists suggest that campgrounds such as Greifenbach acted as the intrusions of both the SED and this "mainstream consensus" into a local community. In sum, vacationers did not retreat into the countryside to pursue hobbies and enthusiasms condemned by the SED. One could claim (as Pauline Bren has done for Czechoslovakia) that the regime purchased the loyalty and acquiescence of vacationers. Alternatively, one could argue, as Görlich does, that the regime had to abandon its goals and adapt to popular desires to avoid social unrest. Even as leisure planners gave into popular desires, however, they did so in hopes of influencing the population and improving their travel habits. The SED and leisure planners alike embraced a vision of the socialist modern, in which all citizens could enjoy comfortable nature outings and futuristic plastic consumer goods. For their part, vacationers sought out comfort and luxury as promised by the regime and as visible in West German media. They did so, however, in a countryside created by the social and political system of the SED; while many campers continued to sing traditional songs and enjoy cabins with friends and family as many had done for decades, the camping culture of East Germany was more than just a nostalgia trip. Together, the SED, leisure planners, and vacationers rejected visions of nature as a space for roughing it. In other words, a new understanding of the nature experience and consumer pleasures began to coalesce within the claustrophobic boundaries of the GDR. More and more, nature became associated with consumer pleasures and dreams of limitless abundance in a countryside that was becoming a hybrid creation of local influences, SED design, and urban consumer desires.

NOTES

1. Erasmus Schröter, ed., *Bild der Heimat: Die Echt-Foto-Postkarten aus der DDR* (Berlin: Schwarzkopf und Schwarzkopf, 2002).

2. Rudy Koshar, "Introduction," in Koshar (2002), 5.

3. Alf Lüdtke, *Herrschaft als sozialer Praxis: Historische und sozio-anthropologische Studien* (Göttingen: Vandenhoeck und Ruprecht, 1991), 13.

4. Judith Kruse, "Nische im Sozialismus," in *Endlich Urlaub! Die Deutschen reisen*, ed. Haus der Geschichte (Bonn: Haus der Geschichte, 1996), 108.

5. Kruse (1996), 106.

6. Martin Bütow, "Abenteuerurlaub Marke DDR: Camping," in Haus der Geschichte (1996), 101.

7. Spode (1996), 19; Bren (2002), 127.

8. Günter Gaus, *Wo Deutschland liegt* (Munich: Hoffmann und Campe, 1983).

9. Dolores L. Augustine, *Red Prometheus: Engineering and Dictatorship in East Germany, 1945–1990* (Cambridge, Mass.: MIT Press, 2007); Raymond G. Stokes, *Constructing Socialism Technology and Change in East Germany, 1945–1990* (Baltimore: Johns Hopkins University Press, 2000).

10. Rubin (2008); Betts (2010).

11. On the history of the SED's embrace of consumer goods and state debt, see Rubin (2008); Betts (2010); Landsmann (2005); Jonathan R. Zatlin, *The Currency of Socialism: Money and Political Culture in East Germany* (Washington, D.C.: German Historical Institute, 2007). On industrial espionage in the 1970s, see Augustine (2007). On the history of GDR consumerism, see Katherine Pence, "'You as a Woman Will Understand': Consumption, Gender, and the Relationship between State and Citizenry in the GDR's Crisis of 17 June 1953," *German History* 19, no. 2 (2001): 218–52; Ina Merkel, "Consumer Culture in the GDR, or How the Struggle for Antimodernity Was Lost on the Battleground of Consumer Culture," in *Getting and Spending: European and American Consumer Societies in the Twentieth Century*, ed. Susan Strasser, Charles McGovern, and Matthias Judt (Washington D.C.: German Historical Institute; Cambridge: Cambridge University Press, 1998), 281–300; Ina Merkel, *Utopie und Bedürfnis: Die Geschichte der Konsumkultur in der DDR* (Cologne: Böhlau, 1999); Paul Betts, "The Twilight of the Idols: East German Memory and Material Culture," *Journal of Modern History* 72, no. 3 (September 2000): 731–65.

12. Görlich (2012), 225–61. Palmowski (2009) also discusses "socialist Heimat," though Görlich does not mention Palmowski in his book.

13. Scott (1998), 5.

14. "Zelten—aber wie?"*Unterwegs* 4 (1958), 1–2; "O Zelten, Zelten, unsre Lust," *Wochenpost* 29 (1956): 14, SAPMO-BArch: DY12 4288.

15. Fritz Menz, Deutsche Bauakademie, "Öffentliche Zeltplätze: Anlage und Ausstattung," February 1, 1958, SäStArchD: BfT 52.

16. "Berichte und Auswertungen zur Zeltplatzordnung im Bezirk Dresden," December 1961, 2, SäStArchD: BfT 50.

17. Dr. Köntopp, "Wandern und Gesundheit," *Unterwegs* 12 (1958), 14–16.

18. Carl (1960), 13.

19. On "false desires," see Jonathan R. Zatlin, "The Vehicle of Desire: The Trabant, the Wartburg, and the End of the GDR," *German History* 15, no. 3 (1997): 363–65.

20. Traute Richter, "Zelten contra Camping!" *Unterwegs* 8 (1958), 15.

21. "Berichte und Auswertungen zur Zeltplatzordnung im Bezirk Dresden," December 1961, 2, SäStArchD: BfT 50.

22. Ibid., 2.

23. L. Geyer, Entwürfsbüro für Gebiets-, Stadt- und Dorfplanung des RdB Dresden,

"Besichtigung der Camping-Artikel auf der Leipziger Herbstmesse 1962," September 22, 1962, 1, SäStArchD: BfT 52.

24. Ibid., 4.

25. Ibid., 8.

26. H. Löbe, "Gedanken zur Problematik der Naherholung," February 1, 1966, 1, BArch: DR5 1037.

27. Dr. Werner Bischoff, "Die Tendenzen der Freizeitgestaltung verschiedener Bevölkerungsgruppen in der DDR," November 30, 1967, 4, BArch: DL102 44.

28. KTW, "Information über einige Fakten der Entwicklung der Touristik im Jahre 1967 in Auswertung der Jahresberichte der BKTW," March 18, 1968, 4, SAPMO-BArch: DY34 5961; Dr. Annelies Albrecht, "Zur Entwicklung des Campingwesens in der DDR—Teilstudie 4, Prognose der Entwicklung des Bedarfs nach Sport und Campingartikeln," 1971, BArch: DL102 629.

29. Staatliche Zentralverwaltung für Statistik, "Statistischer Bericht über die Kapazität und Nutzung der staatlichen Campingplätze, 1979," 10, BArch: DE2 22676.

30. Dr. Annelies Albrecht, "Zu Problemen der Entwicklung des Campingwesens in der DDR—Teilstudie 1, Analyse des Personenkreises der Camper und der Gründe für die Wahl dieser Form der Freizeitgestaltung, 1970," table 7, BArch: DL102 511.

31. *Statistisches Jahrbuch der DDR 1979* (Berlin: Staatsverlag, 1979).

32. *Statistisches Jahrbuch der DDR 1974* (Berlin: Staatsverlag, 1974).

33. "Informationen aus Wiederholungsbefragungen, Befragungszyklus 1974/75," table V/9/11/74, BArch: DL102 880.

34. Dr. Annelies Albrecht, "Die Urlaubsreisetätigkeit der Bevölkerung der DDR von 1971–1980," 18, BArch: DL102 1472. Hasso Spode writes that camping was more expensive than a vacation with the FDGB; see Spode (1996), 19.

35. As Pierre Bourdieu has forcefully asserted, however, the power of objects to re-create individual and group identities is severely limited by established social structures. In this sense, objects often serve to reinforce traditional class differences by acting as objects of distinction. See Pierre Bourdieu, *Distinction: A Social Critique of the Judgment of Taste* (Cambridge, Mass.: Harvard University Press, 1984). See also Jean Baudrillard, "Consumer Society," in *Selected Writings*, ed. Mark Poster (Stanford: Stanford University Press, 2001), 45.

36. Michel de Certeau, *The Practice of Everyday Life* (Berkeley: University of California Press, 1988).

37. Igor Kopytoff, "The Cultural Biography of Things: Commoditization as Process," in *The Social Life of Things: Commodities in Cultural Perspective*, ed. Arjun Appadurai (Cambridge: Cambridge University Press, 1986), 81. See also Koshar (2000); Celia Lury, *Consumer Culture* (New Brunswick, N.J.: Rutgers University Press, 1996); Daniel Miller, ed., *Acknowledging Consumption* (London: Routledge, 1995); Daniel Miller, *Car Cultures* (Oxford: Berg, 2001).

38. For an introduction to the politics of rambling, see Wendy Joy Darby, *Landscape and Identity: Geographies of Nation and Class in England* (Oxford: Berg, 2000); Anne Wallace, *Walking, Literature, and English Culture: The Origins and Uses of Peripatetic in the Nineteenth Century* (Oxford: Oxford University Press, 1993).

39. John Urry, *Sociology beyond Societies: Mobilities for the Twenty-First Century* (London: Routledge, 2000), 52.

40. Urry (2000), 92.

41. Wolfgang Sachs, *For the Love of the Automobile* (Berkeley: University of California Press, 1992), 96–97; a similar point is made in Warren James Belasco, *Americans on the Road: From Autocamp to Motel, 1910–1945* (Baltimore: Johns Hopkins University Press, 1997), 8.

42. Dr. Annelies Albrecht, "Zur Entwicklung des Campingwesens in der DDR," 1971, BArch: DL102 629.

43. Dr. Wolfgang Stompler, "Dokumentation zur Urlaubsreisetätigkeit in den jahren 1969 bis 1972," June 1, 1973, BArch: DL102 725.

44. Dr. Annelies Albrecht, "Zu Problemen der Entwicklung des Campingwesens in der DDR—Teilstudie 1, Analyse des Personenkreises der Camper und der Gründe für die Wahl dieser Form der Freizeitgestaltung, 1970," table 12, BArch: DL102 51; Dr. Annelies Albrecht, "Analyse des Personenkreises der Camper und Meinungen zum Versorgungsniveau auf Campingplätzen," 1978, BArch: DL102 1253; Dr. Werner Bischoff, "Die Tendenzen der Freizeitgestaltung verschiedener Bevölkerungsgruppen in der DDR," November 30, 1967, 17, BArch: DL102 44.

45. On the shortages of automobiles, see Zatlin, "Vehicle of Desire" (1997): 370.

46. For an example of the complexity at play here, consider hot-rodders in post-1945 America. These nonconformers defined their activities as all-American in order to find acceptance and to prove their worth to society. See H. F. Moorhouse, *Driving Ambitions: An Analysis of American Hot-Rod Enthusiasm* (Manchester: Manchester University Press, 1991), 172.

47. "Zelten und Wandern mit Kind und Kegel," *Wochenpost* 29 (1956): 14.

48. Ibid., 14.

49. For discussions of plastics and technology in the GDR, see Rubin (2008); Betts (2010); Eli Rubin, "The Order of Substitutes: Plastic Consumer Goods in the *Volkswirtschaft* and Everyday Domestic Life in the GDR," in *Consuming Germany in the Cold War*, ed. David F. Crew (Oxford: Berg, 2003), 87–120; Raymond G. Stokes, "Plastics and the New Society: The German Democratic Republic in the 1950s and 1960s," in *Style and Socialism: Modernity and Material Culture in Post-War Eastern Europe*, ed. David Crowley and Susan E. Reid (Oxford: Berg, 2000), 65–80.

50. Rubin (2003), 99–100; (2008), 145–48.

51. Rubin (2008), 145. Rubin uses the phrase *roughing it* also, though we came to it independently. I first used it in a paper submitted in 2005 for publication in an essay collection published in 2010: Scott Moranda, "Camping in East Germany: Making 'Rough' Nature More Comfortable," in *Pleasures in Socialism: Leisure and Luxury in the Eastern Bloc*, ed. David Crowley and Susan E. Reid (Evanston, Ill.: Northwestern University Press, 2010), 197–218.

52. Dr. Annelies Albrecht, "Zur Entwicklung des Campingwesens in der DDR—Teilstudie 4, Prognose der Entwicklung des Bedarfs nach Sport und Campingartikeln, 1971," 5, BArch: DL102 629.

53. "Zelten und Wandern mit Kind und Kegel," *Wochenpost* 29 (1956): 14.

54. Rubin (2008), 76.

55. Eberhardt Lange, *Campinghygiene und Erholung* (Berlin: VEB Verlag Volk und Gesundheit, 1974), 25–26.

56. Lange (1974), 39.

57. Lange (1974), 84.

58. L. Geyer, Entwürfsbüro für Gebiets-, Stadt- und Dorfplanung des Rat des Bezirkes Dresden, "Besichtigung der Camping-Artikel auf der Leipziger Herbstmesse 1962," September 22, 1962, 1, SäStArchD: BfT 52.

59. Ibid., 2–7.

60. Urry (2000), 191.

61. Belasco (1997), 82.

62. Dr. Annelies Albrecht, "Zur Entwicklung des Campingwesens in der DDR— Teilstudie 4, Prognose der Entwicklung des Bedarfs nach Sport und Campingartikeln, 1971," BArch: DL102 629.

63. Sachs (1992), 156.

64. Dr. Annelies Albrecht, "Ausstattung und Kaufabsichten der Camping Gemein- schaften bei Freizeitkonsumgütern—Ergebnisse einer Befragung auf Campingplätzen," 1978, BArch: DL102 1251.

65. Ibid., table 2.

66. Dr. Wolfgang Stompler, "Zur Bedarfsentwicklung im Freizeittourismus der DDR Bevölkerung bis zum Jahre 1990," 1976, 34, BArch: DL102 1069.

67. Renate Gräfe and Dr. Anelies Albrecht, "Analyse des Personenkreises der Camper und Meinungen zum Versorgungsniveau auf Campingplätzen: Ergebnisse einer Befragung auf Campingplätzen," 1978, table 9, BArch: DL102 1253. For more on new consumer items making mobility possible, see Anja Dähmlow and Viola Härtel, "Ver- reisen kann jeder, Zelten ist Charaktersache," in *Wunderwirtschaft: DDR-Konsumkultur in den 60er Jahren*, ed. Neue Gesellschaft für Bildende Kunst (Cologne: Böhlau, 1996).

68. Peter Stöckmann and Dr. Annelies Albrecht, "Tendenzen der Entwicklung der Urlaubs und Reisetätigkeit und der damit verbundenen Geldausgaben der Bevölkerung für Waren und Leistungen," 1978, 24–36, BArch: DL102 1252.

69. Such a biography of the tent reflects the approaches to material culture and consumer society advocated by Kopytoff (1986) in his call for a social biography of things.

70. Koshar (2000); Spode (1996).

71. Urry (2000), 58. The car, according to Urry and historian Rudy Koshar, has even reconfigured "civil society" to accommodate "distinct ways of dwelling, traveling and socializing in, and through, an automobilized time-space." See Rudy Koshar, "Germans at the Wheel: Cars and Leisure Travel in Interwar Germany," in Koshar (2002), 215–32.

72. Sachs (1992), 152. According to historian Warren Belasco, auto campers cre- ated a hybrid network of tourists, cars, roads, and nature that transformed the country- side; see Belasco (1997), 30–35.

73. See Sachs (1992); Koshar (2002).

74. Zeller (2000), 230. See also Thomas Zeller, *Driving Germany: The Landscape of the German Autobahn, 1930–1970* (New York: Berghahn Books, 2007).

75. On Grunewald, see Jeffrey K. Wilson, *German Forest: Nature, Identity, and the Contestation of a National Symbol, 1871–1914* (Toronto: University of Toronto Press, 2011); on the Bastei, see Schindler (1999).

76. Bütow (1996), 104.

77. Staatliche Zentralverwaltung für Statistik, "Statistischer Jahresbericht über den Stand und die Entwicklung des Tourismus und Erholungswesens der DDR, 1979," 48, BArch: DE2 22676.

78. Staatliche Zentralverwaltung für Statistik, "Ergcbnisse der Berichterstattung über die staatlichen Campingplätze, 1989," 8, BArch: DE2 20969.

79. Dr. Wolfgang Stompler, "Zur Bedarfsentwicklung im Freizeittourismus der DDR Bevölkerung bis zum Jahre 1990," 1976, 10, BArch: DL102 1069; "Zur Entwicklung der Urlaubsreisetätigkeit der DDR-Bürger," 1979, 6, BArch: DL102 1305; Dr. Annelies Albrecht, "Tendenzen der Entwicklung der Urlaubs und Reisetätigkeit und der damit verbundenen Geldausgaben der Bevölkerung für Waren und Leistungen," 1978, 10, BArch: DL102 1252.

80. Staatliche Zentralverwaltung für Statistik, "Statistischer Jahresbericht über den Stand und die Entwicklung des Tourismus und Erholungswesens der DDR, 1979," 7, BArch: DE2 22676.

81. Ibid., 17. See also Bütow (1996), 104.

82. Abt. Erholungswesen, RdB KMS, "Ausgewaählte Angaben zu Campingplätzen des Bez KMS," Sächsisches Staatsarchiv Chemnitz (hereinafter SäStCh): 30413/138258.

83. Photograph, "Typische Flachmoorgegend am Geyerschen Teich," [1955?], SäStCh: 30413/5329. Another image of early twentieth-century lakeshore in a swampy condition can be seen in "Grosser Teich, Dammteich oder?," *Freie Presse*, August 25, 2001, newspaper clipping in Geyer Turmmuseum Archiv.

84. Lothar Handschack, "Zur Geschichte des 'Geyerschen Teiches,'" date unknown (after 1990), and "An leidvolle Vergangenheit erinnert," *Freie Presse*, December 12, 2003, both in Geyer Turmmuseum Archiv.

85. Rainer Karlsch and Zbynek Zeman, *Urangeheimnisse: Das Erzgebirge im Brennpunkt der Weltpolitik, 1933–1960* (Berlin: Ch. Links Verlag, 2002); Reimar Paul, *Das Wismut Erbe: Geschichte und Folgen des Uranbergbaus in Thüringen und Sachsen* (Göttingen: Verlag der Werkstatt, 1991); Ralf Engeln, *Uransklaven oder Sonnensucher? Die Sowjetische AG Wismut in der SBZ/DDR 1946–1953* (Essen: Klartext Verlag, 2001); Michael Beleites, *Pechblende: Die Uranbergbau in der DDR und seiner Folgen* (Wittenberg: Kirchliche Forschungsheim, 1988); Michael Beleites, *Altlast Wismut: Ausnahmezustand, Umweltkatastrophe und das Sanierungsproblem im deutschen Uranbergbau* (Frankfurt am Main: Brandes und Apsel, 1992).

86. Ing. Sachs, "Aktenvermerk," January 3, 1950, Stadtarchiv Ehrenfriedersdorf (hereinafter StaarchEhr): S IV/e4; Gemeinderat Auerbach, "Besprechung mit Herrn Dr. Sachs," December 20, 1949; Letter from Gemeinderat Auerbach to MLF, Hauptabteilung Wasserwirtschaft, January 10, 1950; and Letter from Gemeinderat zu Auerbach to den Kreisrat, January 13, 1950, StaarchEhr: S IV/e2.

87. See 1962/63 correspondance on Ehrenfriedersdorf and Geyerschen Teich in SäStCh: 30413/27303; Letter from RdK Annaberg (Wasserwirtschaft) to RdB KMS (Wasserwirtschaft), July 29, 1963, SäStCh: 30413/27324.

88. Letter from Ehrenfriedersdorf Bürgermeister to Revierausschuss für das Obergebirgische Bergrevier in Freiberg, July 23, 1947, and Letter from Ehrenfriedersdorf Bürgermeister to VVB Buntmetalle, December 3, 1949, StaarchEhr: S IV/e3; Letter from Rat der Stadt (hereinafter RdS) Ehrenfriedersdof to Wasserwirtschaftsdirektion Obere Elbe Mulde Dresden, October 8, 1963, SäStCh: 30413/27303; Ing. Johannes Sachs, "Stadt Ehrenfriedersdorf: Ordnung der Wasserverhältnisse im oberen Greifenbachgebiet," February 1949, StaarchEhr: S IV/e4.

89. Stadt Ehrenfriedersdorf, "Besprechung," September 14, 1948, StaarchEhr: S IV/

e4; Letter from Gemeinderat zu Auerbach to the Kreisrat and the Sächsisches Strassen und Wasserbauamt, January 13, 1950, and "Übersicht über die gepflogenen Verhandlungen bezüglich der Wasserentnahme aus dem Greifenbachgebiet," March 17, 1952, StaarchEhr: S IV/e2.

90. Letter from Kreisbeauftragter für Naturschutz (RdK Annaberg) to Entwurfsabteilung für Stadt und Dorfplanung (RdB KMS), December 17, 1955, SäStCh: 30413/13338; GO VEB Zinn und Spätgruben Ehrenfriedersdorf, "Protokoll über die Mitgliederversammlung der BPO VEB Zinngrube Ehrenfriedersdorf am 15.2.56," SäStCh: SED Kreisleitung Zschopau (14524) IV 7/1101/1628.

91. Abt. Kommunale Wirtschaft (RdB KMS), "Niederschirft über die am 20.10.54 stattgefundene Besprechung des Beirates für Fragen des Landschafts und Naturschutzes bei der Wasserwirtschaft des RdB," October 20, 1954, and Letter from Abt. Arbeit Bauaufsicht (RdK Annaberg) to Hauptarchitekt (RdB KMS), December 5, 1956, SäStCh: 30413/13338.

92. Letter from Baumann to Kombinatsdirektor (VEB Bleierzgruben "Albert Funk"), February 6, 1968, and Sektion Kanutouristik (DTSB), "Eingabe," January 18, 1974, StaarchEhr: S IV/e24; RdK Zschopau, "Niederschrift über eine Besprechung von Vertretern des Campingbeirates am 12.7.1967 in der Teichschänke am Greifenbachstauweiher," July 18, 1967, KarchMZ: 7074.

93. Horst Mueller, "Greifenbachstauweiher oder Geyerscher Teich?," *Wochenblatt und Anzeiger*, May 1, 2001, 6; Horst Roessler, "30 Jahre später," 1972; Werner Schoenherr, "Weisse Flecken in der neueren Heimatgeschichte?," *Wochenblatt und Anzeiger*, November 19, 1999; "Grosser Teich, Dammteich oder?," *Freie Presse*, August 25, 2001; Mario Ulbrich, "Volkseigene Erholung und der grosse Stress danach," *Freie Presse*, October 6, 2001. All newspaper clippings from Geyer Turmmuseum Archiv.

94. Muenzner, "Landschaftsrahmenpläne Erholungsgebiet Stauweiher Greifenbach: Bebauungskonzeption Touristencampingsiedlung, " June 30, 1969, SäStCh: 30413/128093; Mario Ulbrich, "Volkseigene Erholung und der grosse Stress danach," *Freie Presse*, October 6, 2001; Letter from VEB Naherholung to the RdS, October 23, 1967, StaarchEhr: S IV/e24.

95. RdK Zschopau, "Empfehlung des RdK Zschopau zu Punkt 4 des Tagesordnung," July 30, 1968, StaarchEhr: S IV/e24.

96. Abt. Erholungswesen (RdK Zschopau),"Vorlage für die Sitzung des Kreistages," April 7, 1976, SäStCh: 30413/72446; Letter from VEB Erholungsgebiet Greifenbach to Abt. Jugendfragen, Körperkultur und Sport (hereinafter JKS) (RdK Zschopau), March 27, 1978, SäStCh: 30413/72511; Ständige Kommission Landeskultur und Erholung, "Abschrift," June 13, 1979, SäStCh: 30413/72470.

97. Zuarbeit zur Konzeption des RdB KMS" (no date or author) and "Entwurf: Ordnung über das Campingwesen im Bez KMS (Campingordnung)," SäStCh: 30413/149580.

98. Abt. JKS, "Niederschrift über die Beratung des Campingbeirates am 6.6.1969," June 26, 1969, KarchMZ: 7074.

99. Vorschläge für die Qualifizierung von Campingplatzleitern," SäStCh: 30413/138252.

100. Letter from Abt. UWE (RdK Zschopau) to Abt. Erholungswesen (RdB KMS), June 19, 1981, SäStCh: 30413/149580.

101. Abschlussprotokoll, "Durchführung territorialer Rationalisierungsmasnahmen—Aktiv Naherholung," September 22, 1969, 3, KarchMZ: 7074. In Kreis Zschopau, there were twenty-two *Betriebferienheime* (company vacation homes), though not all of them were at Greifenbach specifically.

102. FDGB Kreisvorstand, Feriendienst, "Bericht über durchgeführte Untersuchungen in den Betriebserholungsheimen innerhalb unseres Kreises und Gebieten zur eventuellen Nutzung der Wochenend und Naherholung," September 8, 1967, KarchMZ: 6118.

103. Abt. JKS, "Niederschrift über die durchgeführte Beratung des Aktivs Naherholung am 1.12.1967," January 4, 1968; Arbietsgruppe territoriale Koordinierung, "Protokoll über die Sitzung am 22.1.1968," January 22, 1968; Abt. JKS, "Niederschrift über die durchgeführte Beratung des Aktivs Naherholung am 1.12.1967," January 4, 1968, KarchMZ: 7074.

104. "Es bestehen wenig Wünsche, die Ferienheime durch die Bevölkerung unseres Kreises auszulasten" (Abt. JKS, "Abschlussprotokoll, Durchführung territorialer Rationalisierungsmasnahmen—Aktiv Naherholung," September 22, 1969, 3, KarchMZ: 7074).

105. Letter from Abt. UWE (RdK Plauen) to Abt. Erholungswesen (RdB KMS), March 15, 1985, SäStCh: 30413/128049.

106. Abt. JKS, "Niederschrift über den operativen Einsatz der Ständigen Kommission JKS des Kreistages Zschopau im Naherholungszentrum Greifenbachstauwieher," August 18, 1969, 2, KarchMZ: 7074.

107. Letter from Folkschor Streckewalde to the Kreiskabinett für Kulturarbeit beim RdK Zschopau, "Urlauberbetreuung Naherholungszentrum Greifensteingebiet," February 3, 1970, KarchMZ: 6117.

108. Letter from G.S. and J.S. to "Kollege Mann," VEB Naherholung, February 22, 1973, KarchMZ: 6117.

109. "Kirchenlager," 1962/63, SäStCh: 30413/5723.

110. RdK Zschopau, Abt. JKS, untitled document (speech detailing the history and development of the reservoir), 2, KarchMZ: 6117.

111. Letter from VEB Naherholung to RdK Zschopau, Abt. JKS, November 20, 1969, 2, KarchMZ: 6117.

112. Letter from RdK Zschopau, Abt. Volksbildung to RdS Ehrenfriedersdorf, July 7, 1964, KarchMZ: 7073; Speech by the RdK Zschopau, Abt. JKS, 7, KarchMZ: 6117; Letter from VEB Naherholung to RdK Zschopau, Abt. JKS, November 26, 1968, 3, KarchMZ: 7074.

113. Dietrich Zühlke, *Zwischen Zwickauer Mulde und Geyerschem Wald* (Berlin: Akademie Verlag, 1980), 6, 129.

114. Letter from RdK Zschopau, Stellvertreter der Vorsitzender to Abt. Handel und Versorgung and Letter from Baumann, RdK Zschopau to the National Front in Karl Marx City (in response to their letter of March 29, 1961, complaining about conditions at the campsite), both April 17, 1961, KarchMZ: 7073.

115. Letter from RdK Zschopau to RdB KMS, Vorsitzenden, July 21, 1961, KarchMZ: 7073.

116. "Vorschlag zum Perspektivplan Naherholung bis 1970," August 8, 1967, KarchMZ: 6093; Abt. JKS, "Information für die Sitzung des Rat der Kreise Zschopau

am 3/7/1968," March 6, 1968, KarchMZ: 7074; Letter to Kreisinspektion Zschopau from RdK, June 14, 1966, 1, KarchMZ: 7073.

117. "Ob das so bleiben soll?" *Neue Zschopauer Zeitung,* July 18, 1963.

118. W. Wappler, "Erholungszentrum wird weiter ausgebaut," *Freie Presse,* January 6, 1966, StaarchEhr: Zeitungsauschnitte 1966; "Vorschlag zum Perspektivplan Naherholung bis 1970," August 8, 1967, 5, KarchMZ: 6093.

119. "Niederschrift aus einer Beratung von Vertretern des RdS Ehrenfriedersdorf and der Stadt Geyer betreffs Campingplatz Greifenbachstauweiher," April 21, 1965, 1, KarchMZ: 7073; Letter from VEB Naherholung Ehrenfriedersdof to the RdK, Abt. JKS, November 26, 1968, KarchMZ: 7074.

120. Abt. Erholungswesen, untitled document, August 5, 1969; "Niederschrift über eine Beratung des Campingbeirates," September 7, 1966; "Niederschrift über die durchgeführte Beratung am 16.8.1968, " September 12, 1968; "Niederschrift aus einer Beratung von Vertretern des RdS Ehrenfriedersdorf and RdS Geyer betreffs Campingplatz Greifenbachstauweiher," April 21, 1965, KarchMZ: 7073; Letter from VEB Naherholung to RdK Zschopau, Abt. JKS, November 26, 1968, KarchMZ: 7074.

121. Dr. Borris (Kreishygienarzt), "Aktennotiz," August 12, 1970, StaarchEhr: S IV/e24.

122. Abt. JKS, "Planerfüllung 1 Halbjahr 1970," July 13, 1970, SäStCh: 30413/5948; Letter from VEB Erholungsgebiet Greifenbach to Abt. JKS (RdK Zschopau), March 27, 1978, SäStCh: 30413/72511; "Ansprache zur Auszeichnungsveranstaltung für die besten Hausgemeinschaften, Freibäder und Campingplätze des Bezirks KMS," 1982, SäStCh: 30413/149571.

123. Letter from Manfred Loeffler to Werner Teucher, no date, SäStCh: 30413/72470.

124. "Ein Paradies für Erholungsuchende," *Freie Presse,* no date, StaarchEhr: Zeitungsauschnitte 1969.

125. Newspaper clippings from StaarchEhr: Zeitungsauschnitte 1969, 1972, 1974, 1978; SäStCh: 30413/128058, 128059, 128080.

126. "Wie klappt während des Campingurlaubs die Versorgung? FP weilte einen Tag lang am Greifenbachstauweiher," *Freie Presse,* August 15, 1977, SäStCh: 30413/128059.

127. Abt. Erholungswesen (RdK Zschopau), "Informationsvorlage über die Entwicklung des Erholungsgebietes Greifensteine/Greifenbach Stauweiher für die Sitzung des Kreistages am 22.4.1976," April 6, 1976, SäStCh: 30413/72446; Letter from Rdk Zschopau to Abt. Erholungswesen (RdB KMS), May 3, 1979, SäStCh: 30413/6552.

128. "Mal Urlaub machen 'gleich vor der Haustür': In Zschopau wurden neue Möglichkeiten der Erholung für kinderreiche Familien geschaffen," *Freie Presse,* August 8, 1978, SäStCh: 30413/128061.

129. "Auf dem Campingplatz wird auf guten Service geachtet," *Freie Presse,* August 27, 1980, SäStCh: 30413/128080.

130. RdB Erfurt, "Konzeption zur Führung des sozialistischen Leistungsvergleiches zwischen den Campingplätzen des Bez Erfurt im Jahre 1979," April 19, 1979, SäStCh: 30413/138252; "Bericht über Wettbewerb 1985 der Campingplätze," SäStCh: 30413/149571; VEB Erholungsgebiet Greifentseine/Greifenbachstauweiher (G/G), "Aufruf der Beschäftigten des VEB G/G an alle Werktätigen der Campingplätze des Bezirkes KMS," April 23, 1986, SäStCh: 30413/138290.

131. VEB Naherholung, "Verbandsvertrag zwischen den VEB Naherholung und den

RdS Ehrenfriedersdorf, Thum, Geyer, und Rat der Gemeinde Jahnsbach und Hermersdorf," [1970?], StaarchEhr: S IV/e24.

132. On the reservoir and its proposed expansion, see SäStCh: 30413/27324, 30455; KarchMZ: 7073; Lothar Mueller, "'Gesetze wurden glatt missachtet' Ex-Wasserbauer Werner Haase: Der Geyersche Teich hätte niemals ein Naherholungsgebiet werden dürfen,",(no date, but newspaper clipping labeled October 2005 by archivist and likely from *Freie Presse*), Geyer Turmmuseum Archiv.

133. See correspondance on Geyersche Teiche in SäStCh: 30413/30455. See also Letter from Abt. Körperkultur, Sport, Erholung (RdB, KMS) to Abt. Volksbildung, July 30, 1964, SäStCh: 30413/5948; Letter from Bezirksnaturschutzverwaltung to RdK Zschopau, "Planung Erholungsgebiet Geyersche Teiche," May 14, 1965, StaarchEhr: S IV/e6.

134. Muenzner, "Landschaftsrahmenpläne Erholungsgebiet Stauweiher Greifenbach: Erläuterungsbericht," June 30, 1969, SäStCh: 30413/128093; Letter from VEB Naherholung to the LPG Helmut Just, August 27, 1970; "Beschluss aus der 24 Sitzung des RdS Geyer," April 20, 1971; and Abt. JKS, "Vorlage für die Sitzung des Rat der Kreise am 11/11/1971," November 3, 1971, KarchMZ: 6117.

CHAPTER 4

A New Environmental Law: Landscape Care, Global Ecology, and Domestic Social Policy

Given the history of landscape care in the 1950s, the SED's approval of a comprehensive conservation law (the Landeskulturgesetz) in 1970 is somewhat of a mystery, especially as it predated many similar laws in Western Europe. *Landeskultur* was a term familiar to West Germans, but it had particular signifiance for East German conservationists who understood it (as introduced in chapter 2) to mean the preservation *and* the expansion of natural resources through ecologically-sustainable and aesthetically-appropriate uses of the land. Rather than protect small preserves, the law called for holistic planning to preserve the integrity of whole landscapes while balancing the needs of industry, agriculture, recreation, and science. Among other provisions, it called for local governments to create positions for environmental protection officers and develop landscape care plans for landscape preserves. Dozens of similar proposals, however, never saw the light of day throughout the 1960s. Why did the SED decide in 1968 that environmental policy merited more attention? Did international politics determine the timing and character of the law, or did domestic concerns motivate the SED? This chapter will attempt to answer these questions and solve the mystery of the East German Landeskulturgesetz and its origins.

Some historians have suggested that the Landeskulturgesetz was just a Cold War ploy to prove the GDR's superiority to capitalist countries at a time of growing international concern about environmental sustainability.[1] Indeed, the law reflected the foreign policy ambitions of the SED when it went into effect in 1970. In speeches and press releases, Werner Titel, future minister for environmental protection and the head of a planning group that prepared the new law, reminded audiences that capitalism ravaged the environment while socialism's central scientific planning allowed for true environmental protection.[2] Moreover, Titel and associates used the occasion to attack the so called convergence theory, which they described as the West's attempt to depict environmental problems as a common problem of all industrialized nations on both sides of the Iron Curtain.[3]

The SED could not help but notice that scientists around the world were giving environmental issues greater attention. Scholars increasingly popularized the notion that the biosphere was an integrated system in which human uses of the land directly or indirectly influenced the stability and health of distant ecosystems. The international push toward systematic planning gained momentum at a groundbreaking 1955 conference of anthropologists, geographers, and ecologists including Carl Sauer, Lewis Mumford, and Clarence Glacken. The conference, which took its inspiration from George Perkins Marsh and his 1864 book *Man and Nature*, investigated the complex environmental consequences of human activity and published key papers in *Man's Role in Changing the Face of the Earth*.[4] During this same period, Julian Huxley (brother of Aldous), an evolutionary biologist and director general of UNESCO (the United Nations Educational, Scientific, and Cultural Organization), established the International Union for the Protection of Nature, which changed its name in 1956 to the International Union for the Conservation of Nature and Natural Resources (IUCN).[5] After its publication in 1962, Rachel Carson's *Silent Spring* became an international sensation and sparked broader public concern about the planet.[6] Scientists later explored the consequences of economic exploitation at summits such as the 1968 UNESCO Biosphere Conference (linked to the International Biological Program's ecological research) and the 1969 UNESCO gathering "Man and His Environment: A View Toward Survival." Later still, the United Nations introduced the Man and the Biosphere research program in 1971, and the European Council named 1970 the year of nature conservation.[7] Against this backdrop of international research and politics, did East German conservationists see the Landeskulturgesetz as merely Cold War gamesmanship and a miserable compromise never intended to alter East Germany's relationship with nature in any fundamental way?

From today's perspective, the law's anthropocentrism stands out, but East German scientists and nature preservationists initially saw it as a hopeful victory after a decade of struggle. The GDR's "conservation bloc" continued to stress *Erholung* and its value to worker productivity, but they were not satisfied with mere tourism planning. Instead, as this chapter will demonstrate, they proposed conservation policies remarkably similar to those included in the Landeskulturgesetz. Conservationists used whatever tool they could to push their agenda, from finding allies among prominent East Germans to linking their work to the latest "world-class" research that revealed conservation's benefits to economic expansion. Historian Sandra Chaney correctly stresses that East German scientists and architects never fully embraced the idea of biocentrism and thus could never sustain a credible critique of the SED before the late 1970s. As she argues, the turn to *Erholung* meant that conservationists failed to question the compatibility of biodiversity and materialism.[8] Yet as this chapter also will show, the IUCN then shared a similar worldview with the leaders of East Germany's conservation bloc. The conservation bloc, with their continued faith in managed yet limitless growth in the 1960s and early 1970s, actually belonged to the mainstream of world's scientists, who at that time rarely imagined hard limits to economic growth as an ecological necessity. In this sense, the 1970 Landeskulturgesetz (which might seem limited from today's perspective) reflected the highest aspirations of East German (and global) conservation. In fact, preservationist Reimar Gilsenbach remarked at the time, "I believe that these ideas are exactly those that we have long discussed."[9]

Compared to the previous decade, the 1960s were, on the surface, more promising for reformers, because the SED now appeared friendly to reform. Throughout its history, East Germany's proximity to the capitalist Federal Republic made comparisons of social welfare and economic success across the Iron Curtain inevitable. The regime responded with a sometimes unpredictable mix of repression and material concessions. With the construction of the Berlin Wall in 1961, the SED introduced an element of stability to their rule. East Germans no longer had the option of "voting with their feet" by fleeing to West Berlin and became increasingly resigned to the notion that the GDR was there to stay. Feeling more secure, Walter Ulbricht began to experiment. In 1963, he introduced a program of cultural and economic liberalization associated with the New Economic System. For example, he encouraged Kurt Turba to compose a youth communiqué in which the SED promised to tolerate a greater variety of free-time activities, including listening and dancing to rock music.[10] Cultural liberalization abruptly came to an end in 1965, with the eleventh plenum of the SED, also known as the Kahlschlag Plenum. Here, Eric Honecker and other SED hard-liners publicly attacked Ulbricht's new tolerance of popular youth culture; Honecker loudly condemned rock fashions and music as degenerate and threatening to the development of enlightened socialist personalities. The regime's later encouragement of the Warsaw Pact invasion of Czechoslovakia during the Prague Spring reflected its nervousness about excessive reform. At the same time, an increasingly influential Erich Honecker endorsed Ulbricht's new attention to popular desires, as long as party functionaries deemed them untainted by Western decadence. As part of the larger project of mollifying popular discontent in the 1960s, the party introduced the five-day workweek, encouraged *Eingaben* (complaint letters), and rewrote the constitution in 1968 through an extensive series of public meetings meant to engage the public in the process. While conservationists hoped that the New Economic System's emphasis on scientific planning might benefit comprehensive landscape care, most of the major SED attempts to satisfy popular desires during this decade did little to benefit conservationists. In fact, by stressing economic success and material desires, they probably did more harm than good.[11]

As this chapter argues, the SED's domestic social agenda and its concerns for popular opinion best explain the timing and content of the Landeskulturgesetz. As will be seen, the text of the Landeskulturgesetz thus connected landscape planning to expanded *Erholung* opportunities for the general public. The SED's social agenda had both benefits and drawbacks for conservationists. On the one hand, conservationists themselves had long been promoting the links between landscape protection and *Erholung*. In this way, the conservation bloc shaped the language of the new law. On the other hand, this focus on *Erholung* threatened to undermine comprehensive reform of land-use planning. Throughout the 1960s, the SED advertised its efforts to increase leisure opportunities to win over a disgruntled population. As a result, the law downplayed ecology and the reform of land-use planning while accentuating how the regime worked to help local governments secure more camping and boating destinations for hardworking East Germans.

In highlighting this domestic agenda rather than foreign policy goals, this chapter again focuses attention on East Germany's fragile "mainstream consensus" about authoritarian planning, limitless abundance, and land use. If the Landeskulturgesetz had been only window dressing conceived in SED offices to enhance the GDR's international reputation and dupe hopeful East German scientists, it would be easier for historians to paint the regime as a totalitarian state standing above its subjects and possessing unlimited power to shape society to its whims. The genealogy of the Landeskulturgesetz, as presented in this chapter, places more emphasis on the limits of dictatorship, the loud and very public grumbling of citizens, and the key concessions the regime made to ensure its popular legitimacy. Later seen as compromised, it could also be understood as a last, brief moment before a vocal minority began to question the compatibility of conservation, limitless consumerism, and dictatorship. Conservationists, even if they noticed warning signs to the contrary, finally had a well-publicized, comprehensive planning law on the books. It reflected their desire to have technical experts manage leisure, agriculture, and nature preservation for the benefit of all. While the law made little room for hard limits on economic uses of the land, most conservationists still believed that economic growth could be managed without such limits. As much as anything, later frustrations with the law reflected dashed hopes that the law could truly make a difference. Vacationers also got what they wanted, in that the law reassured them that the regime meant to provide inexhaustible abundance, which, in this case, meant equal and numerous vacation opportunities in an increasingly crowded countryside. The SED, for its part, composed the law in such a way to ensure that reformers did not limit their ability to grow the economy, maintain low food prices through industrial agricultural methods, and keep the masses happy. In sum, the Landeskulturgesetz had something for everyone. Satisfaction with the law would not last long, however. As the regime publicized the law, as we will see, cracks already began to form in East Germany's "mainstream consensus."

Precursors to the Landeskulturgesetz

The Landeskulturgesetz did not appear out of thin air, and the SED did not merely copy nature protection laws from elsewhere. The vision and perseverance of East Germany's conservation bloc during the 1960s were essential for conceptualizing the Landeskulturgesetz, if not for its final form and approval. Recognizing the limits of their influence in the Ministry for Agriculture, the conservation bloc sought to somehow increase their power and prestige in the 1960s. Attempts at administrative reform first took root in the 1950s, and these efforts at centralization also reflected the hopes held by conservationists as far back as the 1920s in Germany.

Conservationists' basic argument for more central regulatory power remained essentially the same throughout the 1950s and into the 1960s. Even before the 1954 Nature Protection Law went into effect, the ILN and Kulturbund (Culture League) began to fight for more power over land use, demanding their own high-level ministry to oversee economic initiatives. In 1953, Hermann Meusel wrote to the Central Committee of the SED to ask for a central planning office for nature protection, directly responsible to the Ministerial Council (a type of "presidential cabinet" where representatives of each central ministry gathered to coordinate planning and receive their marching orders from the SED). This solution, he highlighted, would correspond best with the precedent set by the Soviet Union, East Germany's supposed role model.[12] At a summit of nature preservationists in Berlin in 1953, the theme of a central, more powerful administration again dominated discussions. Stronger central support for nature protection was so important because local nature protection officers at the district and county level of governance had almost no power to influence local authorities.[13] The Kulturbund and the DAL later presented the SED and the Ministry for Agriculture with two documents to promote administrative and legal reform. The Kulturbund's Nature and Heimat Friends sent the SED their thoughts on "Some Problems in Nature Protection and Landscape Care" in early 1961, and the DAL pushed higher authorities to endorse their new "Guidelines for a Socialist Land Improvement" in 1962.[14] Meusel, Stubbe, and Gilsenbach also began a letter-writing campaign to promote these guidelines, noting, as always, the connections between *Erholung* and landscape care and the need for better and more comprehensive protection of rural landscapes from misguided exploitation.[15] To gain the ear of the SED, they all presented their aspirations as only possible under a socialist regime promoting central planning and cutting-edge science that could overcome narrow economic interests (*Betriebsegoismus*).[16]

Hoping to convince the SED of the need for a new Landeskulturgesetz as early as 1960, the ILN sought the help of Johannes Dieckmann, the president of the Volkskammer (East Germany's parliament) and chair of the Liberal Democratic Party (LPDP), a nominally independent political party tightly controlled by the SED. He was also cofounder of the Kulturbund and president of the Society for German-Soviet Friendship, even though he was not an SED party member. The ILN and its friends often highlighted Dieckmann's support when pushing for reform, hoping that having a prominent ally would help them.[17] In 1963, for example, Reimar Gilsenbach requested Dieckmann's support of a National Park Saxon Switzerland and pleaded, "The effectiveness of an independent journalist is limited. I will provide the press, television, and radio with a whole assortment of articles on this theme. But those can only be helpful suggestions . . . If you, Mr. President, embrace the promotion of these ideas, then much could be accomplished."[18] In 1963, the DAL also requested that Dieckmann create a Committee for Land Improvement within the Volkskammer, possibly an Advisory Board for Landeskultur and the Conservation of Natural Resources within the Ministerial Council, or even perhaps a full Ministry for Land Improvement.[19] Meusel met with a few MPs from the Volkskammer about conservation and reported, "We have been impressed there that, on the side of attending MPs, there was great interest for the issues at hand. A lively discussion highlighted the damage to our landscape."[20] In 1966, Dieckmann composed an article in support of a *Landeskulturgesetz* for *Morgen*, an

LPDP periodical.[21] Dieckmann, furthermore, wrote to the Ministerial Council pushing for a central body to administer and coordinate land improvements.[22]

In the mid-1960s, however, the SED saw no need for a new conservation law. A representative of the State Council wrote to Dieckmann and explained that it would be unproductive to take on these issues, especially since they should only be discussed if linked to the fulfillment of the economic plan. He also asked that the members of the Volkskammer better orient themselves to the established central tasks necessary for the full construction of socialism. In pencil at the bottom of this letter, an annoyed reader, presumably Dieckmann, wrote, "Besides central tasks there are still other tasks!"[23] When Meusel expressed frustration that Dieckmann's aid had not gotten the ILN any further in its reform efforts, the DAL's president told him in early 1965, "[Dieckmann] told me that he had ran into clear reservations and disapproval in many offices, always with the argument that one must concentrate on central tasks."[24]

The ILN's constant agitation for reform often backfired and led to reprisals from authorities during this period. The SED and agricultural planners clearly saw the ILN as a threat to industrial agriculture.[25] SED functionaries in the DAL, including Günter Zillmann from the State Secretariat for Research and Technology (Staatssekretariat for Forschung und Technik), grumbled about political difficulties within the ILN and complained about aggressive criticisms of industrial agriculture voiced by Meusel and friends.[26] The creation of the Ständige Kommission für Landschaftspflege und Naturschutz (SKLN, or Standing Committee for Landscape Care and Nature Protection), with Meusel moving from leadership of ILN to this committee in 1963, might have been an attempt to isolate conservationists within a weak committee ignored by the academy as a whole.[27] Meusel soon complained that the academy's yearbook never reported on the commission's research and that key individuals within the DAL never attended a commission meeting.[28] In 1966, tensions again came to the surface at a meeting where officials from the State Secretariat for Research and Technology attacked the ILN for troublemaking and downplaying economic objectives.[29]

In addition to seeking out allies among prominent politicians, the conservation bloc also tried to win over their opponents by presenting their research as "world-class." For these scientists, the quite similar agenda of the International Union for the Conservation of Nature affirmed their vision for conservation and nature protection—one that moved beyond the protection of relict nature preserves and toward a comprehensive planning of land use to balance economic development and ecological sustainability.[30] When labeled reactionary and unscientific, Meusel countered that his work reflected the cutting edge of global science. He told his superiors, "All over the world nature protection takes on tasks that are important to landscape care and land improvement. Right now at the International Union for the Preservation of Nature conference these questions are being addressed."[31] The Kulturbund's Nature and Heimat Friends noted, "The IUCN . . . deals more and more now with problems of the *Kulturlandschaft*, such as the struggle against soil erosion, against ever-increasing pollution of air and water, and against the depletion of natural resources needed for economic production."[32] In failing to endorse policies promoted by the IUCN and many Eastern European neighbors, another conservationist pointedly suggested that the GDR fell further behind global standards.[33]

The IUCN and East Germany's conservation bloc shared some basic assumptions about conservation and planned economic growth. The IUCN was one of the first postcolonial, international organizations to promote resource conservation. While weak in terms of actual political influence, organizations such as the IUCN lobbied governments and hosted scientific commissions that allowed for transnational cooperation between scientific experts. UNESCO, the Swiss League for Nature Protection, and the French government led the initiative to found the International Union for the Protection of Nature (IUPN) in 1948. Other key players included the New York Zoological Society, the Society for the Preservation of Fauna of the Empire, and the Boone and Crockett Club. UNESCO's director general, biologist Julian Huxley, supported the IUPN, largely because the United Nations had no agency with a specific environmental mission. The initial members of the IUPN included eighteen governments, seven international organizations, and 107 national nature conservation organizations.[34]

The IUPN's name change in 1956 reflected a shift in the organization that appealed to East Germany's conservation bloc. As the International Union for the Protection of Nature, the newborn organization imagined itself as a guardian of endangered species and their critical habitats. Many of the participating nongovernmental organizations fully embraced the preservation of habitats in preserves that excluded all economic activity.[35] At the 1956 Edinburgh General Assembly, however, the IUPN changed its name to the International Union for the Conservation of Nature and Natural Resources (IUCN) and placed greater emphasis on resource conservation that would assist developing nations on their path to sustainable growth. This change reflected the harsh realities of lobbying for nature protection during a period of intense postwar reconstruction and a new global initiative to encourage economic development in the postcolonial world. While the Soviets and East Germans offered development aid to sympathetic governments in Asia and Africa, the United States countered with a Green Revolution to provide the developing world with new agricultural technologies.[36] Complementing the Green Revolution, the IUCN now sought the "restoration, wise use, and administration of natural resources as a basis for development to assure 'the future peace, progress and prosperity of Mankind.'"[37] The organization recognized that its success depended on an appeal to developing nations seeking economic growth.[38] In the culmination of this transition, the IUCN published a handbook in 1973 entitled *Ecological Principles for Economic Development.*[39]

The new emphasis on economic development made the IUCN more attractive, in particular, to the Soviet Union and its allies, with the crucial exception of the SED. At the IUCN's 1960 assembly in Poland, the executive board affirmed its decision to "give more specific attention to the economic aspects of conservation."[40] A Soviet member of the IUCN's executive board, B. N. Bogdanov, applauded the new IUCN, which he thought "much enhanced by further strengthening of its attention to the social and economic aspects of nature conservation."[41] When Soviet conservationist L. K. Shaposhnikov later took over the IUCN's Education Commission, he further encouraged this greater focus on economic development, commenting that "nature conservation is a vital economic and social problem of all nations."[42] Despite the Soviet Union's engagement with the IUCN, East Germany did not fully participate in the organization and viewed links between its scientists and the IUCN with great suspicion. When the GDR had the opportunity to join the IUCN as a full member, agricultural planners overruled East German conservationists.[43] At the same time, the West Germans blocked East German membership, since NATO members did not officially recognize the sovereignty of the GDR.[44]

The aversion of East Germany's agricultural economists to the IUCN had deeper roots, however. Agricultural planners did not approve of a neo-Malthusian worldview shared by Julian Huxley and many prominent IUCN scientists. Neo-Malthusian economic theory blamed poverty and environmental degradation on uncontrolled population growth. Many of the IUPN's original founders came from the Boone and Crockett Club in the United States and the United Kingdom's Society for the Preservation of the Wild Fauna of Empire, which had long sought to protect African and Asian species from native overhunting. As such, postwar conservation maintained a link to the Social Darwinism of empire, in which white Europeans felt the need to instruct supposedly irresponsible nonwhites on the proper management of natural resources.[45] Marxist economic planners may have also distrusted the links of the

IUCN and UNESCO to the "Green Revolution," which was meant to increase grain yields around the world and thus lessen the appeal of "red" revolutionaries to developing nations. In the eyes of neo-Malthusians, the cure for social revolution was prosperity, which required population control combined with scientific innovation to increase food production and maintain natural resources. In this vein, Julian Huxley advocated "birth control in development nations to limit potentially catastrophic increases in human populations."[46] Huxley, specifically, feared the rapid population increase of non-Europeans that threatened "Western" cultural progress, so he endorsed sterilization to slow out-of-control population growth in the developing world.[47] Despite Huxley's neo-Malthusianism, the Soviets and East German conservationists recognized that the organization shared with them certain assumptions about economic planning. Huxley also saw a potential for cooperation. Before World War II, he had even admired the Soviet Union's five-year plans and technocratic planning of agriculture and industry. Unlike more conservative eugenicists, Huxley also recognized that environment often determined behavior as much or more than genetics; as such, he insisted on central planning to improve natural and social environments.[48]

Popular Unrest and the Landeskulturgesetz

Despite the strategies employed by the conservation bloc, the Ministry for Agriculture not only thwarted cooperation with the IUCN but also blocked all attempts to strengthen landscape care in East Germany; nonetheless, the Landeskulturgesetz introduced in 1970 closely resembled the proposals made by the ILN and the Kulturbund in the early 1960s. Most important, the new law reflected the conservation bloc's campaign to link *Erholung* and landscape care, acknowledged the need for comprehensive planning, and insisted on balancing economic development and landscape protections so that economic expansion could continue. The barricades confronting conservation interests suddenly seemed to lower, and one might wonder if the conservation bloc had won. What happened?

While nothing had altered the regime's plans for industrial agriculture, the calculations for securing the political legitimacy of the SED had changed dramatically by the end of the 1960s. While the diplomatic motivations have been considered as an influence on the Landeskulturgesetz, more attention needs to be given to domestic political concerns as a motivation for legal reform. Several key political initiatives in the 1960s can be understood as attempts by a divided SED to acknowledge popular desires without sacrificing its singular powers. The emergence of the Landeskulturgesetz, therefore, cannot be understood without acknowledging its connections to the New Economic System of 1963, new directives to collect *Eingaben* (letters of complaint), and the constitutional reforms of 1968.

Concerns about popular legitimacy and related struggles with economic productivity contributed to two key moments in the genealogy of the Landeskulturgesetz. First, in 1963, Walter Ulbricht announced the commencement of the New Economic System. Protected by the Berlin Wall, Ulbricht welcomed new blood into the planning ministries to implement a program of liberalization, simultaneously calling for a decentralization of cultural and economic decision making and an escalation of scientific planning inspired by new research into cybernetics. Objective scientific planning, it seemed, would now trump crass political maneuvers.[49] The New Economic System led to a rather dull but important step toward the Landeskulturgesetz when the Ministerial Council announced its 1967 Ordinance on the Expansion of Prognostic Work (Beschluss über die Weiterführung der prognostischen Arbeit), which asked planners to predict future needs in ten areas of immediate concern, including energy, electronics, and transportation.[50] Second, the SED pushed for greater integration of *Eingaben*, or complaint letters, into ministry decision making. One 1966 initiative (among many *Eingaben* initiatives over the years) set the goal of better analyzing *Eingaben* and acknowledging their suggestions in ministerial decisions.[51]

Eingaben served as an outlet of popular discontent and also a tool of control. Much like appeals to a monarch under early modern absolutism, the SED intended petitioners to engage in a "private dialogue between individuals and the ruling elite."[52] The public participated in governance in an officially approved and individualistic manner, thus channeling their discontent into private complaints and away from organized forms of protest. Petitions also allowed the regime to monitor public opinion and keep track of economic failures as identified by letter writers. In the absence of a public sphere where discontent could be aired, East Germans by the 1980s wrote at least five hundred thousand petitions every year.[53] The regime encouraged this letter writing and demanded that its bureaucrats respond to each and every letter writer, a task that became increasingly time-consuming. Most East Germans had little fear of reprisal for their complaints unless they provocatively questioned the fundamental ideological tenets of the regime. As a result, most petitioners framed their letters as demands that the regime live up to its material promises.[54]

While the Ministerial Council's Ordinance on the Expansion of Prognostic Work made no mention of nature conservation, recreation planning, or environmental pollution, the steady stream of petitions and complaints changed things. The Ministerial Council's analysis of petitions in the third quarter of 1967 revealed an overwhelming concern among the public for pollution and for the five-day workweek.[55] One petition highlighted in the report stressed the financial consequences of pollution, emphasizing the damage done to collective farms by emissions from chemical or cement factories. The report also acknowledged widespread discontent about the regime's unhealthy obsession with industrial agriculture. Oversized, factorylike livestock stalls, many petitioners insisted, had terrible "effects on the local population."[56] While the analysis of *Eingaben* did not appear officially before the Ministerial Council until November 9, 1967, the council was more than likely aware of the *Eingaben* on October 20, 1967, when it asked Dr. Werner Titel, the minister in charge of the Water Management Agency, and Max Sefrin, minister of health, to contribute to prognostic planning and lead a research group on the relationship of pollution to the overall economy.[57] The Ministerial Council's concerns about popular opinion were clearest when Sefrin complained in June 1968 that the response to *Eingaben* in 1967 "came to too little effect."[58]

Despite the growing number of petitions, the Prognosis Group Landeskultur pursued a pragmatic, rather than reformist, orientation.[59] Titel, also a deputy chair of the Ministerial Council, had received an education in agriculture and had been a member of the central council of the FDJ when younger.[60] Not surprisingly, Titel initially seemed completely unaware of the long-standing discussion of pollution and land-use planning within the ILN or the Kulturbund. His eventual proposals were initially tentative, even offering two very different recommendations to the full Ministerial Council. The first fully reflected an agenda of the conservation bloc, and the second stressed achievable and economically feasible goals oriented toward economic productivity. Titel repeatedly pushed the second recommendation and encouraged his working group to focus on small, technical problems and avoid sweeping regulations. For example, he reminded his associates to focus clearly on the issue of waste products, which might provide economic benefits to industry and budget relief for the state.[61] In the prognosis of over a hundred pages finally produced in September 1968, the working group rarely mentioned strict limitations on pollution and instead stressed the economic rewards of the targeted recycling of chemical and other industrial waste products.[62] The conservation provisions were so weak that they might as well have been written by factory managers. In fact, industrial interests praised in particular the narrow ambitions of the Ministerial Council's proposals.[63]

Titel seemed to be steering conservation reform toward death by commit-tee, but in late autumn 1968 and amid popular unrest across Europe, concerns about popular opinion again intervened. From within the Ministerial Council, a working group dominated by health and leisure experts associated with the conservation bloc made a timely intervention. They insisted that the Prognosis Group Landeskultur had underestimated the seriousness and importance of pollution as a threat to the economy—especially through the effects on public health in heavily industrialized regions. Crucially, the committee pointed out to ministerial authorities that citizens had expressed their intense concern about pollution in public meetings related to constitutional reforms in 1968. They noted, "This enthusiasm must be exploited as soon as possible by the regime and be incorporated into regulations, in order to avoid negative political-ideological effects that . . . would especially have influence on the willingness to participate further in socialist democracy."[64] In other words, the small steps of the Ministerial Council were not enough—especially in the battle for popu-lar legitimacy in the wake of the Prague Spring. Much to the surprise of eco-nomic hard-liners, Titel now pushed for a more dramatic display of the re-gime's commitment to Landeskultur, in the form of the new Landeskulturgesetz. Titel stressed public opinion (specifically, the *Eingaben* analysis of 1967) when he proposed in November 1968 to turn his small research collective from an advisory body into a full, permanent Prognosis Group for Industrial Waste and the Systematic Development of a Socialist Landeskultur.[65] By February 5, 1969, he had created the Permanent Working Group for Socialist Landeskultur, which was directly responsible to the Ministerial Council.[66]

Despite the long history of acrimony between conservationists and eco-nomic planners, the Prognosis Group Landeskultur surprisingly invited a select group of conservation experts to help compose the Landeskulturgesetz. In De-cember 1968, the Bund Deutschen Architekten (BDA, German Architects' League) and the Kulturbund organized a scientific colloquium on "the Evolu-tion of a socialist *Kulturlandschaft* in the GDR." Groups contributing to the resulting report included health technocrats and the ILN—exactly the coalition of conservation and health interests created in the 1950s. It should be noted, though, that the ILN's former leader, Hermann Meusel, only heard after the fact about the BDA and the Kulturbund's contributions to the writing of a *Landeskulturgesetz*.[67] Not surprisingly, the colloquium's suggestions (for-warded to the Ministerial Council in March 1969) resembled earlier reform proposals that had been gathering dust in the Ministry for Agriculture and SED offices since 1960. As previous proposals had, their suggestions to the Ministe-rial Council began with a reminder that key individuals had intended the 1954

Nature Protection Law to be followed by a more comprehensive *Landeskulturgesetz*. They insisted on the need for a coordination of all economic activities that influence the appearance and health of the *Kulturlandschaft* and hoped to overcome all narrow interests (*Zweigegoismus*). At the heart of their vision was this connection between healthy landscapes and *Erholung*—both were inadequately regulated, to the detriment of each. Most important, their proposal called for a unified leadership for Landeskultur, perhaps a State Secretariat for Landeskultur within the Ministerial Council.[68]

The rapid change of course could be read in the alarmed responses from many economic planners. A working group from the State Planning Commission acknowledged the political reasons for the SED to introduce a new *Landeskulturgesetz* but rejected the hasty leap forward. The committee wrote, "In our appraisal of the proposed law on November 21, 1968, we had already established that the writing of a law was unrealistic before July 1969. There exists still no mature vision for the integration of *Landeskultur* into the socialist system." At best, they conceded, they recognized that there may be political reasons to introduce such a law in honor of the thirtieth anniversary of the GDR's creation.[69] The DAL's Division for Forestry, which had fought against the conservation bloc within the Ministry for Agriculture, complained that the law went too far in subordinating economic planning to *Landeskultur*. The foresters wrote, "These [problems] are, in our opinion, a question not just of formulation but, instead, of ideological vagueness. Through [our] participation in divisional meetings [in the DAL] and other meetings, we are aware that scientists and representatives of *Landeskultur* lack the necessary ideological clarity on such questions."[70]

Erholung's Role in the Landeskulturgesetz

The SED's growing nervousness about public opinion also led it to give more attention to *Erholung* and tourism. Statements about *Erholung*'s importance for health and well-being dominated the text of the Landeskulturgesetz, as well as its subsequent promotion in the press. Crucially, the law insisted that landscape planning focus on the development of infrastructure to accommodate an increasing number of vacationers. As we will see, this stress on *Erholung* reflected the SED campaign in the 1960s to respond to popular discontent about material conditions. It also reflected the SED's vision of limitless economic growth aided by contented and healthy workers refreshed by their leisure time. Its interest in *Erholung* thus only increased as it became aware of a public health disaster looming on the horizon (as rates of obesity, heart disease, and respiratory diseases grew). Of course, conservationists had made this link between conservation, *Erholung*, and public health central to their reform campaign and thus influenced the text of the new law. However, *Erholung* became increasingly problematic as the text was completed and as authorities publically promoted the Landeskulturgesetz. Conservationists then began to worry that *Erholung* planning might overshadow genuine landscape care and environmental protection.

Extensive sections of the law and its precursors promoted the setting aside and protection of *Erholung* landscapes to provide for "Happiness and Relaxation" and to help in the "Preservation and Promotion of Health."[71] In the run-up to the new law, a February 1969 Ministerial Council decree ordered district authorities to secure the landscape's value for *Erholung*.[72] The law itself stated, "For the comprehensive fulfillment of our citizens' rights to leisure and *Erholung*, especially through tourism, sport, and physical fitness . . . , as well as for the preservation and promotion of health, the landscape is to be systematically developed, cared for, and sensibly used. To this end, landscape preserves and other spaces, especially forests and lakeshores, are to be developed into *Erholung* parks."[73] A subsequent executive ordinance to compliment the Landeskulturgesetz bore the title "Development and Care of Landscapes for Erholung." The ordinance demanded the prevention of pollution in *Erholung* landscapes and also the development of these regions for the public.[74]

The history of SED social and leisure policy from 1953 to 1970 can help explain the regime's emphasis on *Erholung* in the Landeskulturgesetz. After the 1953 uprising over work norms, the regime continued to promote "productive" proletarian sport, but local concessions to casual leisure interests became more common. In practice, reforms meant to improve productivity provided workers (especially those in strategically important industries) with higher wages and more social welfare benefits, including more vacation days and exclusive access to campsites.[75] In the 1960s, Walter Ulbricht also tentatively downplayed political education and highbrow *Kultur* in official leisure planning. In this way, the party ensured greater participation in cultural activities and organizations that had been largely ignored by most East Germans up to that point. Honecker's 1965 attack on youth culture did not sway the SED from its new attention to popular outdoor recreation. While hiking and camping had earlier been seen as vestiges of bourgeois romanticism, they now were preferable to rock-and-roll lifestyles. At the thirteenth plenum of the Central Committee of the SED in 1966, Erich Honecker recommended the regime pay more attention to the ways in which East Germans enjoyed themselves in the countryside. Honecker told the plenum, "They [workers] wish for an interesting free time, in which they feel happy and are affirmed as creative individuals just like at work . . . More employees spend—especially on their free Saturdays and Sundays—their free time in nature with their families, participate in tourism and sport, undertake excursions, and relax in their gardens . . . Many leaders do not recognize the new circumstances."[76] In a related initiative, the SED introduced the "five-day week every two weeks" in 1966 (in 1967, this became a five-day workweek every week). Changes to the work week led to a series of initiatives where cultural authorities tried to make their organizations more attractive to the general public.[77] The 1968 Constitution, when finally complete, confirmed the importance of *Erholung*. Articles 34 and 35 guaranteed the right to free time and *Erholung*.[78] Honecker's rise to power in 1971 then confirmed that the state's interest in *Erholung*. Honecker promised, "Recreation planning is, in light of the social policies of the socialist state, to be further developed."[79]

To a certain degree, the conservation bloc encouraged these high-level political decisions through their constant arguments about *Erholung* and public health. As Ulbricht raised the profile of cybernetics and social science, his New Economic System led the State Planning Commission to organize working groups or committees to evaluate social and economic trends. As a part of this effort, a group of sociologists, economists, doctors, sports physiologists, and leisure planners met in 1964 to study the problem of *Erholungswesen*.[80] The two most prominent committee members were from the conservation bloc, including the landscape architect Frank Erich Carl from the Bauakademie and Dr. Edelfried Buggel from the DWBV.[81] Preliminary research on living standards at the Planning Commission asserted that longer vacations in the countryside were necessary for "reproducing" labor energy.[82] Recreation, wrote Dr. Alfred Keck of the living standards program, played a very useful role in the "restoration of [workers'] efficiency."[83]

Labor experts had more reasons than ever to pay attention to the conservation bloc's arguments about *Erholung* and planning. After many young skilled workers fled westward in the 1950s, these experts nervously predicted a demographic crisis. They, for example, forecast a labor shortage by 1970 as the East German population aged.[84] Studies also revealed increasing rates of obesity and heart disease (the most common cause of death in the GDR in the 1960s).[85] Automation and a growing number of office jobs, researchers argued, aggravated these health problems. Workers, according to living standards researchers, "spent most of their days in enclosed spaces with artificial climates, [and] changes in the demands of work, noise, and transportation led to overstimulation and thus to nervous stress." "All of these experiences," they suggested, "must be counteracted through a purposeful planning of leisure."[86] Through sport and recreation, experts thus hoped "to lengthen and beautify the lives of our citizens."[87]

In a sign of the times, the DWBV, earlier notorious for ignoring leisurely hiking, now turned its attention to family hikes and outings. Throughout leisure planning offices, the SED gave new importance to family-friendly activities.[88] Dr. Edelfried Buggel led the DWBV on its particular path toward this compromise with popular desires. Opinion surveys conducted by Buggel revealed that half of those surveyed were regularly active in sport or tourism and that most enjoyed sport and leisure on their own or with their families rather than in mass organizations.[89] Beginning in the late 1960s and through the 1970s, DWBV functionaries such as Bernhard Fisch and Wolfgang Bagger abandoned "athletic tourism" to encourage more public hiking events for families, individuals, and the elderly.[90] For example, the DWBV in Leipzig insisted on the development of "public family hikes and factory events for workers."[91] Dresden's district leadership responded to popular demands for more public hikes by better publicizing family hikes hosted by its clubs and sponsoring "people's hikes," short guided hikes, and mushroom-collecting excursions.[92] The emerging public health crisis also informed the DWBV reconciliation with popular leisure practices. Instead of promoting athletic competition, organizers now promoted the Run/Walk for Health (Lauf dich Gesund) campaign to promote jogging and hiking as ways to combat the growing problem of heart disease.[93] Dr. Bernhard Fisch emphasized in *Sportliches Wandern*, "Active tourists retain on average greater physical productivity into old age and greater immunity against many diseases."[94] Fisch thus proposed that local organizers offer "fitness walks," with slogans such as "Hike with—Stay fit!"[95]

Even though they had brought *Erholung* to the SED's attention, the conservation bloc rarely benefited from the SED's new attention to *Erholung* in the late 1960s. The language of the 1968 Constitution stressed the development and expansion of tourist infrastructure, not the conservation of nature for the benefit of tourists. For example, it obligated the state to "systematically develop the network of vacation and recreation destinations" and "plan for improvements to tourism."[96] In a move that must have been disorienting for reformers, even proponents of industrial agriculture began to celebrate popular *Erholung*. At the 1967 Nature Protection Week, industrial forester Fritz Wernicke emphasized the slogan "Our forests—an important component of our natural wealth, provider of raw materials, as well as sites of joy and *Erhol-*

ung."[97] At a December 1968 gathering of this working group, hard-liner Dr. Gerhard Grüneberg (the promoter of large-scale industrial agriculture and collectivization) even made an appearance to advocate for *Erholung* forests.[98]

The story of the highly influential 1966 Landschaftstag, or landscape planning conference, provides a crucial example of this disorienting turn of events that ultimately crushed conservation hopes. Conservationists in the 1960s became increasingly worried about vacationers overwhelming lakeshores and mountain forests. Kurt Kretschmann, for example, led a crusade against the privatization of lakeshores by bungalow owners near Berlin.[99] These concerns, in addition to a long-standing desire to more comprehensively plan land use, led to proposals for a planning conference. But cultural authorities rejected a proposed April 1963 conference on landscape care and *Erholung* as a threat to economic and agricultural priorities. In 1966, however, the regime reversed course and approved the conference proposal of the Nature and Heimat Friends.[100] Dr. Hugo Weinitschke worked to limit discussions at the Landschaftstag to specific tasks related to *Erholung*. He set the agenda when he noted, "For all the breadth of the tasks before nature protection in our Republic, we want in the following days to focus closely on a special area of interest [*Erholung*]. Special attention was given to this problem during the eleventh plenum of the Central Committee of the SED."[101] With the approval of the five-day workweek, the SED recognized a need for more *Erholung* destinations and better coordination of tourism planning. Over the next few years, authorities clearly pushed the landscape planners to focus on the planning of vacation destinations and not to agitate for a broader, more comprehensive reform of environmental policy.[102]

Preservationist Reimar Gilsenbach immediately noticed how the conference threatened nature protection. In his paper, he argued for National Parks, but censors changed the title of his speech in the official program from "Does the GDR Need National Parks?" to "What Is an *Erholungspark*?" Organizers demanded that he not mention national parks in his speech.[103] During his presentation, Gilsenbach despaired at the compromise inherit to the proceedings and complained, "If we are going to worry about *Erholung* landscapes, then we should not forget that *Erholung* is only a part of a much larger and more serious problem."[104] Conservation interests in East Germany had reached a "moment of truth" in their embrace of *Erholung* as a justification for better landscape care and protection. For years, they had used *Erholung* as one of the only rhetorical tools available to them in the fight against the Ministry for Agriculture. Now, the SED cared very much about *Erholung* but used it to silence calls for land-use reform.

As the SED released the Landeskulturgesetz to public review, *Erholung* indeed appeared again and again in official commentaries, speeches, and press coverage, reflecting the law's importance for signaling to the public that the SED cared very much about their leisure desires. Titel proclaimed in a speech, "Nature is a site of *Erholung*, for preserving health, for sport and play. A sensible planning of our natural environment will do justice to this function of nature; an arbitrary use of natural resources, a worsening pollution of water and air, and uncoordinated construction within a landscape reduces the value of nature [for *Erholung*] and damages our society."[105] A reliable SED voice in the Kulturbund noted, "The objective of the law reflects in full the declaration of . . . Walter Ulbricht at the twelfth plenum, where he proclaimed that today the conditions are ripe" for improving living standards.[106] The SED's Volkskammer faction praised the law's stress on continued economic growth and highlighted its importance in providing citizens with *Erholung* opportunities.[107] The Kulturbund celebrated the law for allowing for the multiple use of landscapes by industry, agriculture, and vacationers.[108]

While Gilsenbach increasingly doubted the value of recreation planning for conservationists, his subsequent optimism about the Landeskulturgesetz reflected the complicated and confusing political path the law had traveled before becoming publicized. In numerous ways, the history of the Landeskulturgesetz thus complicates narratives of East German environmental decline and totalitarian silencing of conservation. An exploration of the law's backstory reveals a cacophony of dissenting voices inside and outside of the bureaucracy. In addition, the new conservation law reflected the SED's need to respond to pressures from below. Even as the Ministry for Agriculture blocked their every move, the conservation bloc did not retreat into silence but continued to engage in reform efforts. Accused of economic sabotage, they persisted in letter campaigns to give conservationists greater veto power over economic projects. The conservation bloc initially called attention to the leisure needs of the public (through, for example, the State Planning Commission's working group on living standards). The efforts of the conservation bloc to encourage holistic planning at a landscape scale also succeeded insofar as the new law adopted their own language and definitions of *Landeskultur* (which, of course, resembled the global discussion about the conservation of natural resources), and their own connection of *Landeskultur* to *Erholung* and public health certainly dominated the publicity surrounding the Landeskulturgesetz. When prompted by concerns about popular legitimacy, the SED indeed listened to the reform proposals of the conservation bloc. However, the regime also bluntly ignored key demands of one group of dissenters (the conservation bloc) in the interest of satisfying the recreation desires of a much more important one (the workers and general public). The regime used the research data prepared by the conservation bloc as they saw fit and avoided major administrative reforms that might threaten their control. The Ministerial Council stubbornly refused to introduce a proposed Ministry for Land Improvement (until 1972, when the SED created the Ministry for Environmental Protection as a response to the UNESCO environmental conference in Stockholm) and doggedly insisted on local control over land-use planning. Most important, the Landeskulturgesetz barely acknowledged the concerns about ecosystems and holistic planning circulating among East German scientists. Rather, the SED celebrated *Erholung* and the importance of natural outings to popular desires, worker productivity, and public health. *Erholung* had previously helped conservationists fashion a critique of poor economic planning and wasteful resource exploitation, but it now helped conceal them.

NOTES

1. For example, David Blackbourn (2006) suggests that the law was the result of political gamesmanship. He writes, "In 1970, not coincidentally the same year that the Brandt government was moving ahead in the West, the GDR introduced a comprehensive environmental policy" (338).

2. Dr. Werner Titel,"Umweltschutz in der DDR dient dem Whole des Menschen," December 1, 1969, BArch: DK4 2703; Dr. Werner Titel, "Sozialistische Landeskultur zum Schutz der natürlichen Umwelt—Gemeinschaftsaufgabe alle," January 28, 1971, BArch: DK4 2699.

3. Zillmann, Ministerium für Wissenschaft und Technik, "Bericht über die vorberatung der sozialistischen Länder für die UNO Umweltkonferenz, Stockholm 1972, am 2 und 3. Sept 1971 in Berlin," September 28, 1971, BArch: DK4 2488.

4. Aldo Leopold, *A Sand County Almanac, with Other Essays on Conservation from Round River* (New York: Oxford University Press, 1966); International Symposium on Man's Role in Changing the Face of the Earth and William Leroy Thomas, eds., *Man's Role in Changing the Face of the Earth* (Chicago: University of Chicago Press, 1956).

5. On Julian Huxley and the IUCN, see R. S. Deese, "The New Ecology of Power: Julian and Aldous Huxley in the Cold War Era," in McNeill and Unger (2010), 279–300; Robert Boardman, *International Organization and the Conservation of Nature* (Bloomington: Indiana University Press, 1981); Robert Boardman, *The International Politics of Bird Conservation: Biodiversity, Regionalism, and Global Governance* (Northampton, Mass.: Edward Elgar, 2006); John McCormick, *Reclaiming Paradise: The Global Environmental Movement* (Bloomington: Indiana University Press, 1989); C. Kenneth Waters and Albert Van Helden, eds., *Julian Huxley: Biologist and Statesman of Science* (Houston: Rice University Press, 1992); Martin Holdgate (IUCN), *The*

Green Web: A Union for World Conservation (London: Earthscan, 1999); Alison Bashford, Population, Geopolitics, and International Organizations in the Mid Twentieth Century," *Journal of World History* 19, no. 3 (2008): 327–47; Leif E. Christoffersen, "IUCN: A Bridge-Builder for Nature Conservation," *Green Globe Yearbook*, 1997, 59–69; Kenneth Iain MacDonald, "IUCN: A History of Constraint," February 6, 2003, accessed July 9, 2010, http://perso.cpdr.ucl.ac.be/maesschalck/MacDonaldInstitutional_Reflexivity_and_IUCN-17.02.03.pdf.

6. Rachel Carson, *Silent Spring* (Boston: Houghton Mifflin, 1962). On Carson's influence in West Germany, see Chaney (2008); Dominick (1992).

7. On the history of global environmentalism in the twentieth century, see McCormick (1989); McNeill and Unger (2010); Radkau (2008); Ramachandra Guha, *Environmentalism: A Global History* (New York: Longman, 2000); John R. McNeill, *Something New under the Sun: An Environmental History of the Twentieth-Century World* (New York: W. W. Norton, 2000).

8. Chaney (2005).

9. "Stenografisches Protokoll der Tagung der Kommission Natur und Heimat im DKB am 19.12.1969 zum Landeskulturgesetz," December 19, 1969, 11, SAPMO-BArch: DY27 2771.

10. For more on periodic reform movements in the FDJ and youth policy, see Fenemore (2002); Gotschlich (1994), (1997); Monika Kaiser, *Machtwechsel von Ulbricht zu Honecker: Funktionsmechanismen der SED-Diktatur in Konfliktsituationen 1962 bis 1972* (Berlin: Akademie Verlag, 1997); Mählert (1996); Corey Ross (2000); Dorothee Wierling, "Der Staat, die Jugend und der Westen: Texte zu Konflikten der 1960er Jahre," in *Akten, Eingaben, Schaufenster: Die DDR und ihre Texte; Erkundungen zu Herrschaft und Alltag*, ed. Alf Lüdtke and Peter Becker (Berlin: Akademie Verlag, 1997); Dorothee Wierling, "Die Jugend als innerer Feind: Konflikte in der Erziehungsdiktatur der sechziger Jahre," in *Sozialgeschichte der DDR*, ed. Kaelble et al. (Stuttgart: Klett-Cotta, 1994).

11. On 1960s reforms, see Kaiser (1997); Jeffrey Kopstein, *The Politics of Economic Decline in East Germany, 1945–1989* (Chapel Hill: University of North Carolina Press, 1997); Andre Steiner, "Dissolution of the Dictatorship over Needs? Consumer Behavior and Economic Reform in East Germany in the 1960s," in Strasser et al. (1998), 167–85; Andre Steiner, *Die DDR-Wirtschaftsreform der sechziger Jahre. Konflikt zwischen Effizienz- und Machtkalkül* (Berlin: Akadamie Verlag, 1999); Jörg Roesler, *Zwischen Plan und Markt: Die Wirtschaftsreform 1963–1970 in der DDR* (Berlin: Verlag Weltarchiv, 1991).

12. Letter from Meusel to ZK der SED, Abt. Landwirtschaft, Gen Skudowski, "Betr: Personelle und finanzielle Voraussetzungen zur planvollen Arbeit im Naturschutz der DDR," [1953?], BArch: DK107 77/12.

13. "Naturschutztagung in Berlin am 12 und 13.9.1953: Diskussionsbeiträge," BArch: DK107 39/23.

14. Reform efforts began with a discussion of the Ministry for Agriculture's proposed "Guidelines for Nature Protection" in 1958 and 1959. See Ministry for Agriculture, "Richtlinien des Naturschutzes: Anlage 1," September 28, 1958, BArch: DK1 1039; Letter from Weinitschke, "Betr.: Richtlinien des Naturschutzes," August 15, 1959, BArch: DK1 3754; "Richtlinien des Naturschutzes in der DDR" and "Stenogra-

phische Aufzeichnungen der Sitzung der AG Naturschutz am 9 Dez 1959 in der DAL Berlin," December 10, 1959, BArch: DK107 77/30. Conservationists more assertively pushed for comprehensive landscape care starting in 1961. Letter from Prof. Dr. Meusel to DAL and SKLN, May 3, 1962; SKLN, "Richtlinien für eine Sozialistische Landeskultur," December 7, 1962, BArch: DK107 A9/35; Landesklutur und Grünland (DAL), "Gesichtspunkte zur Ausarbeitung von 'Richtlinien für eine sozialistische Landeskultur,'" May 3, 1962, SAPMO-BArch: DY27 308; Arbeitsausschusses der ZK NuH des Präsidialrates, "Entwurf: An des ZK der SED—Zu einigen Problemen des Naturschutzes und der Landschaftspflege," February 1961, SAPMO-BArch: DY27 3296; "Aufgabenstellung des Zentralen Fachausschusses Landeskultur und Naturschutz für die kommende Zeit," November 26, 1963, SAPMO-BArch: DY27 3506.

15. Letter from Meusel to Stubbe (DAL), October 4, 1961, BArch: DK107 A154/101; Hermann Meusel, "Diskussionsbeitrag auf der Plenarsitzung der DAL am 18/19 Mai 1962," May 18, 1962, BArch: DK107 86/12; "Auszug aus den stenographischen Aufzeichnungen der Sitzung der Ständigen Kommission für Landschaftspflege und Naturschutz im Plensaal der DAL am 28 und 29.11.1962," January 8, 1963, BArch: DK 107 A9/34. See also Letter from Meusel and Mueller to Stubbe, July 5, 1962, BArch: DK107 A132/20; Geschäftsführung Sektion Landeskultur und Grünland, "Zur Information, Betr: Hinweise über die Situation von Landschaftspflege und Naturschutz," May 29, 1964, BArch: DK107 A9/35.

16. Sektion Landesklutur und Grünland (DAL), "Gesichtspunkte zur Ausarbeitung von 'Richtlinien für eine sozialistische Landeskultur,'" May 3, 1962, SAPMO-BArch: DY27 308.

17. Letter from Prof. Dr. Bauer, ILN to Herrn Dr. Roos, Ökonomisches Forschungsinstitut der SPK, Abteil Territorialplanung, July 15, 1966, BArch: DK107 64/85; Letter from Stubbe to Vorsitzenden der Staatlichen Plankommission Schuerer, October 21, 1966; and Letter from Vorsitzende, Staatliche Plankommission, to Stubbe, DAL, August 1, 1966, BArch: DK107 A154/101.

18. Letter from Reimar Gilsenbach to Prof. Dr. Johannes Dieckmann, Präsident der Volkskammer, September 28, 1963; Letter from Prof. Dr. Dieckmann to Reimar Gilsenbach, October 4, 1963; and Letter from Reimar Gilsenbach to Prof. Dr. Johannes Dieckmann, February 29, 1964, BArch: DA1 3377.

19. "Kurzbericht über die 4 Sitzung 1962 der SKLN am 21 und 22 Juni 1962," July 3, 1962, and "Auszug aus den stenographischen Aufzeichnungen der Sitzung der SKLN im Plensaal der DAL am 28 und 29.11.1962," January 8, 1963, BArch: DK107 A9/34; Letter from Dr. Weinitschke to Kanzlei des Präsidenten, Volkskammer, April 6, 1963, BArch: DA1 3377; Letter from Reimar Gilsenbach to Stubbe (DAL), February 26, 1963, BArch: DK107 A154/180.

20. Letter from Meusel to Stubbe, June 4, 1963; Letter from Bauer (ILN) to Stubbe (DAL), June 15, 1966; and Letter from Stubbe (DAL) to Schuerer, July 14, 1966, BArch: DK107 A154/101.

21. Letter from Bauer (ILN) to Stubbe (DAL), June 15, 1966, BArch: DK107 A154/101.

22. According to a letter from Alexander Abusch, Dieckmann wrote to Willi Stoph on July 1, 1966 about creating a committee in the Ministerial Council to lead landscape care efforts. Letter from Alexander Abusch, Stellvertreter des Vorsitzenden des MR to

Dr. Johannes Dieckmann, July 19, 1966, BArch: DC20 19119; Henneberg, Geschäfts-führer der Sektion Landeskultur und Grünland, "Kurzbericht über den Erfüllungsstand der Vorbereitungen des VII Parteitages im ILN," January 13, 1967, BArch: DK107 A64/53.

23. Letter from Gotsche, Sekretär, Staatsrat to Dr. Johannes Dieckmann, Volkskammer, June 7, 1963, BArch: DA1 3377.

24. Letter from Meusel to Stubbe, December 8, 1964, and Letter from Stubbe to Meusel, January 21, 1965, BArch: DK107 A154/180.

25. Letter from Meusel to Stubbe, April 18, 1964, BArch: DK107 A154/101.

26. Letter from Sektion Landeskultur und Grünland (DAL) to P 2, May 4, 1964, BArch: DK107 86/12; SED, "Einschätzung zur politischen Führung des Wettbewerbs in den Instituten der DAL des Bezirkes Halle und Umsetzung der kritischen Hinweise in der Beratung der Bezirksleitung Halle der SED mit den DAL Instituten im Bezirk Halle am 10.9.1970 aus der Sicht der DAL Zentrale," SAPMO-BArch: DY30 IV A 2/7/217; "Kurzbericht über die 2 Sitzung 1965 der SKLN am 1.4.1965," May 3, 1965, BArch: DK107 A9/34; SKLN, "Kurze Einschätzung der Arbeit der SKLN im Jahre 1967 und Schlussfolgerungen für 1968," January 8, 1968, BArch: DK107 64/85. See also Letter from Sektion Landeskultur und Grünland (DAL), January 20, 1965; Letter from Henneberg, Sektion Landeskultur und Grünland (DAL), January 31, 1966; Letter from Sektion Landeskultur und Grünland (DAL) to P 1, November 3, 1967; and Letter from Dr. Reichel, MLF, to ZK der SED, Abt. Landwirtschaft, Genossen Haubold, June 13, 1966, BArch: DK107 A64/53.

27. Letter from Meusel to Prof. Dr. Mueller Stoll et al., September 23, 1960, and "AG der Sektion Landeskultur und Naturschutz," BArch: DK107 A132/20; ILN, "Auszug aus dem Präsidiums Protokoll Nr. 33/1963," October 17, 1963, BArch: DK107 A154/101.

28. Letter from Meusel to Direktor Plachy der DAL, January 30, 1967, BArch: DK107 64/85.

29. "Niederschrift über die Aussprache im ILN der DAL am 26.4.1966," April 27, 1966, BArch: DK107 64/85; Author unknown, "Vermerk an F/1 Betr: Aussprache im ILN über Aufgabenstellung," BArch: DK107 A64/53.

30. Letter from Bauer and Schulmeister to SED ZK, March 29, 1961, SAPMO-BArch: DY27 2947.

31. "Stenoaufzeichnungen zur Sitzung der AG Naturschutz am 3. Mai 1956," May 7, 1956, BArch: DK107 25/13.

32. Arbeitsausschusses der ZK NuH des Präsidialrates, "Entwurf: An des ZK der SED—Zu einigen Problemen des Naturschutzes und der Landschaftspflege," February 1961, SAPMO-BArch: DY27 3296.

33. Letter from Bauer and Schulmeister to SED ZK, March 29, 1961, SAPMO-BArch: DY27 2947.

34. The founding of the IUCN was the culmination of a long struggle to create a true international office for nature protection. See Boardman (2006), (1981).

35. Christofferson (1997), 64.

36. On the Green Revolution, see Angus Lindsay Wright, *The Death of Ramón González: The Modern Agricultural Dilemma* (Austin: University of Texas Press, 2005); John H. Perkins, *Geopolitics and the Green Revolution: Wheat, Genes, and the*

Cold War (New York: Oxford University Press, 1997); Nick Cullather, "Miracles of Modernization: The Green Revolution and the Apotheosis of Technology," *Diplomatic History* 28, no. 2 (2004): 227–54; David A. Sonnenfeld, "Mexico's 'Green Revolution,' 1940–1980: Towards an Environmental History," *Environmental History Review* 16, no. 4 (1992): 28–52.

37. Christofferson (1997), 61. Already in the 1940s, British and American ecologists hoped to move beyond mere preservation. One British ecologist reflected, "The backward looking word, preserve, was used less and less. Another 'ordinary' English word, conserve, took its place . . . There was nothing really new in the idea of statutory land use planning and scientific management of land and natural resources, and yet these were perceived to be the exciting dimensions of post-war reconstruction" (Holdgate [1999], 17; see also Boardman [1981], 68).

38. MacDonald (2003), 7.

39. McCormick (1989), 177.

40. Boardman (1981), 68.

41. Boardman (1981), 69.

42. Boardman (1981), 98.

43. Letter from Dr. Plachy to Skodowski, July 31, 1964; Letter from Skodowski to Dr. Plachy (DAL), August 18, 1964; Sektion Landeskultur und Grünland, "IUCN," November 3, 1967; BArch: DK107 A64/89.

44. Boardman (1981), 75.

45. MacDonald (2003), 5–6.

46. C. Kenneth Waters, "Introduction: Revising Our Picture of Julian Huxley," in Waters and Van Helden (1992), 14.

47. Garland E. Allen, "Julian Huxley and the Eugenical View of Human Evolution," and Elazar Barkan, "The Dynamics of Huxley's Views on Race and Eugenics," in Waters and Van Helden (1992), 216, 230–37.

48. Allen (1992), 196, 217, 220–21.

49. See Kaiser (1997); Steiner (1998), 167–85; Steiner (1999).

50. Ministerrat, "Beschlussprotokoll der 6 Sitzung des MR am 20.Oktober 1967," BArch: DC20I/3 622.

51. Bischoff, "Informationsbericht über die Eingabenbearbeitung im II Quartal 1966," July 28, 1966, BArch: DA1 4387.

52. Zatlin (2007), 288.

53. Zatlin (2007), 293.

54. For more on *Eingaben*, see Jonathan R. Zatlin, "Ausgaben und Eingaben: Das Petitionsrecht und der Untergang der DDR," *Zeitschrift für Geschichtswissenschaft* 10 (1997): 902–17; Ina Merkel and Felix Mühlberg, "Eingaben und Öffentlichkeit," in *"Wir sind doch nicht die Mecker-Ecke der Nation": Briefe an das DDR-Fernsehen*, ed. Ina Merkel (Cologne: Böhlau, 1998), 11–46. See also Port (2007); Betts (2010).

55. Präsidium des Ministerrats, "Bericht über Hauptprobleme der Eingabenarbeit im 3 Vierteljahr 1967," November 9, 1967, 5, BArch: DC20/I/3 626.

56. Ibid., 6

57. Präsidium des Ministerrats, "Beschlussprotokoll der 13 Sitzung des Präsidiums des MR am 20 Oktober 1967," BArch: DC20/I/4 1642; Präsidium des Ministerrats, "Beschluss zum Bericht der Hauptprobleme der Eingabenarbeit im 3 Vierteljahr 1967," November 9, 1967, BArch: DC20/I/3 626.

58. Letter from Vorsitzender des Ministerrats to Stellvertreter des Vorsitzenden des Ministerrats (Sefrin), June 30, 1968, BArch: DC20/I/3 627.

59. Members included Prof. Dr. Neef, director of the Institute for Geography at the Dresden University of Technology; Dr. Weinitschke of the ILN; Gerhard Reiss; of the State Planning Commission; several representatives of the various economic ministries; the Ministry for Health; and Wernicke of the Staatliches Komitee für Forstwirtschaft (who had often been at odds of conservation interests within the ILN).

60. Profile of Dr. Werner Titel, BArch: DK4 2703.

61. Prognosegruppe Abprodukte und sozialistische Landeskultur, "Protokoll über die Beratung der Prognosegruppe zum 1 Entwurf der Hauptprobleme und ersten Schlussfolgerungen," April 26, 1968; Prognosegruppe Abprodukte, "Disposition für die Beratung zur Konstituierung der Prognose Gruppe am 15.3.1968," March 12, 1968; "Konzeption für die Ausarbeitung der Prognose 'Industrielle Abprodukte und planmässige Gestaltung einer sozialistischen Landeskultur in der DDR,'" March 15, 1968, BArch: DC20 19122.

62. "Prognose Industrielle Abprodukte und planmässige Gestaltung einer sozialistichen Landeskultur in der DDR," September 1968, BArch: DK4 1313; Staatliche Plankommission, "Volkswirtchaftliche Einschätzung und Vorschläge für die weitere Arbeit zur Prognose 'Industrielle Abprodukte und planmäsige Gestaltung einer sozialistischen Landeskultur,'" September 2, 1968, BArch: DC20 19122.

63. Prof. Dr. Lilie (Staatliche Plankommission), "Stellungnahme zur Prognose 'Industrielle Abprodukte,'" October 30, 1968, and Letter from Sefrin, Minister für Gesundheitswesen to Willi Stoph, Vorsitzender des Ministerrats, July 24, 1968, BArch: DC20/I/4 1893.

64. Expertengruppe and Staatssekretär Dr. Rost, "Stellungnahme zur Prognose 'Industrielle Abprodukte,'" November 26, 1968, BArch: DC20/I/4 1893.

65. Dr. Werner Titel et al., "Beschlussvorschlag über die planmässige Entwicklung einer sozialistischen Landeskultur in der DDR," November 21, 1968, BArch: DC20 19121.

66. Dr. Werner Titel, "Schwerpunkte für die Ergänzung der Prognose Abprodukte und sozialistische Landeskultur," December 20, 1968, BArch: DC20 19120; Ministerrat, "Beschluss über die planmässige Entwicklung einer sozialistischen Landeskultur in der DDR," February 5, 1969, BArch: DC20/I/3 715.

67. "Kurzbericht über die gemeinsame Sitzung der Sektion Landeskultur und Grünland und der SKLN am 4.10.1968," October 24, 1968, and "Kurzbericht über die 1 Sitzung 1969 der SKLN am 23.1.1969," February 21, 1969, BArch: DK207 64/86.

68. Bund Deutsche Architekten and the Kulturbund, "Vorschläge für ein Landeskulturgesetz und für die Planung und Leitung der Landschaftsentwicklung in der DDR," February 24, 1969, SAPMO-BArch: DY15 113.

69. Arbeitsgruppe Staats- und Wirtschaftsführung, "Stellungnahme zur Vorlage," January 30, 1969, BArch: DC20/I/3 716.

70. DAL Forstwirtschaft, "Zum Entwurf des Gesetzes über die planmässige Gestaltung der sozialistischen Landeskultur in der DDR," July 14, 1969, SAPMO-BArch: DY30 IV A 2/7/239.

71. Dr. Werner Titel et al., "Landeskulturgesetz: Beschluss zum Entwurf des Gesetzes über die planmässige Gestaltung der sozialistischen Landeskultur in der DDR," October 9, 1969, 1, BArch: DC20 19121.

72. Ministerrat, "Beschluss über die planmässige Entwicklung einer sozialistischen Landeskultur in der DDR," February 5, 1969, BArch: DC20/I/3 715.

73. Politbüro des ZK, "Statute 13 (Entwurf: Gesetz über die planmässige Gestaltung der sozialistischen Landeskultur in der DDR)," October 21, 1969, SAPMO-BArch: DY30 J IV 2/2/1247.

74. "Zweite Durchführungsverordnung zum Landeskulturgesetz—Erschliessung, Pflege und Entwicklung der Landschaft für die Erholung, vom 14.5.1970," *Gesetzblatt* 2 (1970).

75. Port (2007). For an overview of the literature on workers, wage incentives, and factory reforms, see Corey Ross (2002), 57–60. Other key works include Kopstein (1997); Peter Hübner, *Konsens, Konflikt, Kompromiss: Soziale Arbeiterinteressen und Sozialpolitik in der SBZ/DDR 1945–1970* (Berlin: Akademie Verlag, 1995); Peter Hübner, "Die Zukunft war gestern: Soziale und mentale Trends in der DDR-Industriearbeiterschaft," in Kaelble et al. (1994), 171–87; Roesler (1994), 144–70.

76. Erich Honecker, "Referat," Thirteenth ZK Tagung, Day 3, 1966, 39–40, SAPMO-BArch: DY30 IV 2/1/347.

77. Esther von Richthofen, *Bringing Culture to the Masses: Control, Compromise, and Participation in the GDR* (New York: Berghahn Books, 2009).

78. Wübbe (1995), 39.

79. Görlich (2012), 102.

80. The research group for Erholungswesen was one of ten collectives under the working circle "Living Standards" within an advisory council for Economic Research. Dr. Alfred Keck, "Zum Forschungsprogramm des 'Arbeitskreises Lebensstandard,'" 1964/1965, 15, BArch: DE1 VA 47634.

81. "Konzeption für Forschungsgemeinschaft zur Entwicklung des Erholungswesens der DDR," May 22, 1964, BArch: DE1 VA 48462.

82. Planning Commission, "Die Grundrichtungen für die Entwicklung einer sinnvollen Freizeitgestaltung (Kultur, Sport, Erholung)," February 1, 1965, 11, BArch: DE1 VA 43571.

83. Alfred Keck, "Soziologische Aspekte und ökonomische Erfordernisse der Gestaltung des arbeitsfreien Zeitbudgets bei der Planung der materiellen und kulturellen Lebenslage der Bevölkerung," May 20, 1964, 37, BArch: DE1 VA 51380.

84. Frank E. Carl, "Beitrag zur Erarbeitung der Perpektive des sozialistischen Erholungswesens in der DDR bis 1970, für die Staatliche Plankommission, Abteilung Kultur, Volksbildung, Gesundheits und Sozialwesen," October 9, 1963, 3, BArch: DH2 II/09/10; Helmut Böhme, "Systematische körperliche Betätigung für alternde Menschen als mittel des Leistungserhalts und der Gesundheitsförderung," June 1, 1965, 1, BArch: DR5 681.

85. Dipl.-Gärtner Horst-Udo Schultze, "Grundlagen für eine rationale Nutzung der natürlichen und baulichen Reserven der DDR für Erholungszwecke," 1967, BArch: DH2 II/09/14.

86. Arbeitskreis Lebensstandard, "Plan zur Ausarbeitung wissenschaftlicher Grundlagen für die planmässige Entwicklung des Lebensstandards und der Formen der Bedürfnisbefriedigung," 1965/66, 14, and H. Löbe, "Gedanken zur Problematik der Naherholung," February 1, 1966, BArch: DR5 1037; Arbeitskreis Lebensstandard, "Die Grundrichtungen für die Entwicklung einer sinnvollen Freizeitgestaltung (Kultur,

Sport, Erholung)," February 1, 1965, 10, BArch: DE1 VA 43571. For more on the importance of public opinion surveys in the GDR, see Heinz Niemann, *Meinungsforschung in der DDR* (Cologne: Bund Verlag, 1993) and *Hinterm Zaun: Politische Kultur und Meinungsforschung in der DDR; Die geheimen Berichte an das Politbüro der SED* (Berlin: Edition Ost, 1995).

87. State Planning Commission, "Die Grundrichtungen für die Entwicklung einer sinnvollen Freizeitgestaltung (Kultur, Sport, Erholung)," February 1, 1965, 10, BArch: DE1 VA 43571; Helmut Böhme, "Systematische körperliche Betätigung für alternde Menschen als mittel des Leistungserhalts und der Gesundheitsförderung," Material zum Tagesordnungspunkt 3 der Sektionstagung Volkssport am 9.6.65, June 1, 1965, 1, BArch: DR5 681.

88. Görlich (2012), 173–80.

89. Dr. Erbach and Dr. Edelfried Buggel, "Bericht über die sportsoziologische DDR-Erhebung 1965," 18, BArch: DR5 1105; Untitled report on a research trip to the Soviet Union, 28, eco-Archiv: DWBV box 6. See also Arbeitsgruppe Erholungswesen, *"Programm zur Entwicklung des Lebensstandards bis 1970 (Teilkonzeption, Nr. 20)*: Konzeption für die Entwicklung des Erholungswesens im Zeitraum des Perspektivplanes," April 15, 1965, BArch: DH2 II/09/09.

90. Fackkommission Wandern, DWBO, "Protokoll der Tagung am 26.1.1974," Bernhard Fisch Collection; Interview with Dr. Wolfgang Bagger on March 9, 2002; and "Presseinformation über den 'Leipziger Wanderkatalog 1986,'" December 19, 1985, eco-Archiv: Leistungsvergleich.

91. Bezirk Leipzig, "Rechenschaftsbericht 1970–1974," March 1, 1974, eco-Archiv: Verbandstag V.

92. "Jahresprogramm 1969—FK Wandern," *Wandern und Bergsteigen* 2 (1969); "Rechenschaftsbericht für die Wahlperiode 1970–1974 des Bezirksfachausschusses des DWBO Dresden," March 19, 1974, eco-Archiv: Verbandstag V; "Bemerkungen zur genärtigen Situation des DWBO im Bezirk Dresden," October 31, 1976, Schindler Collection: Protokolle—DWBO Dresden, 1970–80.

93. "Lauf dich gesund!" *Der Tourist*, August 1967, 4.

94. Bernhard Fisch, *Sportliches Wandern* (Berlin: Sportverlag, 1977), 10.

95. Fisch (1977), 10; Bernhard Fisch, "Richtlinie über die Klassifizierung für Sportwanderer," *Der Tourist*, May 1976, 5–9.

96. Wübbe (1995), 39.

97. Oberforstmeister Fritz Wernicke, "Naturschutz in der DDR," 1967, SAPMO-BArch: DY27 2699; Arbeitsgemeinschaft Erholungswald (SKLN), "Protokoll der Gründungsversammlung der Arbeitsgemeinschaft Erholungswald im Rahmen der SKLN der DAL Berlin," January 17, 1968, BArch: DK107 A64/87.

98. Arbeitsgruppe Erholungswald (SKLN), "Kurzprotokoll über die 2 Sitzung der AG Erholungswald am 11.12.1968," December 11, 1968, BArch: DK107 A64/87. For more on Gerhard Grüneberg, see Nelson (2005).

99. Auster (1996), 44.

100. "Beschlussprotokoll der Beratung des Arbeitsausschusses der Kommission NuH des Präsidialrates des DKB," May 30, 1962, September 13, 1962, January 29, 1963, April 4, 1963, and October 9, 1964, SAPMO-BArch: DY27 3296. Gilsenbach complained that authorities interfered with a second conference attempt in 1965. "Pro-

tokoll der Beratung des Arbeitsausschusses der Kommission NuH des Präsidialrats des DKB am 24.9.1965," SAPMO-BArch: DY27 3296; Letter from Bauer (ILN) to Stubbe (DAL), April 6, 1966, BArch: DK107 A154/101.

101. Hugo Weinitschke, "Die Mitwirkung der NuH bei der Erschliessung und Pflege von Erholungsgebieten," in *Landschaft, Erholung und Naturschutz: Eine Auswahl von Referaten des Landschaftstages des DKB 1966* (Berlin: Kulturbund, 1967), 14.

102. "Kurzbericht über die gemeinsame Sitzung der Sektion Landeskultur und Grünland und der SKLN am 4.10.1968," October 24, 1968; "Kurzbericht über die 1 Sitzung 1969 der SKLN am 23.1.1969," February 21, 1969; "Kurzbericht über die 2 Sitzung 1969 der SKLN am 19 und 20 März 1969," April 3, 1969, BArch: DK207 64/86; "Stenografisches Protokoll der Tagung der Kommission Natur und Heimat im DKB am 19.12.1969 zum Landeskulturgesetz," SAPMO-BArch: DY27 2771; Minutes from the December 19, 1969 meeting, SAPMO-BArch: DY27 3296.

103. Gilsenbach (2001) wrote, "Dem Vortrag, den ich als Mitglied der ZK NuH halten soll, habe ich den provokanten Titel gegeben: 'Braucht die DDR Nationalparke?' Im Tagungsprogramm steht statt dessen eine entschärfte Version 'Was ist ein Erholungspark?'" (540).

104. Reimar Gilsenbach, "Was ist ein Erholungspark?" in Weinitschke (1967), 62; Gilsenbach (2001), 540–41.

105. Dr. Werner Titel, "Bedeutung und Verwirklichung des Landeskulturgesetzes: Vorlesung—Lehrgang Nationale Front," January 21, 1971, BArch: DK4 2699.

106. "Stenografisches Protokoll der Tagung der Kommission Natur und Heimat im DKB am 19.12.1969 zum Landeskulturgesetz," 33, SAPMO-BArch: DY27 2771.

107. "Material zur Stellungnahme der SED Fraktion der Volkskammer zum Landeskulturgesetz," 1969, SAPMO-BArch: DY 30 IV A 2/7/239.

108. "Stenografisches Protokoll der Tagung der Kommission Natur und Heimat im DKB am 19.12.1969 zum Landeskulturgesetz" 40, SAPMO-BArch: DY27 2771.

CHAPTER 5

Real Existing Socialism:
Nature, Social Inequalities, and
Environmental Consciousness

In 2003, the movie *Good Bye Lenin!* highlighted the sudden and traumatic disappearance of an entire material culture and the equally overwhelming spread of West German consumer goods into every nook and cranny of East Berlin after 1989. The movie's climactic scene unfolds, interestingly, at an East Berlin family's bungalow retreat in the countryside. This choice of setting reflected the important role that bungalows came to play in the everyday life of many East Germans.[1] The film presents the bungalow as an idyllic retreat where the family seems (at first, anyway) to escape their troubles in a niche untouched by the recent upheaval. This staging of the scene may not have been coincidental. Indeed, scholars concerned with bungalows, cottages, or dachas in Eastern Europe often orient their analysis around the so-called niche society of Eastern Europe. According to Lovell, Soviet authorities believed that "the dwellings that stood on *dacha* plots were profoundly alien to the Soviet communal ethos: they represented enclaves of unsocialized existence that were impervious to the penetrating collective gaze."[2] Lovell argues that *dachas* created relatively independent social niches within Soviet society: "[*Dachas*] infused people's lives with new meanings, gave them new opportunities to pursue 'private' activities, yet also enabled them to cultivate a sense of community that was largely independent of party-state institutions."[3] Paulina Bren, alternatively, argues that cottage vacations were "a decidedly state-endorsed escape, whereby a person in fact participated in 'normalization' and the government's desire for 'the quiet life.'"[4]

The bungalow retreat nostalgically remembered in *Good Bye, Lenin!* was, however, hardly idyllic in reality; instead, angry disputes, or "horizontal conflicts," between everyday Germans characterized everyday life at most vacation destinations as much or more as vertical conflicts between citizens and the state. In an earlier chapter on camping culture, I shifted focus away from discussions of an East German niche society in which East Germans retreated from and struggled against government intrusion; this current chapter will go a step further and argue that vacationing just as often pitted East German against East German. A close look at bungalows and rural destinations reveals that these exurban retreats were more than escapes from socialist mobilization. They were also a space of noisy arguments and conflicts between neighboring vacationers. As Andrew Port has argued, these "horizontal conflicts" have not received enough attention from scholars of East German history. The political stability of the GDR hinged in important ways on the inability of many East Germans to focus their frustrations on the SED; instead, they turned to the regime to intervene in disputes with their neighbors and coworkers.[5]

Erich Honecker's "real existing socialism" in the 1970s and 1980s only exacerbated these disputes. The regime now ignored fundamental structural reforms that had preoccupied bureaucrats in the 1960s. Instead of utopian transformations, planners focused on immediate and tangible abundance. In practice, the regime's corroding factories and inefficient supply networks could not provide that abundance, so it indebted itself at an epic scale to increase wages, subsidize low food and housing prices, and provide more consumer goods. As Jonathan Zatlin has written, "[T]he GDR was not simply living beyond its means, but consuming its future—eating oranges instead of buying capital equipment to boost exports and pay for the oranges."[6] Honecker's wage increases also created inflationary pressures. With more money to spend but not enough commodities to purchase, the costs of those scarce goods began to rise.[7] In this context, vacationing must have only increased its prestige in the eyes of the SED, as it could soak up excess currency without costing too much to the government. To compensate for its growing debt and to alleviate shortages, Honecker also worked diligently to bring hard currency (i.e., West German marks) into East Germany. To meet consumer demand, the regime created new special shops selling high-end consumer goods or luxury Western-made products. *Intershops* sold luxury Western goods to foreign visitors or East Germans with access to foreign currency, and *Exquisit* and *Delikat* shops sold expensive (and rare) consumer goods to East Germans who could afford it. While offering a possible solution to pent-up consumer demand, the expensive goods at these shops only highlighted social inequalities in a country ostensibly founded to eliminate class differences. Citizens with ties to West Germany (and thus to hard currency), individuals with tradable skills, or those with connections to power now emerged as a new elite.[8]

Returning to the case study of Greifenbach Reservoir begun in chapter 3, this chapter argues that these "horizontal conflicts" also owed much to the particular way that the SED managed its vacation destinations. As will be demonstrated, the SED committed few resources to managing natural landscapes and did little to restrict unplanned development. Its unwillingness to introduce strict regulation reflected both a fear of administrative reform that would threaten established power relations and a worry that local authorities would be handicapped in their ability to offer material incentives to a potentially unhappy population. Haphazard bungalow construction exposed widespread social inequality within a state that promised to erase class differences. In an individualistic fashion, citizens scrambled to obtain green spaces in which they could rejuvenate, and vacationers often had to depend on their connections and ingenuity to secure access to those spaces. As a result, many vacationers often demanded greater state intervention to prevent privileged groups from building bungalows in nominally public spaces. Vacationers and local residents accepted campgrounds and bungalow colonies as a component of everyday life in the SED welfare dictatorship and not as an escape from the regime; in fact, they expected the regime to live up to its promises of limitless abundance and questioned the regime's legitimacy. In this sense, the visit to a family bungalow in *Good Bye Lenin!* did not recall an East German niche society offering refuge from the SED as much as it provided a return to a lost GDR space (mutually created by state and society, stamped with SED power, and usually characterized by much bickering) that was then being erased by the radical transformations of 1990.

This chapter, finally, argues that a strong sense of citizen and consumer rights in a failing social welfare state influenced how vacationers enjoyed the nature experience. In overcrowded nature retreats, vacationers increasingly understood nature as a precious commodity. The regime's promises of improved public health, material comfort, and increasing living standards all made nature outings an entitlement expected by East German citizens. Ideal nature retreats, however, became increasingly rare as factories belched pollutants, campgrounds produced litter, and privileged bungalow owners blocked access to a lakeshore. As the state failed to provide satisfactory *Erholung* experiences because of its mismanagement of rural landscapes, nature retreats joined a long list of denied pleasures that included the banana, the automobile, and high-end consumer electronics. Unlike many politically engaged environmentalists, vacationers thus understood landscape planning as a compliment (not an antidote) to consumerism. Even when complaining of shortages, they participated in a larger mainstream consensus shared by the SED, economic planners, and even some conservationists who thought about natural landscapes in terms of economic growth, quality of life, and improved living standards from the 1960s and onward.

Planned Planlessness

At Greifenbach Reservoir and elsewhere in the GDR, the construction of leisure facilities unfolded in a very haphazard fashion, as seen in chapter 3. As a result, vacation destinations such as Greifenbach often appeared chaotic and outside of state control, often to the detriment of East Germans lacking connections or cash. In truth, however, the unscripted and unapproved activities of vacationers were unexpected consequences of the SED's very power. To understand this, it is important to investigate a basic contradiction at the heart of SED planning. On the one hand, the regime hoped to prove its concern for popular desires. On the other hand, any bureaucratic reform meant to better respond to those desires could not threaten key centers of SED control.

In most cases, no clear rules indicated which government authorities should administrate a recreation district that crossed county or town lines. Greifenbach Reservoir and its watershed, for example, included land within three counties, or *Kreisen*: Annaberg, Zschopau, and Stollberg. In addition, the local landscape preserve fell under the jurisdiction of the town councils in Ehrenfriedersdorf, Geyer, and Thum. In addition, regional mining concerns or water resource authorities had some authority over the lakeshores, since they operated the dams. At Greifenbach, the number of voices calling for landscape conservation varied in each administrative district, so that advocates of more careful planning in Ehrenfriedersdorf stood by helplessly as Annaberg or Geyer ignored their directives and approved camps and bungalows.[9]

While the FDGB's Feriendienst might have coordinated and managed such leisure spaces that crossed administrative borders, it lacked the funds and the SED's support for further centralization in the 1960s and 1970s. In the 1950s, the regime hoped to regulate vacationing by placing all working-class vacations under the central control of the Feriendienst. In 1960, however, the SED allowed individual firms to build their own vacation homes.[10] The regime thus encouraged miscommunication and overlapping jurisdictions as individual firms planned vacations for their employees and negotiated with counties and towns for prime lakeshore or mountain properties, with some industries receiving preferential treatment. Firms usually built bungalows, boathouses, and campgrounds exclusively for their employees. Essentially, public spaces became reserves for a small group of citizens, especially since firms rarely communicated with each other to share resources.[11] While the FDGB Ferien-dienst facilities had a reputation of being shabby and overcrowded when com-pared to employer-operated facilities, its administrators did claim to represent all East German workers. Individual firms, on the other hand, prioritized their own interests over the concerns of local authorities or vacationers not under their direct employ. In 1962, the Feriendienst operated 420 vacation homes, but employers had built 620, many of which were small bungalows.[12] By 1979, the Feriendienst hosted over 21 million overnight visits, but facilities owned or leased by employers hosted over 40 million overnight visits.[13]

As administrative confusion worsened in the 1960s, it seemed that the regime might intervene to protect tourist interests. The problem of lodging caught the attention of East Germany's highest official in the mid-1960s, when Walter Ulbricht condemned employers that did not share their vacant beds and called for better planning of recreation and tourism. In 1964, the SED then passed an ordinance calling for the improvement and simplification of leisure planning in the GDR. Planning reform began at Oberhof, a skiing resort and training center for Olympic athletes. On January 10, 1967, the SED introduced an ordinance supported by the FDGB Feriendienst that called for a new economic system in the planning and leadership of tourism (*Erholung-swesen*), by which a single VEB Naherholung responsible to the local county or district officials oversaw the construction and use of a popular destination's vacation homes. In this way, the Feriendienst meant to reassert authority over vacationing.[14]

Ultimately, the "Oberhof system" failed to recentralize tourism planning, partly because the SED still feared any administrative reform that threatened the power of local SED representatives, youth functionaries, or the powerful industries essential to the GDR economy. As the head of the FDGB admitted in 1967, the Feriendienst steered clear from conflict with powerful industries essential to the GDR economy.[15] The Oberhof system also helped the SED deflect more disruptive reforms proposed by technical experts associated with the "conservation bloc." Conservationists who had attended the 1966 Land-schaftstag hoped for a central state Institution for Tourism Planning that had the power to pressure local governments to improve tourist infrastructure to benefit the general public.[16] Leisure reformers in the State Committee for Physical Culture and Sport in 1967 also demanded the creation of a Ministry for Recreation in Berlin to coordinate the development of vacation districts and provide noncompetitive sport and leisure for the public. In response, the FDJ and sports authorities rather aggressively punished the plan's spokesper-son by quickly reassigning him to lesser responsibilities.[17] All planning had to originate in local governments dominated by SED party members and their economic planners.

An additional factor limiting general public access to vacation facilities was the SED's desire to use tourism as a way to alleviate its debt crisis. Throughout most of the history of the GDR, travel restrictions made it very difficult for foreigners to travel within East Germany, but the state's growing debt and desperate need for hard currency changed things. In 1972, the regime relaxed travel restrictions for West Germans, which led "to a level of Western tourism unprecedented for a Soviet bloc country," according to Jonathan Zatlin. The state even demanded that Western travelers exchange a minimum of twenty deutsche marks (later thirteen) per day to ensure that their money stayed in the GDR.[18] To accommodate these travelers, local governments began to build new infrastructure for foreigners. For example, Greifenbach built a section of bungalows specifically meant for foreign tourists, and district officials in Karl Marx City told planners to expect more vacationers from West Germany.[19] Any hope of closely regulating the development of vacation landscapes for the general public stood little chance in the face of these immense pressures to solve an economic crisis through the expansion of facilities exclusive to foreigners.

The development of the Greifenbach campground reflected these broader trends in tourism planning. Zschopau's county authorities quickly created the VEB Naherholung in January 1967—just days after the SED and the FDGB proposed the Oberhof system. This VEB Naherholung pushed firms to report their unused capacity so that bureaucrats could then distribute those beds to needy vacationers.[20] Due to the SED's focus on decentralized planning, however, the VEB Naherholung at Greifenbach lacked real power to regulate the development and use of this recreational space, even though it had been created by the Oberhof system specifically to improve coordination. Firms and local town councils largely ignored the VEB Naherholung. The town of Ehrenfriedersdorf, for example, did not give up revenues to the VEB Naherholung so that it could fund its own athletic and cultural programs, and one local firm only relinquished its boat rental operation to the VEB Naherholung after considerable resistance.[21]

Rather than regulate and impose limitations, the VEB Naherholung generally found it easier to grow the campground to meet the demands of employers, especially as financial power remained in the hands of individual firms. Employers received "social and cultural funds" from the state to spend on cultural and athletic programs, facilities, and equipment. In general, benefits to workers increased in the 1950s and 1960s as the regime sought to placate

Fig. 1. Greifenbach Reservoir in the 1980s. In the woodlands and meadows surrounding the lake, vacationers relaxed in bungalows and at campgrounds. "Am Stauweiher." Postcard. VEB Foto-Verlag Erlbach i. V. Foto: Hoffmann. A3—III/26/13.

workers in key industries and cement its legitimacy.[22] Across the GDR, firms used up to half of these subsidies to pay for vacation homes and summer camps.[23] For their part, villages and districts had fewer financial resources. Admission fees and lottery earnings from Karl Marx City, for example, did not cover all of the VEB Naherholung's expenses, so it had to rely on help from the vacationers (and their employers) whom it supposedly oversaw. The VEB Naherholung thus required each bungalow owner to sign a contract obliging them to contribute to the maintenance and improvement of the lake and its environs. In 1970, for instance, authorities signed thirty-five contracts with different enterprises to provide labor or goods for park improvements, and six businesses in 1967 contributed twenty thousand marks toward the construction and improvement of public swimming pools.[24] In turn, firms that helped in the construction of campgrounds and bungalows must have benefited through looser restrictions on building their own vacation homes in public recreation landscapes.[25] By the 1970s, enterprises or government entities controlled most bungalows built at Greifenbach. Over two hundred firms used Greifenbach, including firms such as the motorcycle factory in Zschopau, the Sachsenring automobile factory in Zwickau, and SDAG Wismut (the joint East German–Soviet uranium mine); all made agreements to provide material contributions to camp development.[26] Such contracts further confirmed that the SED cared more about managing the distribution of privileges to certain firms and employees than about rational landscape planning.

Holidays for All? Bungalows and Social Inequality

Partly because of planned planlessness, unregulated bungalow development at Greifenbach and throughout the GDR increasingly made many vacationers aware of persistent social inequalities. East Germans did not just grumble about the SED regime; they also bickered with each other and asked the regime to interfere to address those growing social inequalities. In these complaints, vacationers revealed not only that they shared with the regime a hope in limitless abundance through careful management but also that they became increasingly disillusioned about the possibility of achieving that goal. In addition, they increasingly understood their love of nature in terms compatible with their sense of consumer rights and social justice.

In the 1950s, landscape architects and other leisure planners remained internally divided about bungalows. Reinhold Lingner, the architect responsible for the Landscape Diagnosis (discussed further in chapter 2), believed that rustic bungalow settlements offered a preferred alternative to wild campgrounds crowded with automobiles and awash in consumerism.[27] In the early 1960s, the Bauakademie even produced architectural drawings for bungalows resembling fairy-tale cottages with shingles, shutters, and flowerpots.[28] Not everyone agreed about the benefits of bungalows, however. Landscape architect Frank Erich Carl, for example, saw bungalows as a threat to landscape preserves.[29] Both the FDGB Feriendienst and the Bauakademie instead advocated for the construction of immense, multistory hotels, which they hoped would help the regime save money, resources, and open land.[30] Ideologically, bungalows represented a holdover of "bourgeois" leisure practices; and financially, it cost less per vacationer for the FDGB to centralize, build a few large structures, and create economies of scale.[31] In this way, the SED hoped for tourism to parallel planning for heavy industry—the bigger, the better.[32]

Nonetheless, bungalows continued to proliferate in the 1960s. In some districts, bungalows became conspicuous at campgrounds—especially in Suhl (where they comprised 46 percent of beds at campgrounds), Gera (36 percent), and Dresden (22 percent). Conservationists repeatedly complained of lakeshores dominated by private cottages.[33] Back in Greifenbach, popular demand for these structures never seemed to cease. In the mid-1960s, vacationers built approximately fifty illegal cottages (it was technically illegal to construct private residences on public land if done without prior approval of authorities), and thirty more citizens applied for permits to legally build structures. In the late 1960s at Greifenbach, seventy-four individuals or organizations had built bungalows.[34] Once the illegal cottages had been built, little could be done to remove them, because owners often had connections with local officials; bungalow owners with cash simply paid fines imposed by authorities for the transgression of the law.[35] In December 1966, authorities in Zschopau placed a ban on construction near the lake, but administrators on the Annaberg side of the lake ignored the new regulations.[36]

The construction of bungalows elicited numerous complaints about social inequalities across the GDR. In 1972, one citizen wrote to the Ministry for Environmental Protection to criticize construction along lakeshores in general. If not accessible by the public, he argued, "nature" (in this case, lakeshores and riverbanks) was "changed" (*umfunktioniert*). This individual identified public accessibility to the public as a key characteristic of "nature." He wrote, "Directly on the lakeshores of the *Erholungsgebieten* stand various types of weekend homes, which sometimes reach the size of fully functioning suburban homes [*Siedlungshäuser*] with garages. Even the landscape preserves that are designated by local authorities are not spared. Even if individual needs should not be ignored entirely, current policy only maximizes benefits for a few citizens."[37] He hoped to open up the *Erholungsgebiete* to all citizens and not just to the "privileged." This letter was not an isolated case. The Ministry for Environmental Protection noticed a trend in letters of complaint in 1977 toward a critique of the development and parceling of public land.[38]

An incident at Greifenbach Reservoir in 1973 led to especially bitter complaints about the conspicuous consumption of a few privileged bungalow owners. The initial spark to this incident was the eviction of some "long-term campers" from the campground by the VEB Naherholung.[39] These campers, who had volunteered for work brigades and had helped build out the camp infrastructure, felt slighted by the privileged treatment of the new bungalow owners or users (often managers or bureaucrats from Berlin or other larger cities). One vacationer wrote, "Before the [lake] was 'discovered,' before even the masses had any idea that one could rejuvenate and relax there, our family belonged to those who had reconstructed the lake."[40] According to one vacationer from Karl Marx City, other veteran campers (*Dauerzeltlern*) had not received eviction notices, even though they too had resided at the campground the previous four summers. He wrote, "I believe that it is not in the spirit of the Eighth Party Conference . . . to introduce such differences between campers."[41] This petitioner obviously mimicked official party rhetoric, but his frustration with unequal treatment was genuine nonetheless. "After closer inspection," another camper noted, "you have arranged special privileges for distinct groups within the population." He believed that the promises made by the regime to provide *Erholung* and health had been violated. "I must confirm," he added, "that blue- and white-collar workers from collectivized firms [*volkseigene Betriebe*] . . . did not retain their permit for a campsite." "What happened to the concerns about working people and the class consciousness of our socialist leaders?" he asked.[42] A petitioner from Bad Freienwalde wrote in 1974, "Everywhere offers the same picture. At an always-increasing tempo, the most beautiful terrain is removed from the public domain by the construction of bungalows by individuals and firms." He continued, "The egoism of a few groups triumphs." [43] One woman, "Marta," aggressively commented, "Of course—and to this you should give some thought—there are no time limits for cottages at the lake. These [vacationers] may, regardless of how many years they were already there or how long they want to remain, pursue their leisure. It is, as always, the little man who only has a tent that is easiest to drive away."[44]

The evolution of an unofficial "market" for bungalows reinforced the notion that citizens with better access to cash and materials appropriated natural spaces for themselves. A visitor to Rügen on the Baltic Coast, for instance, suggested that the construction of illegal bungalows continued because of minor fines (i.e., bribes) paid by individuals and institutions to the local government.[45] Numerous reports in the Erzgebirge revealed that local governments approved bungalow construction in landscape preserves, despite efforts of nature preservationists to bulldoze illegal weekend homes.[46] In cash-strapped local governments, moreover, the opportunity to approve illegal bungalows and then fine owners (in other words, to sell the plot) was, more than likely, hard to resist.[47] An investigation by the district of Karl Marx City even revealed a growing rental market. Some landowners seemed to build bungalows on speculation; they built on their property and then found an enterprise to pay a yearly user fee for the cottage. Bungalow owners also advertised sublets in newspapers across the GDR, in the hopes of renting to more privileged residents of Berlin or other cities. An ordinance in 1983 attempted to end this speculation and private trade in bungalows by insisting that contracts for the use of a cottage be coordinated by local officials.[48]

As vacationers complained about social inequalities, they did not reject consumerism outright; rather, they treated nature destinations as scarce consumer commodities. A campsite was another consumer good that hardworking citizens of a modern socialist state deserved. In connecting their nature enthusiasm to consumerism, vacationers reimagined *Erholung*. They agreed with landscape architects, leisure planners, and the SED that workers needed *Erholung* for their health and well-being, but they altered the meaning of *Erholung* to emphasize entitlement. While authors of these complaints astutely quoted party rhetoric, they still gave that rhetoric new meanings—especially by imagining their citizenship as including the right to consumer comforts (something the SED had often disparaged as a superficial distraction from political struggle but now promoted). One vacationer tactically established in his letter a narrative of a respectable "worker" losing his right to consume and enjoy leisure. He wrote, "When one has worked day after day for eighteen years as I have, a person looks forward to when they can relax [*erholen*] after a work shift at a nearby campground."[49] In a similar fashion, a master mechanic from Langebrück argued that his employees with large families had as much right as any other individual to enjoy "nature."[50] One family from Karl Marx City quite openly described themselves as scorned consumers. They described at length their investment of money and time into their *Stabilzelt*, an all-weather tent set up for the entire camping season. Campsites, they suggested, were rare commodities to be cherished and preserved, since they were not easily acquired. Once in possession of one, the family held on to their "piece of nature" tenaciously and scoffed at suggestions from the VEB Naherholung that they easily could find another campsite elsewhere in the vicinity of Karl Marx City.[51] Another nature enthusiast (the "Marta" previously mentioned) explicitly linked her health, happiness, and enjoyment of nature to consumer satisfaction. She worked hard to consume camping equipment and create her own "nature experience" and wondered why wealthier consumers should fare better than her. Marta wrote, "We do not earn our money so easily that we can make purchases and then simply leave a tent unused in a corner."[52]

All of these complaints about privileged vacationers reflected real social differences that were increasingly difficult to ignore by the 1980s. Certain cash-rich East Germans enjoyed better access to nature than others; connections to SED power often determined these privileges, but other factors came into play as well. District authorities in Karl Marx City observed that intellectuals, craftsmen, and influential personalities built excessively large and elaborate bungalows. Authorities, for example, noted, "For example, an employee of the Mining Academy in Freiberg claims a bungalow of fourteen-hundred square meters." In another case, "A bungalow built out to the size of a single family home by the county doctor in Aue has led to discussions among the residents."[53] Most bungalow owners at Greifenbach were artisans, white-collar workers, managers, or skilled workers such as welders or electricians. Few, if any, less-skilled workers from the regionally important mining industry owned a bungalow. In fact, it appeared that not a single unskilled worker from heavy industry owned a cottage at Greifenbach Reservoir.[54] In general, bungalow access seemed to depend on education and connections (among white-collar workers and managers) and access to construction materials or cash (among artisans, welders, and electricians). Plumbers or electricians may have traded services for favors; artists and artisans may have been able to sell their goods in the West for cash. Other cash-rich East Germans included families with relatives in the West and individuals active in the black market. Individuals with relatives and friends in high party offices or other advantageous connections—known as "vitamin B" (referring to *Beziehungen*, or "connections")—enjoyed more privileges, and residents of Berlin (often well-placed in the party apparatus) had better connections and more cash than residents of other party districts.[55] The complaints among East Germans that some citizens had privileged access to nature would appear to hold true; in leisure and tourism, the SED had not eradicated social differences, even if those differences did not always map onto historical class structures.

As nature became a scarce commodity desired by East German consumers, they insisted on greater state intervention (not less) to address the problem. The regime just needed to develop (rather than preserve) nature landscapes for their individual enjoyment. Complaints about bungalows and weekend homes often expressed a belief in socialism's ability to control development for the "good of the people," which meant creating spaces for individual nature experiences. "Marta" from Greifenbach wrote, "We recognize that others need a possibility for recreation—but not at the cost of others. The grounds [at the lake] are big enough; they only need to be developed."[56] She criticized the privileged, but she merely wanted to extend the ideal nature experience (currently available to bungalow owners) to all citizens, and to this end, she demanded better management by authorities. Another camper suggested that the lake and its surrounding landscape should be an accessible space distributed evenly to all citizens.[57] For these critics, nature should be preserved not for its own sake but for the sake of the average consumer. A petitioner from Bad Freienwalde also suggested better planning. Socialism itself had not prevented a "well-connected" class of individuals from developing the landscape, but better planning might. New regulations, he argued, could work against the "tendency—noticeable everywhere—that families with the largest homes in the quieter sections of the city, with the highest incomes, autos, and other comforts, now also lay claim to a bungalow, a boathouse, and a sailboat in the most precious spots."[58]

East German authorities did make some effort to regulate "wild" bungalow construction and address concerns about inequality, but the regime usually insisted that private pleasures could expand without limits as long as coordination and planning improved. In 1967, Greifenbach's VEB Naherholung pressed for more legal action against *Schwarzbauten* (illegally constructed structures).[59] Officials at the district level, however, mainly worried about the proliferation of "unsightly" bungalows that did not "fit" the local landscape.[60] Planned regulations called for the restriction of private construction but also provided permits for bungalows in designated areas.[61] In Karl Marx City's district offices, planners introduced a revised and friendlier ordinance on bungalows and other weekend homes in 1975. This document attempted to prevent construction along lakeshores and in nature preserves, but it did not outright condemn bungalows as authorities more often did in the 1950s.[62] Another attempted solution was the establishment of bungalow "interest communities" (*Interessengemeinschaften*), where individual greed would not triumph over collective well-being.[63] Since the simultaneous endorsement of private pleasures and collective consciousness proved ineffective, officials called for another revision in 1979.[64]

In these bungalow colonies, the state focused less on eliminating class differences and increasingly more on helping East Germans cultivate private pleasures. East Germans cherished the privacy of a bungalow where they "disappeared on weekends," and as one informant told historian Paul Betts, his bungalow was "his own individual piece of the people's property."[65] This informant's comments on the "people's property" hints, at the same time, that many East Germans expected the state to provide for their private desires. Vacationers hoping to protect their private nature experiences insisted that the SED not only further develop campsites and tourist infrastructure but also fulfill its promises to protect private property rights. As the local governments eased restrictions on bungalow construction, popular magazines increasingly featured bungalows in photo spreads and advertisements.[66] Eventually, the 1975 Civil Code guaranteed the right to a weekend home, as the regime further acknowledged the validity of individualistic consumer desires; and a 1981 brochure on civil law rights later informed owners of bungalows and homes of their personal property rights and responsibilities.[67]

More and more, frustrated consumerism influenced expectations for the nature experience. Nature outings became associated with bitter struggles for more camping equipment, for prime campsites, for private property rights, or for raw materials needed to build a bungalow. In a country known for consumer scarcity, vacationers wanted to enjoy their purchased camping equipment in the mountains or at the beach, and they complained that some privileged consumers had access to more peaceful or enriching nature experiences. Greifenbach vacationers, as some of the above complaints suggested, did not just understand natural landscapes as spaces needing protection from development, but rather as scarce commodities owed to citizens of a socialist state. If the state promised improved public health and high living standards, it needed to develop the countryside more rationally for everyone's enjoyment. On the one hand, many East Germans shared a faith in managed economic growth evident in their demands for better administration of lakeshores and other vacation destinations. On the other hand, growing "horizontal conflicts" over unequal access to the countryside led to angry complaints that the regime failed to live up to the promises made by the SED, landscape architects, and doctors. By the end of the 1970s, vacationers essentially found themselves scrambling for more and better "nature experiences" at the expense of publicly-accessible open space. In this way, interactions with the countryside became acquisitive, and anything that interfered with opportunities to obtain private "green spaces" became an aggravation and a source of broader discontent.

Popular Environmentalism

An analysis of *Eingaben* (complaint letters) sent to the Ministry for Environmental Protection in the 1970s and 1980s confirms that popular demands for nature protection often became intertwined with hopes for more private pleasures and leisure opportunities. Letter-writers repeatedly linked environmental problems to the regime's promises of more *Erholung* opportunities. Pollution threatened trees and wildlife, but it also made the scramble for healthy and relaxing green spaces even more challenging. The letters suggest a popular environmentalism oriented around leisure desires and shaped by a rhetoric cultivated by the conservation bloc in the 1960s and seemingly embraced by the regime in its Landeskulturgesetz.

Two types of complaint letters typically arrived at the offices of the environmental protection ministry from 1972 to 1975 and from 1980 to 1983 (the two periods selected for closer analysis). One type of letter directed the ministry's attention to specific pollution points—a factory, farm, or neighbor. These could also be described as NIMBY (not-in-my-backyard) complaints. Letter writers wanted, above all else, to prevent their homes or families from suffering the negative consequences of nearby pollution. Another type of letter questioned the broader trends in East German economic policy; in other words, some East Germans looked beyond their neighbors and wondered what the ultimate consequences of statewide industrial production might be for their individual quality of life. A significant number of complaints (from a quarter to half) addressed one or more of the following more wide-reaching problems: outdoor recreation, public health, and the fate of the *Erzgebirge*.[68] Among cases where a copy of the original complaint was available in the archive, 41 percent specifically mentioned pollution's threat to *Erholung*, or "recreation," in their complaint. Indeed, non-NIMBY complaints referred to *Erholung* more often than to any other issue.[69]

The concern for *Erholung* was not trivial. While complaints about specific polluters revealed the carelessness of the regime, arguments about a citizen's right to *Erholung* insisted that the regime needed to promote general well-being and reserve spaces for nature enjoyment. Asking authorities not just to protect lives but to make those lives pleasant demanded much more from the ministry. In 1972, one East German complained to the ministry about the haphazard construction of industrial facilities in the forests near Leipzig. He insisted, "The forest landscape would still provide for *Erholung*, if only it was brought into proper order."[70] Another 1972 letter writer complained, "One cannot build such poison pits in the immediate vicinity of such worthwhile local recreation spaces." He reminded the ministry of the benefit of this recreation area for the well-being of local citizens.[71] Likewise, a doctor from Dessau complained that the railroad's plans for construction in a recreation landscape contradicted the regime's dedication to living standards and quality of life.[72] *Erholung* also informed many complaints about dying forests in the Ore Mountains, or *Erzgebirge*. As one *Erzgebirge* resident wrote to the ministry in 1982, "Many millions have been invested to develop the area into an *Erholung* and vacation district. Hotels, guesthouses, and other facilities have been built." But, he asked, "Who will have any desire to seek out *Erholung* in such a contaminated area?"[73] Many other letter writers wondered how the state could allow a renowned recreation district to degenerate. In a sample of ninety-six letters that addressed the problem of the *Erzgebirge* between 1980 and 1983, nearly half specifically mentioned threats to *Erholung*.

An environmentalism oriented toward *Erholung* had distinct advantages as well as disadvantages. On the plus side, these letters spoke a language the regime could understand. At the same time, this popular environmentalism sent

mixed messages about materialism, economic development, and their consequences for natural beauty. While letters sometimes demanded the protection
of untouched *Erholung* spaces where vacationers might retreat from lives dominated by materialism, pollution complaints oriented around *Erholung* often
linked environmentalism to dashed hopes for economic expansion and improved material living standards. If the state wanted to invest in crowded vacation districts to address shortages of campgrounds or hotels, how could it tolerate environmental threats to those regions? Complaints about limited *Erholung*
opportunities thus could lead to better pollution regulations, but they also
pushed the regime develop landscape preserves for more vacationers.

The environmentalism revealed in these letters differed from one type of
environmentalism then becoming prominent in West Germany. As in the GDR,
West Germans traveled to the local countryside in increasing numbers, but a
growing movement of citizens raised questions about the consequences of their
individual consumption. Some West Germans even made radical demands for
limits to growth.[74] In a society of scarcity, however, East Germans may have
been more aware of their desire for goods and leisure than they were of the
consequences of their consumption. Many citizens critiqued environmental
policy without necessarily questioning consumerism or wondering if improved
living standards might require less development. Such material desires did not
mean that East Germans remained ignorant of and unconcerned about society's
negative impact on the environment. Nonetheless, it was very difficult to separate the fate of vacation spaces from individual consumer satisfaction (as will
be further explored in the next chapter). Seemingly sharing with the regime a
belief in limitless abundance guaranteed by rational planning, many vacationers sought private enrichment in nature and avoided a more radical critique of
the status quo. Instead, they insisted the regime quit avoiding fundamental reforms and live up to its promises.

The complaint letters in this chapter shared a vocabulary determined in
part by the GDR's unique economic and political history, but the popular environmentalism expressed in the letters may not have been completely unique to
the East. Not all West Germans critiqued consumption; many wanted a "light
green society" with both material abundance and better environmental protections. As those West Germans did, many East Germans complaining to environmental authorities dreamed of a "light green society." In fact, activist environmentalists in many societies often demand greater economic sacrifices than
the mainstream might tolerate. Throughout postwar Europe, expressions of
environmental concern always took diverse forms, ranging from the more radical to the more moderate. But, how did radical demands for simpler, less ma-

terialist lifestyles create unique challenges for the East German environmental movement in the 1980s? The next chapter will attempt to answer that question.

NOTES

1. *Good Bye Lenin!* (Culver City, Calif.: Sony Pictures Classics, 2004).
2. Stephen Lovell, "Soviet Exurbia: Dachas in Postwar Russia," in Crowley and Reid (2002), 106.
3. Lovell (2002), 110.
4. Bren (2002), 127. For other discussions of Eastern European vacation cottages, see Karin Taylor, *Let's Twist Again: Youth and Leisure in Socialist Bulgaria* (Vienna: Lit, 2006); Karin Taylor, "My Own Vikendica—Holiday Cottages as Idyll and Investment," in *Yugoslavia's Sunny Side: A History of Tourism in Socialism (1950s–1980s)*, eds. Hannes Grandits and Karin Taylor (Budapest: Central European University Press, 2010), 171–210.
5. Port (2007), 277–83.
6. Jonathan Zatlin, "Consuming Ideology: Socialist Consumerism and the Intershops, 1970–1989," in *Arbeiter in der SBZ-DDR*, ed. Peter Hübner and Klaus Tenfelde (Essen: Klartext, 1999), 560.
7. Zatlin (2007), 226.
8. Zatlin (2007), 267–85.
9. Letter to Annaberg from RdB Karl Marx Stadt, February 28 1965, KarchMZ: 7073.
10. Görlich (2012), 123.
11. Frank Erich Carl et al., Institut für Städtebau und Architektur der Deutschen Bauakademie, "Untersuchungen und Empfehlungen zur Rekonstruktions und Neubautätigkeit im Erholungswesen der DDR," March 1965, BArch: DH2 A 442; Hans Thiele, "Über die Entwicklung der Erholungsgebiete in Mitteldeutschland" (speech), BArch: DH2 II/09/10.
12. Görlich (2012), 119–20.
13. Staatliche Zentralverwaltung für Statistik, "Statistischer Jahresbericht über den Stand und die Entwicklung des Tourismus und Erholungswesens der DDR, 1979," 7, BArch: DE2 22676.
14. FDGB Feriendienst, "Analyse über die Ergebnisse der Untersuchungen in Oberhof zur Vereinfachung und Verbesserung des Erholungswesens in der DDR," 1967, 1, SAPMO-BArch: DY34 5963; FDGB Feriendienst, "Durchsetzung des neuen ökonomischen Systems der Planung und Leitung im Feriendienst der Gewerkschaften," 1967, SAPMO-BArch: DY34 5954.
15. Görlich (2012), 124, 141.
16. Auster (1996), 47.
17. The State Committee for Physical Culture and Sport agitated for the reform. See "Stellungnahme des Stako beim Ministerrat der DDR zu Problemen der zentralen staatlichen Leitung des Erholungswesens in der DDR," 1966/67, 1, BArch: DR5 1177; Staatliche Komitee für Körperkultur und Sport, "1.Entwurf—Einbringung eines Beschlusses über die staatliche Leitung des Erholungswesens—Begründung," September

21, 1967, BArch: DR5 427; "Schriftswechsel mit der ZK der SED: Vorlage für das Sekretariat des ZK," September 30, 1967, BArch: DR5 1138; FDGB Feriendienst, "Protokoll über die am 30.8.1967 stattgefundene Beratung beim Stako," August 30, 1967, 1–3, SAPMO-BArch: DY34 5953. For the harsh response from authorities, see Letter from Hellmann to Honecker, December 8, 1967, SAPMO-BArch: DY 30 IV A 2/18/5. For more on proposals to create a central ministry for recreation, see the following archival folders: SAPMO-BArch: DY 30 IV A 2/18/5, 2/18/39, 2/18/6; BArch: DR5 1177, 1087, 1138, 427; SAPMO-BArch: DY34 5953.

18. Zatlin (2007), 250.

19. "Internationale Campingplätze in der DDR," 1987, SäStCh: 30413/13825; "Bebauungskonzeption: Touristencampingsiedlung Stauweiher Greifenbach," May 1, 1973, SäStCh: 30413/128093; "Kurzprotokoll von der Beratung des Arbeitsausschusses der Bezirkskommission NuH am 30. 1.1976," SäStCh: 32682/164.

20. "Vorschlag zum Beschluss über Erfassung und Sicherung zusätzlicher Übernachtungsmöglichkeiten für Erholungsuchende," January 3, 1967, KarchMZ: 6118. Similar sentiments are expressed in "Niederschrift der Beratung des Aktives Naherholung am 20.6.1967," June 22, 1967, KarchMZ: 7074.

21. Abt. JKS, "Information für die Sitzung des Rat der Kreise Zschopau am 7.3.1968," March 6, 1968, KarchMZ: 7074; Abt. JKS, Speech transcript, KarchMZ: 6117.

22. On the power of workers in negotiations over wages and other benefits, see Port (2007), 164–94 and Jeffrey Kopstein, *The Politics of Economic Decline in East Germany, 1945–1989* (Chapel Hill: University of North Carolina Press, 1997), 29–58. For more on Culture and Social Funds as workers' benefits, see Zatlin (2007), 161–66.

23. Görlich (2012), 123.

24. Letter from Abt. JKS, Aktiv Naherholung addressed to VEB des Kreises, January 21, 1970, KarchMZ: 7074; Abt. Umwelt und Erholung, "Auswertung der Saison im Naherholungszentrum Greifenbachstauweiher/Greifensteine im Jahre 1970," KarchMZ: 6117.

25. StaarchEhr: Zeitungsauschnitte 1970; Letter from Bürgermeister Ehrenfriedersdorf to Mann (VEB Naherholung), April 25, 1972, StaarchEhr: S IV/e24. The SED received a quick response when it requested a plot for bungalows in 1972, as did the Mayor of Ehrenfriedersdorf when he requested cabins for exchange with a partner city in Czechoslovakia.

26. RdK Zschopau, "Baugenehmigungen," March 27, 1974, StaarchEhr: S IV/e11; RdK Zschopau, "Bootshaus," March 28, 1974, StaarchEhr: S IV/e17; "Dem Gebiet der Naherholung gehört unsere ganze Aufmerksamkeit," *Freie Presse*, [1978?], StaarchErh: Zeitungsauschnitte 1978; Letter from VEB Erholungsgebiet to Abt. JKS (RdK Zschopau), March 27, 1978, SäStCh: 30413/72511; VEB Erholungsgebiet Greifensteine/Greifenbachstauweiher, "Wettbewerbsprogramm 1987," January 26, 1987; VEB Erholungsgebiet Greifensteine/Greifenbachstauweiher, "Erläuterung zum Bewertungsbogen," September 7, 1987; and VEB Erholungsgebiet Greifensteine/Greifenbachstauweiher, "Erläuterung zum Bewertungsbogen für den sozialistischen Wettbewerb, 1989," SäStCh: 30413/150992.

27. Reinhold Lingner, "Beispielsentwurf für eine Feriensiedlung am Wasser," September 6, 1958, 2, SAPMO-BArch: DY34 3001.

28. SAPMO-BArch: DY34 3002.

29. For example, F. Carl, "Gebiets und landschaftsplanerische Gesichtspunkte zum Problem der Erholungsplanung in der DDR," November 21, 1962, BArch: DK 107 A9/34.

30. Aktenvermerk, "Betr: Antwort auf die Thematik für den Bericht über die Planung von Erholungsgebieten, von Orten und Einrichtungen der Erholung und Touristik," June 19, 1963, SAPMO-BArch: DY34 3001; Frank Erich Carl et al., Institut für Städtebau und Architektur der Deutschen Bauakademie, "Untersuchungen und Empfehlungen zur Rekonstruktions und Neubautätigkeit im Erholungswesen der DDR," BArch: DH2 A 442. On FDGB financial difficulties, see Görlich (2012).

31. FDGB Feriendienst, "Stellungnahme zum Bau einer Feriensiedlung," November 18, 1958, 3, SAPMO-BArch: DY34 3001.

32. FDGB Feriendienst, "Zum Bau von Bungalows," 1967/68, 1–2, SAPMO-BArch: DY34 5952.

33. Auster (1996), 43–44.

34. Abt. JKS, Speech transcript, 5, KarchMZ: 6117.

35. "Niederschrift über eine Beratung des Campingbeirates am Mittwoch, dem 7.9.1966," KarchMZ: 7073.

36. RdK Zschopau, Abt. JKS, "Vorschlag zum Perspektivplan Naherholung bis 1970," August 8, 1967, KarchMZ: 6093.

37. Letter from K.D. to Ministry for Environmental Protection (Ministerium für Umweltschutz, hereinafter MfU), August 1, 1972, BArch: DK5 4393.

38. Abt. Umweltschutz, "Eingabenanalyse 2. Halbjahr 1977," 2, BArch: DK5 71.

39. In response to numerous complaints, however, officials eventually reversed course and gave permits to campers for at least another year. Altogether, I found a dozen letters at the Marienberg Kreisarchiv about this specific incident.

40. Letter from M.T. to VEB Naherholung, February 18, 1973, KarchMZ: 6117. Letter from G.S. and J.S. to VEB Naherholung, February 22, 1973, KarchMZ: 6117.

41. Letter from H.P. to VEB Naherholung, February 18, 1973, KarchMZ: 6117.

42. Letter from H.A. to VEB Naherholung, February 14, 1973, KarchMZ: 6117.

43. Letter from K.K. of Bad Freienwalde to MfU, January 3, 1974, BArch: DK5 4506.

44. Letter from M.T. to VEB Naherholung, February 18, 1973, KarchMZ: 6117.

45. Letter from J. W. von W. (Dipl.-Psych. und Ind.-Soz. from Berlin) to MfU, September 12, 1979, BArch: DK5 71.

46. Letter from RdK Plauen to Bezirksnaturschtzverwaltung, March 14, 1966, and Herklotz (Sek des RdB KMS), "Betr: Entwurf eines Schreibens an Herrn Felix Clauss, Höhnstein wegen des geforderten Abbruchs seines Wochenendhauses," 1967, SäStCh: 30413/32398.

47. Letter from L.K., Vorsitzender des VKA Plänterwald im Kreiskomitee der ABI Berlin-Treptow, "Bericht über die Ergebnisse einiger Kontrollen zum Landeskulturgesetz, dei während der Monate Juni-Juli-August-September 1972 zeitweilig auf der Insel Pöl vorgenommen wurden," October 5, 1972, BArch: DK5 4393.

48. Ständigen Kommission Landeskultur und Erholungswesen, "Niederschrift über die Beratung am 28.3.1979," March 28, 1979, and Ständige Kommission Landeskultur und Erholung, "Abschrift," June 13, 1979, SäStCh: 30413/72470; RdB KMS, "Ordnung

zur bezirklichen Regelung privater Vermietung von Zimmern und Wochenendhäusern (Bungalow Erholungsbauten)," March 7, 1983, and Clipping from classified advertisements, offering rental of bungalows in various areas including Erzgebirge, SäStCh: 30413/150993.

49. Letter from K.S. to VEB Naherholung, February 13, 1973, KarchMZ: 6117.

50. Letter from H.H. to VEB Naherholung, February 11, 1973, KarchMZ: 6117.

51. Letter from H.A. to VEB Naherholung, February 14, 1973, KarchMZ: 6117.

52. Letter from M.T. to VEB Naherholung, February 18, 1973, KarchMZ: 6117.

53. Ständige Kommission Landeskultur und Erholungswesen, "Abschrift," June 13, 1979, SäStCh: 30413/72470; Abt. Erholungswesen (RdK Zschopau), "Vorlage für die Sitzung des Kreistages: Betr: Die weitere Entwicklung von Körperkultur und Sport sowie Naherholung im Kreis Zschopau," April 7, 1976, and Abt. Erholungswesen (RdK Zschopau), "Informationsvorlage über die Entwicklung des Erholungsgebietes Greifensteine/Greifenbachstauweiher für die Sitzung des Kreistages am 22.4.1976," April 6, 1976, SäStCh: 30413/72446.

54. This overview of bungalow ownership at the reservoir came from the "Zusammenstellung der Bauwerber für Wochenendhäuser am Geyer'schen Teich auf der Grundlage der Standortbesichtigung vom 25.6.1967," KarchMZ: 6117.

55. Zatlin, "Vehicle of Desire" (1997), 370.

56. Letter from M.T. to VEB Naherholung, February 18, 1973, KarchMZ: 6117.

57. Letter from W.L. to VEB Naherholung, February 12, 1973, KarchMZ: 6117.

58. Letter from K.K. of Bad Freienwalde to MfU , January 3, 1974, BArch: DK5 4506.

59. "Festlegung der Begrenzung des Naherholungsgebietes Greifenbachstauweiher Ehrenfriedersdorf," July 22, 1967, KarchMZ: 7073.

60. See SäStCh: 30413/72470.

61. Städtebauliche Bestätigung, "Form for Errichtung eines Wochenendhauses am Greifenbachstauweiher in Geyer," KarchMZ: 6117.

62. Abt. Erholungswesen (RdB KMS), "Massnahmen zur Gewährleistung einer einheitlichen Verfahrensweise zur Flächennutzung beider Errichtung von Erholungsbauten (Wochenendbauten),"April 15, 1975, and Ständigen Kommission Landeskultur und Erholungswesen, "Niederschrift über die 13 Sitzung der Ständigen Kommission Landeskultur und Erholungswesen am 17.5.1978," May 17, 1978, SäStCh: 30413/72470; Stellvertreter des Vorsitzenden für Umweltschutz (RdB KMS), "Beschlussvorlage: Massnahmeplan zur Gewährleistung einer einheitlichen Verfahrensweise zur Flächennutzung bei der Errichtung von Erholungsbauten (Wochenendbauten) im Bez KMS," April 15, 1975, SäStCh: 32682/149; Kreistag Annaberg, "Rede zur Begründung der langfristigen Konzeption Erholungswesen," September 30, 1976, SäStCh: 30413/72425.

63. "Orientierung für die Bildung und die Arbeitsweise von Interessengemeinschaften ohne den FDGB zur Errichtung und Nutzung von Wochenendhaussiedlungen für die Erholung," September 11, 1978, SäStCh: 30413/72454.

64. Abt. Erholungswesen (RdB KMS), "An werter x," July 30, 1979, SäStCh: 30413/72470.

65. Betts (2010), 143.

66. Betts (2010), 143.

67. Betts (2010), 156, 171.

68. Of the 1,080 letters received by the ministry during these years, 37 percent referred to these general problems, and of the letters kept in the archival files (461 for the years I researched), 48 percent did not cite a specific offender. In addition, many petitions about specific offenders linked the offense to a broader issue (40 percent worried about public health). For these *Eingaben*, see BArch: DK5. I used the following files for closer research: signatures 68–72, 2426, 2487, 3310, 3472, 3524, 2644, 4390–94, 4400, 4506, 4507, 4509, 4514, 37888.

69. Of the archived letters that cited no specific offender, nearly half (45 percent) complained about an infringement on their right to recreation in unspoiled nature (compared to 36 percent of archived letters that cited a specific offender).

70. Letter from E.K. to MfU, March 30, 1972, BArch: DK5 4393.

71. Letter from Jagdgesellschaft Fambach to MfU, June 6, 1972, BArch: DK5 2487. Similar sentiments occur in Letter from Kommission Sozialistisches Landeskultur beim Rat der Gemeinde Insel Hiddensee to MfU, June 20, 1972, BArch: DK5 4393.

72. Letter from Obermedizinalrat Professor Dr. W.B. to MfU, September 4, 1972, BArch: DK5 2487; Letter from G.K. to the MfU, July 28, 1972, BArch: DK5 4393. For other correspondence from city council members or organizations, see Letter from W.F. to Ministerrat, November 1, 1972, BArch: DK5 4393; "Abschlussbericht der Arbeitsgemeinschaft 'Luftreinhaltung bei der Sulfatzellstoffproduktion' in Dresden," May 8, 1973, BArch: DK5 4514; Letter from TSG Oberschöneweide (Sektion Allgemeine Körperkultur) to Vorsitzenden des RdK Königs Wusterhausen, September 1, 1973, BArch: DK5 3524; Letter from Station der Jungen Naturforscher und Techniker of Halle (Saale) to the MfU, August 23, 1974, BArch: DK5 3644.

73. Letter from B.L. to Ministerrat, February 3, 1982, BArch: DK5 72.

74. For more on West German environmentalism, see Chaney (2008); Dominick (1998); and Frank Uekötter, "Eine ökologische Ära? Perspektiven einer neuen Geschichte der Umweltbewegungen," *Zeithistorische Forschungen* 9, no. 1 (January 2012): 108–14.

CHAPTER 6

The Limits of Growth and the New Environmentalism

During the GDR's lifetime, East Germany's Ore Mountains (Erzgebirge) suffered from decades of sulfur dioxide poisoning from coal-fired electrical plants located in both the GDR and Czechoslovakia. In response, angry local residents wrote numerous letters of complaint (or *Eingaben*) to the Ministry for Environmental Protection (Ministeriat für Umweltschutz, or MfU). While *Eingaben* had channeled discontent into individual complaints throughout most of the GDR's history, organized groups began to compose petitions in the 1980s. For example, in 1981, the evangelical church in Annaberg-Buchholz reminded authorities of the consequences of air pollution for parishioner health. The congregation's leaders wrote, "Our forests are being destroyed, our water polluted, the air overwhelmed with noxious matter, insects and bird species go extinct, and the health of our people is endangered." They warned, "Public anger is growing."[1]

The dying Erzgebirge forest was just one example of the numerous economic and ecological problems plaguing East Germany by the 1980s. Despite its approval of the Landeskulturgesetz, the SED soon returned to repressing environmental reformers with renewed vigor. The SED Politburo, for example, ordered the Ministerial Council to discontinue its regular environmental reports and stripped the annual Land Improvement Week festivities and conferences to nearly nothing in 1974.[2] The regime, even as it made gestures toward environmental protection, never seriously rethought production methods, and by 1982, the state ordered all environmental data secret and off-limits to public consumption. To the growing frustration of a younger generation of technocrats and party members, Honecker's generation ignored Mikhail Gorbachev's warnings to reform and continued business as usual right up to the peaceful revolutions of 1989. In part due to Erich Honecker's continued need to appease consumer desires, state debt also continued to grow. Scarce financial resources and rising oil prices meant that the regime had little money available to replace aging factories or to lessen its reliance on domestic supplies of sulfur-rich brown coal. Even the Chernobyl catastrophe in 1986 did little to shake the SED from its lethargy; while the regime tolerated individual complaints, any organized critique of the regime's economic or energy program led to harassment by the Stasi.[3]

As the above letter from Annaberg-Buchholz highlights, churches played an increasingly important role in environmental protests against the SED. At the heart of the new environmental movement of the 1980s was a small group of nonconformists who had found a home within the Protestant church. They advocated for human rights, peace, and environmental protection and demanded both democratic reform and a return to a simpler, less materialistic lifestyle. In their critique of consumerism, activists were seemingly at odds with the many East Germans who looked enviously to the wealth of the capitalist West.

Rather than looking for early influences on the movement, most histories of this new environmentalism really only begin with the new opportunities and ideas emerging out of the Protestant churches in the late 1970s.[4] Often scholars note the important connections between East German activists and their counterparts prominent in Western Green politics or at least highlight the ways that environmental literature from Western Europe made its way eastward.[5] We thus know most about intellectuals such as Rudolf Bahro and grassroots activists organized around institutions such as the Environmental Library in Berlin.[6] In his work, Nathan Stoltzfus has argued that a true public sphere only emerged inside East Germany when these young activists initiated local public demonstrations and mobilizations in the 1980s.[7] While he points out that the regime and the church had already injected the environment into official discourse, the unintended implication here is that only a small nonconformist minority had the awareness and courage to critique East German industrial and environmental policy.[8] Nikola Knoth similarly asserts that desire for material security among workers discouraged them from criticizing the regime's use of nature.[9] As shown in the previous chapter, however, desires for material security sometimes did lead to criticisms of environmental pollution. For Jan Palmowski, popular discontent with environmental decay escalated not because the regime ignored natural and cultural landscapes but, rather, because official attention to environment and socialist Heimat stood in stark contrast with the "individual experience of socialism in everyday life."[10] As Palmowski puts it, the public transcript of the socialist Heimat looked increasingly hollow in the face of environmental catastrophe.[11] In Palmowski's narrative, a small group of better-informed church-affiliated activists rejected the Society for Nature and Environment (Gesellschaft für Natur und Umwelt, or GNU) of the Kulturbund (Culture League) and broke radically from this public transcript. This transgression immediately provoked alarm among state authorities, especially in a Stasi that began to infiltrate church-based organizations and tried to channel discontented citizens into official organizations.[12]

This chapter uniquely contributes to this growing historiography of East Germany's new environmentalism of the 1980s. It places the new environmentalism within its domestic historical and social context and seeks to contrast the goals and assumptions of the new environmental movement with previous attempts at conservation and environmental criticism in the GDR. The new environmentalists, I argue, were not just appalled at the hypocrisy and lies of the SED and its representatives in the Kulturbund; they also rejected a mainstream attitude toward nature and planning that the SED, conservationists, and East German vacationers all once shared—specifically a faith in limitless but managed economic growth (as long as planners properly managed land uses). As the previous chapter demonstrated, a popular critique of environmental policy could emerge out of GDR-specific notions of economic growth and social justice. The activists of the 1980s were thus not the first to critique the regime for its environmental policies, but they did pioneer an alternative rhetoric for criticizing SED policies. As Sandra Chaney has written about West Germany, "Highlighting the rebellious rhetoric and sensational protests associated with modern environmentalism overshadows more subtle shifts in language, thought, and daily activity that had occurred within the conservation tradition prior to the 1970s."[13] Just as West German environmental consciousness had roots in the activities of architects, urban planners, and engineers working in the 1960s, East Germany's new environmentalism had roots in an earlier period. But it also was a specific rejection of earlier East German efforts and dreams.

This chapter thus begins by exploring how much of the daily practice of conservation and environmental criticism in the 1970s and early 1980s continued to accept a "mainstream consensus" about growth, material desires, and social justice. A doctrine of multiple use, informed by this consensus, dominated conservation practices. Multiple use refers to land-use policies that try to balance growing demands on resources with little thought given to the ecological limits to continued use. No matter the scale of the problem, conservationists sought to establish landscape care plans that balanced the interests of different stakeholders. Multiple use, remember, was not just an imposition by the SED and economic planners; conservationists in East Germany had long insisted that experts could manage a landscape to balance economic uses, human needs, and nature protection. While they may have wanted to limit extreme cases of pollution and overbuilding, they themselves believed rational planning helped the land sustain economic development. As this chapter will show, complaint letters to the Ministry for Environmental Protection also accepted uncritically the notion of planned management for multiple use.

The chapter will then show that many conservationists gave up hope for balancing the interests of industry and tourism with nature protection and sought out new ways of thinking about conservation. The story of biologist Horst Heynert, in particular, reveals how the SED quite intentionally promoted *Erholung* at the expense of ecology in the 1970s. The SED's use of *Erholung* planning to silence ecology made increasingly pointless the long-standing but faltering attempts of the "conservation bloc" to justify conservation as a boon to public health and worker productivity. While the Landeskulturgesetz had initially given the conservation bloc hope, early misgivings about a law that stressed *Erholung* were only confirmed and led some conservationists to join more radical environmentalists organized within the churches.

As I argue in the last section of this chapter, the political environmentalism of the 1980s made a significant break from East Germany's mainstream discourse about nature, central planning, and economic growth. Health and public welfare continued to preoccupy the minds of church-based environmentalists, but they rejected the notion that authoritarian planners and scientific experts in their white lab coats could manage health and landscape; instead, health (physical, social, and psychological) depended on grassroots activism, ethical choices, and simpler lifestyles. Activists of the 1980s thus did not simply ally with the downtrodden to topple a dictatorship. They told everyday East Germans who were famously frustrated with an anemic economy and consumer scarcity that they should actually consume even less. The SED was their greatest enemy, but they also insisted on a fundamental transformation of mainstream culture. The general public, they insisted, shared some of the blame for the East German ecological and spiritual catastrophes.

Multiple Use and Environmental Protection

Building on their own natural tendencies and bullied by a nervous SED, conservationists in the 1970s increasingly emphasized the "multiple use" of the countryside. Conservationists had always had faith in expert planners to balance land uses to encourage sustainability. As the genealogy of the Landeskulturgesetz of 1970 revealed, the SED and its economic planners never intended for the law to restrict economic growth, and the institutional arrangements to enforce the law in the 1970s and 1980s reflect that legacy. All economic and public uses of the land could coexist, officials in the Ministry for Environmental Protection insisted, as long as the government and industrial firms coordinated and planned together. The SED, furthermore, quickly silenced any approach to conservation that did not embrace multiple use.

The idea of multiple use was not new to the conservation bloc, but it became even more prominent in the late 1960s. In Dr. Hugo Weinitschke's address to the Kulturbund's 1966 Landscape Conference, the prominent nature preservationist focused on the demands vacationers made on physical environments. Weinitschke defended all recreation practices and insisted that proper planning satisfy all leisure needs, arguing, "We must keep all [of these forms] in mind when we plan *Erholung* facilities and districts."[14] "I believe," he insisted, "to each his own! *Erholung* can be imagined in many forms, and the psychological facets [of *Erholung*] may differ from person to person."[15] Weinitschke demanded multiple use and warned against strict limits to the use of landscape preserves. "There is nothing wrong with 'amusement parks,' as long as 'quiet zones' are also available," he suggested, "so that everyone can recreate according to his or her own needs." Weinitschke demanded better planning and management, to protect a landscape's integrity; he recommended scientifically analyzing vacationer behavior and channeling activities into regulated and approved development. Any landscape could withstand the pressure exerted by vacationers and other users, if "great care is taken to prevent the *unorganized* overdevelopment of the landscape."[16]

In the 1970s, Weinitschke's doctrine of multiple use guided the conduct of landscape conferences, or *Landschaftstage*, which became increasingly common in vacation districts. By the end of the decade, regions with landscape conferences included Saxon Switzerland, Thuringia, the Harz Mountains, the Neubrandenburg lakes district, and the Erzgebirge. In 1985, 123 landscape conferences convened across the GDR, during which twenty thousand participants discussed landscape protection and tourist provisions.[17] *Landschaftstag* participants, who were stakeholders living and working in or near landscape preserves, helped craft landscape care plans for their preserves, as the Landeskulturgesetz had mandated.[18] Looking back, these conferences offered an intriguing model for cooperative planning. Some East Germans insisted that these conferences at least initially led to positive interventions in local landscape use, as participants raised important questions about the environmental impact of agriculture and industry.[19] Nonetheless, conservationists rarely dictated the content of a *Landschaftstag*, since district officials and high-level Kulturbund representatives hosted the events, controlled the composition of landscape care plans, and insisted on continued economic development of these lands. After all, the future prosperity of local firms preoccupied the minds of local governments.[20] To further compromise conservation, high-placed agricultural and industrial officials, such as SED Politburo member and agricultural minister Gerhard Grüneberg, often intervened to override landscape care plans.[21] Details from the first *Landschaftstag* in Saxon Switzerland in 1977 confirm that these conferences prioritized compromise and multiple use over strict limits and regulations. Participants and speakers in Dresden included not just leisure planners but also representatives of industrial enterprises, agricultural collectives, and the state forestry service. District officials, in their mission statement, identified the conference as an opportunity to "ensure a sensible and rational use of the landscape preserve, especially for recreation uses."[22] During a field trip, conference participants visited locales chosen to demonstrate the virtues of "socialist land use [*Landeskultur*]" and "the planned multiple use of the landscape."[23]

In the years in between these conferences, environmental protection officers at the county and district level also promoted multiple use on a daily basis. The Landeskulturgesetz called for districts and counties to appoint environmental officers, who advised local authorities on environmental problems and possible solutions. Unlike earlier in the GDR, these officials were no longer housed within the Ministry for Agriculture and Forestry, but they worked closely, as earlier, with the Kulturbund and the Institute for Landscape and Nature Protection (ILN). Just as when Meusel and the ILN offered their expertise in the national park debate, scientists provided technical advice to local preservationists. In part, preservation officers had to defend "multiple use" for practical reasons, as communities depended on local enterprises for cultural funds and often for infrastructure improvements. Local well-being and, thus, vacation opportunities and other welfare benefits depended on the continued growth of local businesses.[24]

The lack of a central environmental ministry with real teeth (as conservationists had tried to create in the 1960s) only made it more difficult to limit economic and popular uses of landscapes, as these users had many local backers with a vested interest in preserving the status quo. No higher authority backed these preservationists against local economic interests, as conservationists quickly recognized. In a *Wochenpost* interview in 1969, Gilsenbach pushed authorities responsible for composing the Landeskulturgesetz about the issue of administration—asking who would put pressure on factories to actually change their polluting practices and wondering who would really control industrial planning. He also insisted that some decisions made locally might have negative consequences far from their source.[25] One conservationist from Karl Marx City understood the lack of a new ministry as the law's greatest weakness. In a few local districts, authorities might have enthusiastically enforced the law, but "where the administrative had no sympathy, [nature protection] is not particularly good."[26] The eventual creation of a Ministry for Environmental Protection did little to ease their fears.

In their collaboration with the Society for Nature and Environment (GNU), environmental protection officers further wedded themselves to state economic interests. The SED created the GNU in 1980 to undermine environmental activism within the church. It imagined that it could depoliticize ecological awareness by creating a home for ecologists and other conservationists informed by new ideas about ecosystem and biosphere protections. This organization especially attracted Kulturbund members with scientific expertise. Whatever the SED's intentions, the GNU cannot be dismissed out of hand as a tool of repression. The organization's outlook and methods owed as much to how its members understood conservation as to what the SED allowed them to do.[27] Among other activities, members conducted surveys of species distribution and identified the environmental impacts of local land use, and the organization had over fifty-seven thousand members by 1987.[28] On the whole, the GNU remained (with the exception of the "city ecology" groups who had a greater appeal to nontraditional ecological activists) a bastion of conservative scientists that preferred to cooperate with authorities to implement incremental change.[29] As environmental protection officers did and the conservation bloc had long done, they retained a faith in limitless abundance and tried to balance a variety of land uses, including recreation, manufacturing, and agriculture.[30]

East Germany's most common form of legal complaint also encouraged multiple-use solutions to environmental problems. Since written *Eingaben*, or petitions, channeled discontent into individualistic complaints to a paternalistic state, letter writers all expected the regime to accommodate their individual desires and thus, by default, expected landscapes to be managed for multiple users. Responses to petitions further encouraged the practice of multiple use. In more than one response to complaint letters about infringements on protected nature, the Ministry for Environmental Protection or its local representatives pushed for intensified use of preserves by many different users. In the town of Kleinmachnow, for example, various residents complained about the construction of a swimming pool in a protected landscape, but the district officials in Potsdam responded that the pool satisfied the *Erholung* "needs of the population."[31] When a Berlin engineer criticized a motorbike track within a local landscape preserve, local authorities in Berlin-Köpenick responded that young bikers had their own rights to *Erholung*.[32] Elsewhere, the Ministry for Environmental Protection approved the expansion of a garden colony into a protected landscape despite the complaints of nature lovers.[33] Land-use planners had to accommodate popular desires as best they could, and no one use of a landscape preserve could justify denying another resident his private pleasures.

Earlier, conservationists promoted *Erholung* as a means to protect landscapes, but now *Erholung* justified uses of the land that threatened protection efforts. The example of motorboating reveals how malleable *Erholung* had become, as it served to justify bans on motorboats as well as to endorse continued boating in landscape preserves. In 1972, the residents of Motzen, represented by several prominent citizens, wrote directly to head of state Erich Honecker to complain that the "natural conditions for *Erholung*" at local lakes had been tarnished by motorboat traffic. On Lake Motzen alone, they reminded Honecker, over thirty thousand workers from Berlin and the region vacationed every year. They asked, "Should these . . . vacations once again be denatured through motor noise, oily water, and noxious exhaust fumes, just because, to put it crassly, there are a few party functionaries who regard the protection of motorboat enthusiasts as more important than protection of the working populations' health and vitality as guaranteed in the constitution?" The citizens of Motzen asked, "How long will you allow these citizens, at the cost of others, to pursue their hobby, which has nothing at all to do with real *Erholung* or sport?"[34] While the Ministry for Environmental Protection did implement new regulations at Lake Motzen in 1975, some vacationers themselves joined authorities in insisting that all uses of local landscapes could be sustained.[35] One citizen, for instance, defended enthusiasts of water-skiing—a "lovely" sport that he believed helped "preserve physical and mental vitality." He doubted that enough boaters existed to truly pollute the water, but more important, he believed, "A ban on water-skiing was incompatible with the GDR's expressed wish to promote sport."[36] Another boating enthusiast disagreed with the proposed restrictions and questioned the state's commitment to providing every citizen a "more beautiful and also more comfortable" life. In his opinion, boating encouraged healthy, "active" recreation in nature.[37] These citizens agreed with authorities that preserves could be managed or developed for multiple use. Hard limits to human uses of nature did not exist in their worldview.

Growing Doubts about Growth

The futility of conservation wedded to a doctrine of multiple use and endless economic expansion became increasingly obvious to conservationists such as Horst Heynert. Heynert had a degree in biogeography from Jena and began his career studying forests in the Erzgebirge of southern East Germany. In several guides to East German botany published in the 1970s, he—like his counterparts in the Kulturbund and in landscape architecture—made a connection between protected natural landscapes and *Erholung*. He wrote in 1970, for instance, that vegetation and the climate of the mountains had a powerful psychological effect and promoted good health and *Erholung*.[38] He thus proposed that planners exploit scientific knowledge about plant geography to restore habitats to their former beauty, and he insisted that plant geographers could help optimize vacation experiences by using their findings to enhance a forest's *Erholung* function.[39] As far as his writings revealed, therefore, Heynert manipulated *Erholung* rhetoric to advocate more "natural" land-use policies. Society and nature, with the proper scientific knowledge, could be fine-tuned for maximum and endless productivity and happiness.

In the 1970s, however, Heynert discovered what Reimar Gilsenbach already had suspected at the time the regime endorsed the Landeskulturgesetz. The Kulturbund leadership cynically promoted *Erholung* at the expense of ecology. Heynert's dispute with Kulturbund leadership began soon after the introduction of the new Landeskulturgesetz. In May 1972, perhaps hopeful about the law's potential to transform the East German economy, Heynert proposed the Working Group Erzgebirge, to bring together scientists from different disciplines with a common interest in better landscape care.[40] He also promoted the idea of a *Landschaftstag* for the Erzgebirge, with presentations, excursions, and a press conference.[41] Complaining that Karl Marx City still had not created a proper department for environmental protection, he organized a workshop titled "Ecology and Environmental Protection," featuring several lectures focused on ecological issues.[42] Heynert hoped to discuss, in particular, the threat of industrial agriculture to the local ecosystem.[43] He and his colleagues repeatedly questioned the wisdom of the regime's obsession with ever larger farms.[44]

Heynert immediately began to face intense scrutiny from political functionaries. His primary opponent was Dr. H. H. Kasper of the Mining Academy in Freiberg, who had been first introduced to the Oversight Committee of Karl Marx City's local Nature and Heimat Friends to "improve leadership" in 1968.[45] Kasper demanded that Heynert's working group focus more on regional culture and history and less on ecological science that might lead to more criticism of socialist industry or agriculture.[46] He did not cancel Heynert's delayed ecology workshop but did insist that a leading district Kulturbund official give a lecture to emphasize political concerns.[47] In the meantime, Kasper organized a competing workshop under the title "Man and the Environment" (*Mensch und Umwelt*).[48] Papers given at the workshop stressed the economy, tourism (*Erholung*), and political education—without a single title referring to ecological science or pollution problems.[49] Kasper also delayed Heynert's proposed *Landschaftstag* for many years, and when it did finally happen in 1978, he insisted that it focus almost entirely on legislation to improve tourism in the Erzgebirge region.[50] Describing the *Landschaftstag* goals, functionaries identified the conference as an opportunity to better provide vacation opportunities to the local working population and organize lodging for foreign tourists.[51] Organizers even prepared a keynote speech that stressed the growing demand for *Erholung* among East German workers and the resulting need for the multiple use of important landscapes.[52] Little serious reference was to be made to pollution problems.[53]

In the face of such scrutiny, Heynert became increasingly wary of the promises of authoritarian scientific planning. He already hinted at this wariness in a 1971 speech presented at the Club for Intelligentsia in Freiburg. Heynert explained how simple changes (i.e., limits) in daily lifestyle could help the environment.[54] He stressed that the enforcement of the new Landeskulturgesetz would be a long-term project requiring new attitudes, not just new plans.[55] By 1977, he insisted about nature conservation, "It is not only necessary to have adequate state laws, but a transformation in the attitude and conscious acts of each and every person is also needed."[56] Advancements in public health and social progress, he argued, required more than scientific, socialist management of society and nature; it required a new humanism built on ecological science and a respect for the nonhuman world. Society would need to become less anthropocentric and more humble in its interactions with nature. For Heynert, expert authority no longer was enough; in fact, the attack on ecology may have convinced him and others that the attractions of a potent authority paled in comparison to its dangers.

Did the conservation bloc abandon its cooperation with authorities as its frustrations grew? It is unclear how many older conservationists actually joined the church-based environmental groups, but the daily experiences of conservation practice must have made them appealing. Heynert's call for new attitudes and a new consciousness certainly echoed the church-based environmental movement's worldview, which will be outlined shortly. Despite the likely misgivings of individuals such as Heynert, however, many scientists joined the GNU, where they continued to work with authorities for incremental change. They thus continued the reformist tradition long established by the conservation bloc and avoided the confrontational style of young nonconformists.

Reimar Gilsenbach, a prominent advocate of a national park and a prominent member of the Kulturbund's Nature and Heimat Friends, provides one important example of a conservationist joining the new environmentalism. Gilsenbach had served as editor of the monthly magazine *Natur und Heimat* in the 1950s and later became a member of the German Academy for Agricultural Science (DAL). In his autobiography, Gilsenbach presents himself as a nonconformist who pushed the Kulturbund and the DAL to better protect the environment. In many ways, though, he fit well within the general culture of the conservation bloc. In his writings, he called for comprehensive planning where experts considered the consequences of each and every planned use of nature. While Gilsenbach often stood out for his advocacy and overtly critical remarks, he did not seem to give up on state planning. He kept working within the system even in the 1980s, as he joined the national leadership of the GNU and continued to participate in the Nature and Heimat Friends and the DAL.

As with Heynert, Gilsenbach's frustrations with the Kulturbund revolved around the problem of *Erholung* and the SED's increasing interest in its promotion. While his early works connected the demand for a national park to the popular need for leisure and recreation, he increasingly identified tourists and vacationers as a threat to protection efforts. Already in 1964, he complained in *Wochenpost* about bungalows and vacation homes. He wrote, "Nature is being parceled up; its beauties becoming privately owned."[57] Looking back on his work with the Kulturbund, he expressed particular regret about his endorsement of a project to create the Müritz Seen Park through the DAL. The park's planning, he complained, focused almost entirely on the efforts to promote tourism, bungalow colonies, and campgrounds.[58] Indeed, the landscape plan for Müritz Seen Park adhered to the policy of multiple use and continued economic development. Multiple use was intended to balance nature protection, tourism, and agriculture; in reality, multiple use meant pig barns located immediately next to lakeshore campgrounds.[59] Over the years, Gilsenbach also witnessed, as Heynert did, increasing censorship. He noted that one conservationist and local county council member successfully negotiated with agricultural collectives to create a landscape care plan but that she lost her speaking privileges at council meetings. Functionaries had tried to silence Gilsenbach himself at the 1966 Landscape Conference, as described in chapter 4. Reading his own Stasi file after 1990, Gilsenbach discovered that he was under surveillance from 1984 to 1988. The Stasi believed that Gilsenbach encouraged a "radical cell" of scientists within the Eberswalde GNU.[60] By 1986, however, he decided that he "no longer saw any sense in participating" in the GNU, and he later regretted his collaboration in state planning. Gilsenbach began to participate in church environmental seminars, developing a working relationship with Carlo Jordan at the Environmental Library in Berlin and helping with the Ark environmental network in the mid-1980s.[61]

Not all disgruntled conservationists followed exactly in Gilsenbach's footsteps. Born in 1941, Michael Succow trained as a biologist and actively participated in conservation efforts in the 1960s and 1970s. Succow resigned from his university position in 1969 due to his opposition to the Warsaw Pact invasion of Czechoslovakia to end the Prague Spring. Later in his life, he became a professor in the DAL and traveled to the Soviet Union and Mongolia on research. He also joined the GNU and became one of the more prominent leaders of that largely conservative organization in the 1980s. While he thus followed a well-worn path of collaboration with the regime, Succow eventually gave up on engagement with authorities. According to Lebrecht Jeschke, Succow concluded that "Growth-Ideology, the SED's monopoly of power, science's failures, and the lack of an ethical relationship to nature were at the root of [the GDR's] disastrous [environmental record]."[62] In 1989, ecological protesters supported Succow's appointment as deputy minister for nature conservation, ecology, and water management of the GDR. Taking advantage of the confusion after the Berlin Wall fell, his office very quickly established several national parks, including the elusive park in Saxon Switzerland.[63]

In contrast to her older colleagues, Annette Beleites early on enthusiastically embraced church-based environmentalism and a critique of materialism. As Heynert did, she identified individual responsibility and personal engagement as the keys to environmental change, but what had been a belated realization for an older generation became a basic starting point of discussion for this younger generation. While she continued to work as a biologist for the State Office for Environment and Nature in Schwerin, she wrote often on environmental themes in church publications, led an "Ecological Circle," and organized a series of ecological seminars, including one in 1988 that caught the attention of the Stasi.[64] She believed that "the environmental theme cannot be left only to conferences and organizations. Every single one of us is obliged to not only to consider the causes and consequences of environmental destruction but also to undertake fully concrete steps to work against this destruction."[65] Through church newsletters, she advocated for simpler lifestyles with a lower ecological impact. "Our tables our already richly stocked," she wrote, continu-

ing, "Our homes are comfortable, our clothes are modern."[66] She added elsewhere, "In our country, we have plenty to eat."[67]

The Environmental Movement of the 1980s

Beleites and her critique of consumerism neatly captured the mood of the
1980s environmental movement more generally. As Beleites did, these activists first gathered within the spaces of the Protestant church, though they initially did so for practical reasons. The church's importance could be traced
back to two key moments in GDR history. Earlier in the GDR, the regime aggressively discriminated against citizens who openly practiced their religious
beliefs.[68] In 1964, however, the regime made a key concession to Christians
who sought an alternative to military service. These new "construction soldiers," or *Bausoldaten*, could fulfill their conscription obligations without car-
rying weapons. According to historian Nathan Stoltzfus, these *Bausoldaten*
formed the core of the emerging peace movement in East Germany that over-
lapped with and supported the environmental movement. Later, a March 1978
agreement between church leaders and Erich Honecker put an official end to
the regime's public antagonism toward religion. The regime now acknowledged the legitimacy of the church; in turn, the church put an end to its uncom-
promised opposition to the SED. In exchange, the church received greater
freedom to govern itself and the right to provide a quasi-public sphere for the
discussion of apolitical topics within church walls. For example, the church
had relatively independent control over its own media and theological institutes. Of course, the SED and the church disagreed about what constituted
apolitical topics. The church insisted, for example, that peace and ecology
were religious affairs, while the regime identified these as political threats to
"real existing socialism."[69]

Activists also gravitated toward the Protestant church because of its increasing attention to environmental issues. Already in 1971, church leaders
asked the Ecclesiastical Research Center in Wittenberg to explore the relation-
ships between Christianity, ecology, and environmentalism. Dr. Hans-Peter
Gensichen commenced the center's activities in 1974, and soon the center published *Die Erde ist zu Retten* (The earth is ours to save) as well as an environmental newsletter known as *Briefe zur Orientierung im Konflikt Mensch Natur.*
The center organized lecture series, brought traveling exhibitions to small towns
across the GDR, and gave support to local environmental groups across the

state. Crucially, the church identified the environment as a "matter of ethics and social responsibility" and not just a technical problem, as the regime insisted.[70]

Environmental activists first organized within church walls around 1980. An ecological research group formed at Dresden's Kreuzkirche; before long, activists had established between fifty-nine and one hundred small groups across the republic. Examples of key environmental happenings included bicycle demonstrations, in which participants toured environmentally damaged landscapes or advocated for car-free days. A 1983 example in Halle brought over 140 participants to the chemical factories surrounding the town center, where one cyclist carried a poster asking at what cost the regime should fulfill Walter Ulbricht's promise "Chemicals Bring Beauty, Prosperity, and Bread." In another case, around one hundred residents of Schwerin planted trees and inspired similar tree plantings across the GDR.

After Chernobyl, environmental activists began to form more visible and more provocative institutions. Berliners such as Carlo Jordan established an Environmental Library in 1986 at the Zion Church, where they collected data on the threat posed by Chernobyl and nuclear energy in general. As the library grew, it also welcomed books and pamphlets on topics such as peace and human rights and became a key center for opposition. The library provided visitors a café, held seminars, distributed a newsletter, and hosted strategy meetings. Building on their success, some of these Berliners then created the Green Ecology Network the Ark (Grün Ökologisches Netzwerk Arche) in 1988 to connect fledgling environmental libraries throughout the GDR. Members of the Ark even produced a grainy documentary on Bitterfeld (*Bitteres aus Bitterfeld*) and distributed research on the GDR's uranium mines.[71]

The new church-based activism provoked strong reactions from authorities. The Stasi disrupted the distribution of newsletters and other mailings and also employed a growing number of informants to foster division and distrust among environmentalists.[72] Both the Ark and the Environmental Library in Berlin came under intense Stasi scrutiny, with the Berlin library enduring nighttime raids as it widened its contacts with peace activists and West Germans. New forms of protests quickly became outlawed. Police warned Halle bicycle demonstrators that their action was criminal; indeed, police arrested many participants as they rode past Buna Chemical Works. In another example, the Stasi prohibited tree plantings as illegal assembly.[73] At the same time, the church itself discouraged overly provocative demonstrations, as it preferred discreet letter writing or behind-the-scenes negotiations.[74]

Too much attention to these high-profile encounters between activists and the Stasi, however, distracts our attention from the subtle but profound challenges to conventional wisdom posed by these church-based environmentalists. They employed a rhetoric that directly questioned the dreams of limitless growth and doctrines of multiple use at the heart of the mainstream consensus voiced by both the regime and its subjects. In a land of relative scarcity where many residents longed for bananas and other exotic foodstuffs, these activists boldly proclaimed, "In our country, we have enough of everything and eat well enough."[75] They demanded that East Germans, instead of waiting for the state to fix a problem, should wake from their apolitical slumber or materialistic stupor and go out and do something about the world's problems.

Throughout church newsletters, activists repeatedly despaired over East German consumer desires. Commenting on material needs, Wittenberg researchers insisted, "Such pseudo and mistaken [material] desires cannot compare to actual needs. They only alleviate stress briefly and create new unhappiness and further pretensions."[76] Instead of consuming more, they argued, East German citizens might want to consider finding happiness through engagement with community.[77] In a set of ecological commandments, Wittenberg theologians included the following commandment: "Thou shall not covet what your neighbors have . . . We must recognize that material comforts are not the true path to a fulfilling or meaningful life."[78] At one rally, banners simply proclaimed that "consumption costs lives."[79] Frustrated activists elsewhere commented, "A person cannot live from bread alone, but also needs God's encouragement."[80] Nobody, they complained, considered the effects of their comfort on the environment.[81]

In other words, these Christians and allied nonconformists demanded that East Germans abandon dreams of limitless growth and change their lifestyles to reflect ecological limits to growth. Many churches across the GDR promoted simpler living as Annette Beleites did. Such pleas can be found throughout the newsletters and pamphlets published by church activists and collected today at the Archive of GDR Opposition at the Robert Havemann Society in Berlin. In a set of "ten commandments," for example, Wittenberg authorities recommended that citizens use fewer household chemicals, drive personal vehicles less often, avoid pesticides in their gardens, and stop building private bungalows in exurban areas. Other commandments pushed for an end to daily showers and overheated apartments, while requesting greater use of public transportation. Church activists recommended that young people should stop purchasing cheap and fashionable goods and should instead choose durable and more expensive products.[82] Some activists promoted vegetarianism.[83] In other cases, desk calendars and seminars provided advice on environmentally friendly lifestyles, with tips for earth-safe laundry detergents and natural cosmetics.[84] In a country where many East Germans longed for an automobile, organizers of the Berlin Environmental Library noted, "Among party leaders there is talk that Trabants and Wartburgs will soon become less expensive." In response, the activists exclaimed, "Actually, they already have become much too cheap!"[85] Elsewhere activists argued that growth does not have to mean "more automobiles"; they instead promoted travel by bicycle and public transit.[86]

One form of consumerism—tourism or vacationing—posed particularly vexing problems for these new environmentalists. Tourism had been the most viable justification for landscape preservation in the early days of the regime. On the one hand, 1980s activists insisted on the health benefits of outdoor recreation. Turning economic priorities from quantity to quality meant transforming a world from gray comfort and mindless consumption to colorful creativity and increased spirituality. Many church-based actions sought to protect tourist destinations from development and thus continued a long East German tradition of tying conservation to public health, recreation, and well-being. On the other hand, tourism—like many forms of consumption—gave a priority to material comforts and private pleasures rather than critical engagement. Tourism, in this sense, symbolized the mainstream consensus about limitless growth. These conflicting attitudes toward tourism appeared throughout the environmental newsletters of the 1980s.

Often, environmentalists depicted tourism or vacationing as a positive alternative to other forms of consumerism. Jaunts into the countryside, church groups insisted, were vital for overcoming an alienation from nature. Weekend hikes, community gardens, country cottages, and nature films reflected a popular desire to reconnect with "wild nature" that could be directed toward more serious environmentalism.[87] It was better to go for a hike than to watch more television, insisted the Ecclesiastical Research Center in Wittenberg.[88] One contributor to the Berlin journal *Umweltblätter* sought to redefine measures of economic growth to better account for nonmaterial pleasures, such as longer weekends or an increase in annual vacation days.[89] *Anstösse*, another samizdat publication, published an article despairing that an invitation to a Saturday nature hike only attracted ten participants from a city of twenty-five thousand, while a popular television show airing on Saturday evening could gain viewers among 80 percent of the population.[90] Alongside demands for pollution control, church groups in Halle asked government officials to better protect and provide for recreation areas.[91] Critics of air pollution in Saxony often noted that vacationing in these increasingly degraded areas was essential to public health.[92] Elsewhere, the journal *Arche Nova* directly linked a collapse of natural landscapes with social problems not unlike those identified by the conservation bloc in the 1950s. The author wrote, "Environmental destruction has social consequences: a spiritual poverty among the people, especially the youth, is obvious. Alcoholism, sadism against fellow humans, animals, and landscape is everyday. Productivity and even creativity is fading away."[93]

Yet activists also despaired over a leisure culture that treated nature as a scarce commodity to be enjoyed individualistically. For church environmentalists, the proliferation of bungalows in the countryside clearly revealed the dangers of escapism. The Wittenberg Ecclesiastical Research Center referred to these cottages in their environmental "ten commandments." The second commandment called for intrusions in nature to be done in the most ecologically friendly manner. Specifically, individuals needed to avoid a partitioning of ecosystems into private gardens and bungalow plots.[94] Concerns about selfish individualism and unequal access to scarce vacation destinations also informed a 1984 initiative to organize summer camps for children from Halle suffering from that city's intense air pollution. Promoters commented on the parceling out of vacation lands that often ignored the needs of those most affected by pollution.[95] The Berlin environmental library in 1989 despaired over new legislation to expand the area around Berlin dedicated to bungalow development. The Berlin activists insisted, "The last undeveloped spaces (and thus the last untouched biota) should not be built upon."[96] These cottages represented, above all else, a flight into individual irresponsibility and a spiritual barrenness.[97] This privatization of public space furthermore appeared to be an obstacle to environmental activism. Personal engagement fell to the wayside, one architect argued in the pages of *Umweltbrief*, as social life was privatized into a world of garden plots, bungalows, and family vacations.[98] Wittenberg leaders described the retreat into private spheres (including the bungalow) as "the increasing checking out from social life and retreat into the private sphere [that] creates resignation and deadly silence."[99]

To overcome resignation and "deadly silence," the new environmentalists stressed the necessity of critical and positive engagement, as modeled in tree plantings. According to *Arche Nova*, "The worst thing is the apathy and a fear of doing something about [the environment]."[100] Repeatedly, activists and church leaders preached hope and encouraged activism. One of Wittenberg's more famous publications, *Die Erde ist zu Retten*, had a title with double meaning: "It radiated optimism (to be saved means it can be saved) but also implied that it was ecologically imperative . . . The earth MUST be saved."[101] In fact, Christian environmentalists took special pride in promoting the "courage to change something" and providing the "strength to be active in society."[102] One activist wrote, "The degeneration into complacency and lethargy, in my opin-

Fig. 2. Rather than a faith in scientific planning, the new environmentalism of the 1980s celebrated personal engagement as the key to land improvements and environmental protection, as seen in this cartoon's depiction of a lone individual's hopeful perseverance despite her dismal and hopeless surroundings. Drawing from Nikolaus Voss's reader assembled for the tree planting initiative in Rostock, October 24–26, 1980: Robert-Havemann-Gesellschaft/AB 08.

ion, is one of the greatest sins of today. I am not willing to let myself coast along with the current of resigned citizens. To live conscious of the environment means today to swim against the current."[103]

Some church environmentalists insisted, moreover, that faith helped them overcome the mainstream consensus about materialism. It was no accident that Noah and the ark (from which *Arche Nova* got its name) became key symbols for the movement. Noah served as an example of an individual who took action in the face of a hopeless situation. Noah, moreover, provided a model of a minority figure sacrificing his personal comfort for the good of the planet—all the more encouraging for Christian activists in East Germany who faced popular resignation. In *Die Erde ist zu Retten*, Wittenberg theologians concluded about Noah, "The engagement of the individual and the tiny minority is sensible even when everything speaks against it." Religion provided hope; without hope, the obstacles appeared too great. They added, "A Christian perspective on environmental problems is never hopeless—and it is not only a perspective but also leads to transformative acts."[104] Images such as a cartoon depicting a woman planting a tree amid seemingly hopeless concrete towers reflected this optimism.[105]

These doubts about material culture and the mass consumption were, of course, not new. Despite the important discontinuities evident in the new environmentalism's break from East Germany's conservation bloc and from mainstream nature enthusiasm, 1980s activists also shared many attitudes with their predecessors in the German conservation movement. They still framed much of their discussion around the SED state's duty to protect public health and guarantee spaces for *Erholung*. Even their engagement with ecology was not new in the 1980s; many East German scientists, planners, and architects embraced ecology in the 1960s. The greatest continuity, however, could be found in the attitude of environmentalists toward the general public. Even as 1980s environmentalists now rejected scientific planning of a "bigger" and "better" future, they continued to distrust everyday East Germans and their consumer and touristic practices, just as landscape architects in the conservation bloc did throughout the entire history of the GDR. A recognition of these discontinuities and continuities helps explain, I argue, the distance of many of those intellectuals and reformers from the crowds they led into the revolutions of 1989. It may also explain many activists' continued hope (even as the crowds began to clamor for German reunification) for reform within a surviving East German state that would offer a third way to the SED and to the consumer society of West Germany. Moreover, the rapid collapse of East German environmental groups after 1989 may have owed a debt to this disconnect between church-based environmentalists and the consumer-oriented public.

The new environmentalism did, however, break from tradition by developing a critique of both potent authority and notions of limitless growth. Earlier conservationists in the GDR questioned the wisdom of unplanned or poorly planned exploitation of natural resources, but they retained a faith in central planning and authoritarian rule, as these things could help experts manage growth forever into the future. East German conservationists had already lost some faith in managed growth because of their experiences of censorship and powerlessness in the 1970s. After the Landeskulturgesetz raised their hopes, it became increasingly obvious that the regime turned conservationists' arguments about *Erholung* and landscape planning against them. Moreover, the everyday practice of multiple use mocked their belief that rational planning could balance many different land uses. As Reimar Gilsenbach suggests in his autobiography, the new environmentalism became attractive not because conservationists were radical nonconformists but because the new environmentalism offered an alternative way to think about and discuss nature protection. It offered hope for increasingly disillusioned reformers. Working within the system was no longer attractive; cooperation was now only a cruel reminder of their very powerlessness. It is unclear how many older conservationists and scientists followed in the footsteps of Heynert and Gilsenbach to rethink their approach to nature protection or, as Gilsenbach did, to join groups such as the Environmental Library in Berlin. At minimum, it is unlikely those two were alone in their intellectual awakening. As for younger scientists, they now had available to them a new way of talking about and enacting environmental change.

NOTES

1. Letter from Evangelisch-methodistische Kirche, Pastorate in Crottendorf, Annaberg-Buchholz, Königswalde und Cranzahl to the Ministry for Environmental Protection (hereinafter MfU), November 30, 1981, BArch: DK5 71.
2. Auster (2001), 496.
3. Palmowski (2009), 207; Stoltzfus (2003), 390.
4. For one example, see Jones (1993).
5. Maier (1997) and Fulbrook (1995), for instance, mentioned ecological initiatives only in the context of the peace and human rights movements and thus paid attention primarily to their immediate political goals. Hermand (1991) limited his discussion to intellectual dissenters who, like many of their Western counterparts in the green movement, were critical of consumption.
6. The literature on GDR environmentalism includes Goodbody (1994); Jones (1993); Halbrock (1992); Joan DeBardeleben, "'The Future Has Already Begun': Environmental Damage and Protection in the GDR," in *The Quality of Life in the GDR*, ed. Marilyn Rueschemeyer and Christiane Lemke (Armonk, N.Y.: M. E. Sharpe, 1989), 144–164; Hans-Peter Gensichen, "Zur Geschichtsschreibung der kirchlichen Umweltbewegung in der DDR," in *Umweltschutz in Ostdeutschland und Osteuropa: Bilanz und Perspektiven,* ed. Fritz Brickwedde (Osnabrück: Steinbacher, 1998), 181–191; Ehrhart Neubert, *Geschichte der Opposition in der DDR* (Berlin: Ch. Links, 1998); Dieter Rink, "Ausreiser, Kirchengruppen, Kulturopposition und Reformer: Zu Differenzen und Gemeinsamkeiten in Opposition und Widerstand in der DDR in den 70er und 80er Jahren,"

in *Zwischen Verweigerung und Opposition: Politischer Protest in der DDR 1970–1989,* ed. Detlef Pollack and Dieter Rink (Frankfurt am Main: Campus, 1997), 54–77.

7. Stoltzfus (2003), 386.

8. Stoltzfus (2003), 387.

9. See Knoth (1992).

10. Palmowski (2009), 187.

11. Palmowski (2009), 188.

12. Palmowski (2009), 217–19.

13. Chaney (2008), 3; see also Cioc (2002).

14. Hugo Weinitschke, "Die Mitwirkung der Natur und Heimatfreunde bei der Erschliessung und Pflege von Erholungsgebieten," in Weinitschke (1967), 15.

15. Weinitschke (1967), 15.

16. Weinitschke (1967), 24 (emphasis mine); Hugo Weinitschke, "Schlusswort," in Weinitschke (1967), 143.

17. Palmowski (2009), 208–9.

18. Auster (1996), 50, 109.

19. Hermann Behrens, introduction to Auster (1996); Auster (2001), 491.

20. Auster (2001), 493, 510.

21. Hermann Behrens, "Landschaftstage in der Deutschen Demokratischen Republik—am Beispiel des Bezirks Neubrandenburg," in Brüggemeier and Engels (2005), 69.

22. "1. Landschaftstag S. Schweiz," 1977, SäStArchD: RdB Dresden/Umwelt 48660.

23. Ibid.

24. An example of this in Palmowski (2009), 215.

25. Reimar Gilsenbach, "Ein Wochenpost Gespräch mit dem Stellvertreter des Vorsitzenden des Ministerrates Dr. Werner Titel," December 21, 1969, 6, BArch: DK4 2703.

26. Ibid., 13.

27. Auster makes a similar point about the GNU; see Auster (2001), 505.

28. Lebrecht Jeschke, "Naturschutz der Wendezeit in der DDR," in Kreuter (2003), 247.

29. William T. Markham, *Environmental Organizations in Modern Germany: Hardy Survivors in the Twentieth Century and Beyond* (New York: Berghahn Books, 2008), 144–45.

30. Palmowski (2009), 209–11.

31. Letter from M.P. to MfU, October 2, 1973; Letter from MfU to M.P., November 5, 1973; Letter from RdK Potsdam to MfU, November 19, 1973; and Letter from RdB Potsdam to MfU, December 13, 1973, BArch: DK5 4391.

32. Letter from Dr. R.K. of Berlin, December 21, 1982, and Letter to Dr. R.K. from Rat des Stadtbezirks Berlin-Köpenick, June 29, 1982, BArch: DK5 68.

33. Letter from S. and others from Schenkendorf-Potsdam to Rat der Gemeinde and MfU, August 17, 1980, BArch: DK5 72.

34. Letter from Residents of Motzen to Erich Honecker, April 6, 1972, BArch: DK5 2426; Letter from H.F. of Berlin to Honecker, September 12, 1972; and Letter from H.F. to *Neues Deutschland,* September 20, 1971, BArch: DK5 4390.

35. Letter from K. family to MfU, October 21, 1974, BArch: DK5 4507.

36. Letter from M.K. of Karl Marx Stadt to Ministry for Verkehrswesen, May 22, 1975, BArch: DK5 4400.

37. Letter from H.C. to MfU, June 20, 1972, BArch: DK5 4390.

38. Horst Heynert, *Blühende Bergheimat* (Leipzig: Urania Verlag, 1970), 7.

39. Heynert (1970), 50.

40. "Kurzprotokoll von der Beratung des Arbeitsauschusses der BK NuH am 18.8.1971" and "Kurzprotokoll von der Beratung des Arbeitsauschusses der BK NuH am 12.10.72," SäStCh: 32682/164.

41. Horst Heynert, "Wie können wir auf der Grundlage des Kommuniques des Ministeriums für Umweltschutz und Wasserwirtschaft und des Präsidums des Kulturbund Aufgaben der sozialistischen Landeskultur und des Umweltschutzes im Bezirk lösen helfen?" SäStCh: 32682/149.

42. Themes included ecosystems, air and water pollution, the electric car, the biosphere, nature protection, and the problems of the hydrosphere. See "Einladung zum Symposium: Ökologie und sozialistische Landeskultur," SäStCh: 32682/149; "Konzeption für die Gestaltung einer wissenschaftlichen Tagung des Arbeitskreises 'Sächsisches Erzgebirge' zu Problemen des Umweltschutzes und der sozialistischen Landeskultur and Kurzprotokoll von der Beratung des Arbeitsauschusses der BK NuH am 12.10.72," SäStCh: 32682/164.

43. "Kurzprotokoll von der Beratung des Arbeitsauschuses der BK NuH am 25.1.1972," SäStCh: 32682/164.

44. "Protokoll von der Beratung des Arbeitsausschusses der BK NuH am 20.6.73," SäStCh: 32682/164.

45. "Kurzprotokoll von der Beratung des Arbeitsauschusses der BK NuH am 25.1.1972," "Kurzprotokoll von der Beratung des Arbeitsausschusses der BK NuH am 18.8.1971," and "Protokoll von der Beratung des Arbeitsausschusses der BK NuH am 18.7.1968," SäStCh: 32682/164.

46. "Aktennotiz von dem Erfahrungsaustausch und der Exkursion der Mitglieder des Arbeitsausschusses der BK NuH mit Freunden der Bezirkskommissionen NuH aus Dresden und Leipzig am 7.9.74 im Kreis Marienberg," September 10, 1974; "Notizen von der Beratung des Arbeitsausschusses der BK NuH am 6.7.1972" and "Aktennotiz von der Besprechung des Arbietsausschusses der BK NuH am 23.5.1972," SäStCh: 32682/164.

47. "Protokoll der Sekretariatssitzung vom 11.3.1974," SäStCh: 32682/46.

48. "Vorlage für den Arbeitsausschuss am 23.5.1974," SäStCh: 32682/164.

49. "Einladung: Zum Kolloqium Mensch—Umwelt—Persönlichkeit—Lebensweise am 3.7.1975," June 13, 1975, SäStCh: 32682/164.

50. "Kurzprotokoll von der Beratung des Arbeitsausschusses der Bezirkskommission NuH am 30.1.1976," "Beschlussprotokoll der Beratung des Arbeitsauschusses der BK NuH am 4.4.75," "Beschlussprotokoll der Beratung des Arbeitsausschusses der BK NuH am 14.2.1975," "Arbeitsplan der Bezirkskommission und des Arbeitsauschusses der Bezirkskommission NuH der Bezirksleitung des KB bis zum IX Bundeskongress 1977," and "Beschlussprotokoll von der Beratung des Arbeitausschusses der Bezirkskommission NuH des KB der DDR am 8.7.1977," SäStCh: 32682/164. "Kurzprotokoll von der Beratung des Bezirksfachausschusses Landeskultur und Naturschutz am 15.1.1976 im Bezirkssekretariat des KB KMS," SäStCh: 32682/149.

51. Bezirkskommission NuH, "Entwurf: Grundkonzeption für die Gestaltung von Landschaftstagen in Bez. KMS," SäStCh: 32682/149.

52. Arbeitsausschusses der Bezirkskommission NuH, "Beratung am 17.7.1975 and Beschlussprotokol von der Beratung des Arbeitsauschusses der Bezirkskommission NuH am 29.10.1976," SäStCh: 32682/164; "Durchführung des 1 Landschaftstages des Bezirkes KMS am 20. und 21.10.1978" and "Einladung zum 1 Landschaftstag," SäStCh: 30413/72474.

53. "Beschlussprotokol von der Beratung des Arbeitsausschusses der Bezirkskommission NuH am 29.10.1976" and "Beschlussprotokoll von der 4 Beratung des Arbeitsausschusses der Bezirkskommission NuH am 27.5.1977," SäStCh: 32682/164.

54. "Kurzprotokoll von der Beratung des Arbeitsauschusses der Bezirkskommission NuH am 8.4.1971," 7, SäStCh: 32682/164.

55. Ibid., 2.

56. Horst Heynert, *Botanische Kostbarkeiten: zwischen Ostseestrand, Böhmerwald und Tatra: Vegetationsskizzen mitteleuropäischer Landschaften* (Leipzig: Urania Verlag, 1977), 11.

57. Reimar Gilsenbach, "Sommer, Urlaub, Reisen—Grosses Plädoyer für Berge, Wälder und Wasser," *Wochenpost*, no. 15 (1964), quoted in Auster (2001), 479–80, and in Gilsenbach (2001), 539.

58. Gilsenbach (2001), 538.

59. Behrens (2005), 68.

60. Gilsenbach (2001), 543–45.

61. Reimar Gilsenbach, *Wer im Gleichschritt marschiert, geht in die falsche Richtung: Ein biografisches Selbstbildnis* (Berlin: Westkreuz Verlag, 2004), 202–4.

62. Lebrecht Jeschke, "Naturschutz der Wendezeit in der DDR," in Kreuter (2003), 248. See also Markus Rösler, "Nationalparkinitiativen in der DDR bis zur Wende 1989," in Auster und Behrens (1999), 547–60.

63. Ulli Kulke, "Beschützte Landschaften," *Welt am Sonntag*, September 30, 2012.

64. From the Stasi file of Annette Beleites, "OPK Biologe," February 26, 1988, Archiv der DDR-Opposition at the Robert-Havemann-Gesellschaft (hereinafter RHG): AB 12.

65. Annette Beleites, *Der Zerstörung entgegenwirken*, June 7, 1987, RHG: AB 01.

66. Annette Beleites, *Erhaltung der Schöpfung*, October 4, 1988, RHG: AB 04.

67. Ibid.; Annette Beleites, *Vor und nach der Ernte: Über Folgen unserer Ernährungsgewohnheiten*, 1989, RHG: AB 01.

68. Betts (2010), 50–73; Jones (1993), 239.

69. Stoltzfus (2003), 392.

70. Stoltzfus (2003), 392.

71. Stoltzfus (2003), 394–99; Jones (1993), 246, 256.

72. Jones (1993), 259; Stoltzfus (2003), 399–400.

73. Jones (1993), 246; Stoltzfus (2003), 396.

74. Stoltzfus (2003), 394.

75. Annette Beleites, *Vor und nach der Ernte: Über Folgen unserer Ernährungsgewohnheiten*, 1989, RHG: AB 01.

76. Kirchlichen Forschungsheim Wittenberg (hereinafter KFW), *Die Erde ist zu Retten: Umweltkrise, christlicher Glaube, Handlungsmöglichkeiten*, 1982, 39, RHG: PS 033.

77. Iring Fetscher, "Alternative Zivilisation," in *Nicht nur Hunde Brauchen Bäume*, ed. Nikolaus Voss, October 26, 1980, RHG: AB 08.

78. "Ökologischer Kateschismus," *Briefe zur Orientierung im Konflikt Mensch Natur*, October 1984, RHG: KFH 22.

79. Stoltzfus (2003), 395.

80. KFW, *Die Erde ist zu Retten*, 35, RHG: PS 033.

81. Ökologischen Arbeitskreises der Dresdner Kirchenbezirke, *Saubere Luft für Ferienkinder*, RHG: AB 07.

82. KFW, *Die Erde ist zu Retten*, 41–45, RHG: PS 033.

83. KFW, *Anstösse* no. 5 (March 1983): 1–2, RHG: PS 3/1.

84. KFW, *Kalendar*, 1988, RHG: Ki 18/01.

85. "Eier und Tomaten auf neuen Wartburg," *Umweltblätter no. 10* (1988), 2, RHG: Umweltbibliothek Berlin.

86. "Tschernobyl Wirkt Überall," *Umweltblätter no. 6* (1986), RHG: Umweltbibliothek Berlin; Eva Storrer, "Mobil ohne Auto am Weltumwelttag," *MUZ*, June 18, 1989, RHG: AB 08.

87. KFW, *Die Erde ist zu Retten*, 32, RHG: PS 033.

88. "Fernsehen: Denkanstösse zu einer genehmigten Droge," *Anstösse*, no. 12 (September 1984), RHG: Anstösse.

89. Umweltbibliothek Berlin, "Tschernobyl Wirkt Überall," *Umweltblätter* , no. 6 (1986), RHG: PS 107/06.

90. KFW, "Fernsehen: Denkanstösse zu einer genehmigten Droge" *Anstösse*, no. 12 (September 1984), RHG: PS 3/7.

91. Ev Kirchenkreis Halle, "Ein Vorschlagskatalog aus der ökologischen Arbeitsgruppe beim Ev. Kirchenkreis Halle," *Briefe zur Orientierung im Konflikt Mensch Natur* 19 (1989), RHG: KFH 23.

92. Ökologischen Arbeitskreises der Dresdner Kirchnbz, *Saubere Luft für Ferienkinder*, RHG: AB 07; "Frische Luft?" *Lausitz-Botin*, RHG: Lausitz-Botin PS 064.

93. "Reportage über Bitterfeld," *Arche Nova* 1 (1988), RHG: PS 9/1.

94. KFW, *Die Erde ist zu Retten*, 42, RHG: PS 033.

95. Ökologischen Arbeitskreises der Dresdner Kirchnbz, *Saubere Luft für Ferienkinder*, RHG: AB 07.

96. Christian Halbrock, "Berliner Datschenradius wird vergrössert," *Umweltblätter* no. 6 (1988), RHG: PS 107/1—107/10.

97. KFW, *Die Erde ist zu Retten*, 15, RHG: PS 033. See also "Andreas Reimann," in *Nicht nur Hunde Brauchen Bäume*, ed. Nikolaus Voss, 13, RHG: AB 08. On the battle against cottages in nature preserves, see "Aus Leserbriefen," *Briefe zur Orientierung im Konflikt Mensch Natur*, February 1983, RHG: KFH 22.

98. Dr. Joachim Heinrich, "Stadtökologie, Umweltschutz und persönliches Engagement," *Umweltbrief* 5/6 (1987), RHG: PS 108/01.

99. KFW, "Persönliches Umweltengagement?" *Kalendar,* 1988, RHG: Ki 18/01.

100. Gerd Breitfeld, "1 Teil des Vortrages zur ökumenischen Versammlung der Christen und Kirchen für Gerechtigkeit, Frieden und Bewahrung der Schöpfung; Dresden, 12.2–15.2.1988," *Arche Nova* no. 2 (1988), RHG: PS 9/2.

101. KFW, *Die Erde ist zu Retten*, 1, RHG: PS 033.

102. "Christliches Umweltseminar—Leipzig," *Umweltbrief*, RHG: PS 108/02.

103. Nikolaus Voss, "Unsere Verantwortung für unsere Umwelt und Zukunft des Menschen—auf der Such nach der Identität unseres Engagements," Referat am Winterseminar 19–21.2.82 in Schwerin, 3, RHG: AB 10; Nikolaus Voss, ed., *Nicht nur Hunde Brauchen Bäume*, 2, RHG: AB 08.

104. KFW, *Die Erde ist zu Retten*, 22, 25, RHG: PS 033.

105. Nikolaus Voss, ed., *Nicht nur Hunde Brauchen Bäume*, 3, RHG: AB 08.

Conclusion

For all that was new about East German environmentalism in the 1980s, it is remarkable how vital tourism remained to debates about nature and nature protection in East Germany. Tourism and nature protection had long been linked in German history, at least as early as the homeland protection movement of the 1890s. East Germany's particular history only made that link stronger, as the regime's need to secure popular legitimacy made tourism a safe arena for engaging in negotiations with the dictatorship. In questioning consumerism and economic growth, however, the new environmentalists struggled to reconcile the contradictory meanings of tourism. In many ways, they had stumbled upon an essential but perplexing characteristic of East German socialism. By the 1980s, the everyday work of socialist rule had given birth to a socialist individualism that simultaneously reinforced and undermined the ruling party.

If they traveled to other socialist states, these new environmentalists might have discovered tourism developing along similar paths throughout the Soviet bloc. Throughout much of *The People's Own Landscape*, I have focused on the longer continuities of German history. While East German conservationists inherited views about tourism and nature protection shaped by the particularities of German history, the emerging literature on Eastern European tourism points to remarkable similarities across the Soviet bloc. All socialist regimes, for example, connected tourism to purposeful leisure, which helped mold socialist personalities. Of course, Eastern Europeans differed little in this respect from bourgeois tourism experts in Western Europe, where guidebook authors and state-sponsored tourist agencies also hoped to nudge tourists toward higher and better tourist practices. Naturally, the nature of dictatorship gave Eastern European tourism experts much more power over everyday tourists. Nonetheless, the historical scholarship emphasizes the limits of dictatorship in almost every socialist state. The individualistic practice of tourism always meant that tourism planners never fully controlled the behavior of vacationers. Christian Noack's discussion of "wild tourism" on the Black Sea, for example, reveals

that the Soviets shared with East German tourism planners the challenge of
regulating or eliminating unofficial and undesired camping activities. Moreover, the relationship of almost all Eastern European regimes to their vacationers changed over time, just as it did in the GDR. By the 1970s, almost everywhere, consumerism became more and more a part of the socialist tourist
experience. Finally, historians of Eastern European and Soviet tourism suggest
that, despite the individualistic experiences of tourists and despite the limits of
dictatorship, tourism sometimes encouraged identification with these regimes
and their projects of socialist modernism.[1]

Broader Eastern European trends might be best appreciated through some
brief comparisons between East Germany and Yugoslavia. At first glance, Yugoslavia's history points to that country's distinctiveness. For example, Patrick
Hyder Patterson concludes that Yugoslav tourism fit well into that government's unique promise to "deliver to its people a Yugoslav version of the Good
Life, a modest and moderated but nonetheless satisfying approximation of the
consumption-driven abundance that had remade the capitalist West."[2] While
noting similarities across Eastern Europe, Patterson positions Yugoslavia's
tourist history as an outlier, when compared to tourism in "more restrictive
polities" such as East Germany.[3] In this way, Patterson reinforces generaliza-
tions about a totalitarian, Soviet-dominated Eastern Europe by identifying Yugoslavia as truly exceptional, even though his conclusions about Yugoslavia's
moderated "consumption-driven abundance" could easily be applied to other
socialist states, including East Germany. Christopher Görlich, for example, argues convincingly that East Germany's FDGB Feriendienst transformed itself
from an institution for molding socialist personalities into a socialist travel
agency tending to customer demands.[4] *The People's Own Landscape* similarly
has shown how the SED and tourism planners increasingly focused on consumer pleasures to secure its legitimacy, as East Germans pressured the regime
to live up to its own promises for a good life, or material abundance. While
certainly distinct in its openness to the West, Yugoslavia may not have been as
much of an outlier as it might first have seemed. A review of the recent histories of Eastern European states suggests instead that tourism provided a unique
opportunity for Eastern Europeans in many different states to negotiate with
their ruling regimes over the good life.

While joining other historians of tourism in rethinking the history of leisure and everyday life under socialist dictatorships, *The People's Own Landscape* also calls for a reconsideration of Cold War Eastern Europe's environmental history. Without a doubt, one cannot tell the history of environmental
collapse without considering the often violent social agendas of Marxist dicta-

torships. Any history of Eastern Europe must recognize the nature of power in a communist dictatorship. The Stasi's repression of the new environmentalists reminds us of the SED's grip on power. Throughout this book, conservationists encountered the heavy hand of authorities censoring and threatening the careers of overly vocal critics of economic development and SED authority. Moreover, the popular enthusiasm for outdoor recreation and nature outings reflected notions of social justice and private pleasure that are only comprehensible when we recognize how the regime monopolized power, discouraged collective action, and rewarded political loyalty with material benefits.

While any explanation of Eastern European environmental destruction certainly must start with the decisions made at the top of these regimes, it must also account for the actions of socialist citizens who sometimes evaded the state and sometimes pushed the powerful to appease popular desires. In the end, I have argued in this book, state incompetence and terror, on their own, cannot fully explain the transformation of East Germany's countryside. The new environmentalists of the 1980s fundamentally challenged assumptions about limitless economic growth and a faith in central planning, but it is not clear that such a program stood a chance of being embraced by mainstream East Germans. While preservation for the benefit of popular *Erholung* may have been anthropocentric and contradictory, it had a popular resonance that environmentalism informed by theories of ecological limits often lacked. Citizens writing letters to the Ministry for Environmental Protection did not just manipulate the regime's rhetorical promises of a better quality of life in order to get their letters read. They seemed to share with the regime a faith in limitless growth and a desire for higher living standards defined by material acquisition. For a time, vacationers, youth educators, the "conservation bloc," and economic planners all joined the SED in dreaming of abundance in a state with limited space. They proposed architectural schemes to better distribute resources, introduced technological fixes to increase productivity, and complained that authorities did not plan well enough to provide both abundance and green spaces. As Greifenbach Reservoir demonstrated, they even collaborated in the dramatic transformations of the East German countryside. Bitter local residents after 1989 correctly identified the campground as an SED space, but they ignored the crucial role that everyday East Germans played in reworking the landscape and pushing the regime to respond to their consumer desires.

Once these complexities of socialist rule are recognized, communist dictatorship and liberal capitalism begin to look more similar. While liberal democracies allowed environmentalists much greater freedom to critique environmental policy, both systems sought to maximize growth and overcome fears of resource scarcity. People on both sides of the Iron Curtain desired lives that were richer with consumer comforts. Both systems also inherited modernization models meant to produce material abundance and ensure social stability. Whether early modern scientific foresters, colonial adventurers, or Nazi racial planners, central Europeans had long dreamed that state authority, science, and technology might generate limitless abundance. While East Germany's new environmentalists operated in a unique environment shaped by the SED and its social welfare programs, they joined their western counterparts in calling for limits to growth. In other words, environmentalists throughout Europe questioned modernization models common on both sides of the Iron Curtain.

1989 did not prove a watershed moment that led governments to accept hard limits to growth or Europeans to reject consumerism in any fundamental way. New environmentalists seemingly won few followers among East Germans.[5] Most East Germans craved more, not fewer, consumer goods, and West Germany offered a more enticing solution—a market capitalism that seemed to offer the limitless horizons that socialism had failed to provide. Democracy triumphed over dictatorship, but the collapse of communism did not mean that dreams of limitless abundance disappeared. While West German capitalism appeared friendlier to the planet than America's consumer society, its "light green society" never fully embraced the notion of limitations. As Helmut Kohl unified Germany in 1990, he actually promised former East Germans a future of abundance and greater economic opportunities. These promises were never clearer than in his speeches promising "blooming landscapes" in a newly unified Germany. As Kohl celebrated national unification as a key to both environmental recovery and robust economic growth, he thus ironically echoed the hopes and dreams of landscape architects in 1950s East Germany. Even as the economy boomed, the land would bloom.[6]

NOTES

1. Grandits and Taylor (2010); Gorsuch and Koenker (2006), 14; Gorsuch, (2011); Koenker (2003); Christian Noack, "Coping with the Tourist: Planned and 'Wild' Mass Tourism on the Soviet Black Sea Coast," in Gorsuch and Koenker (2006), 281–304.

2. Patrick Hyder Patterson, "Yugoslavia as It Once Was: What Tourism and Leisure Meant for the History of the Socialist Federation," in Grandits and Taylor (2010), 367.

3. Patterson (2010), 372.

4. Görlich (2012).

5. Anja Baukloh and Jochen Roose, "The Environmental Movement and Environ-

mental Concern in Contemporary Germany," in Goodbody (2002), 98. See also Ingolfur Blühdorn, "Green Futures? A Future for the Greens?," in the same volume.

6. In an interview, Kohl promised, "Through a collective effort we will succeed soon enough in transforming Mecklenburg-Vorpommern, Sachsen-Anhalt, Brandenburg, Saxony and Thuringia once again into blooming landscapes, where it is worthwhile living and working." *Fernsehansprache zur Währungsunion zwischen BRD und DDR am 1. Juli 1990; Das Erste, 20:15 Uhr (im Anschluss an die Tagesschau).*

Bibliography

ARCHIVAL COLLECTIONS

Archiv der DDR-Opposition in der Robert-Havemann-Gesellschaft e. V. (RHG)
Bundesarchiv in Berlin-Lichterfelde (BArch)
    DC20   Ministerrat
    DE1   Staatliche Plankommission
    DE2   Staatliche Zentralverwaltung für Statistik
    DH2   Deutsche Bauakademie
    DK1   Ministerium für Land- und Forstwirtschaft (MLF)
    DK5   Ministerium für Umweltschutz (MfU)
    DK107 Deutsche Akademie der Landwirtschaftwissenschaften (DAL)
    DL102 Institut für Marktforschung
    DR2   Amt für Jugendfragung
    DR5   Staatliches Komitee für Körperkultur und Sport
eco-Archiv (affiliated with the Arbeiterkultur und Ökologie e.V)
Geyer Turmmuseum Archiv
Kreisarchiv Marienberg-Zschopau (KarchMZ)
    Rat des Kreises Marienberg/Abteilung Körperkultur und Sport
    Rat des Kreises Zschopau/Abteilung Wasserwirtschaft, Umwelt, und Erholung
    Rat des Kreises Zschopau/Abteilung Erholungswesen
Sächsisches Hauptstaatsarchiv Dresden (SäStArchD)
    Rat der Bezirkung (4811)
    Bezirkstag/Rat des Bezirkes (25664)
    Büro für Territorialplanung (BfT)
Sächsisches Staatsarchiv Chemnitz (SäStCh)
    Rat des Bezirkes (30413)
        Abteilung Wasserwirtschaft
        Abteilung Erholungswesen
        Abteilung Umweltschutz
        Abteilung Körperkultur, Sport, und Erholung
        Abteilung Land- und Forstwirtschaft
    Kulturbund (32682)
    SED Kreisleitung Zschopau (14524)
Stadtarchiv Ehrenfriedersdorf (StaarchEhr)

Stiftung Archiv der Parteien und Massenorganisationen der DDR im Bundesarchiv
    (SAPMO-BArch)
    DY12   Deutscher Turn und Sportbund (DTSB)
    DY24   Freie Deutsche Jugend (FDJ)
    DY27   Kulturbund
    DY34   Freie Deutsche Gewerkschaftsbund (FDGB)
    DY30   Zentralkomitee der SED
Umweltbibliothek Neubrandenburg

PRIVATE COLLECTIONS

Wolfgang Bagger
Bernhard Fisch
Joachim Schindler

PERIODICALS

Der Tourist
Freundschaft: Werbeschrift der Sektion Touristik
Natur und Heimat
Skisport und Touristik
Sportecho
Theorie und Praxis der Körperkultur und Sport
Unterwegs
Wandern und Bergsteigen
Werbeschrift (BSG Empor)
Wochenpost

PUBLISHED PRIMARY SOURCES

Aust, Gerhard. "Gründung einer Naturkundlichen Arbeitsgemeinschaft." In *Jahrbuch
    für Touristik 1954.* Dresden: BSG Empor-Löbtau, 1954.
Bäseler, Horst. *Campingplätze: Grundsätze und Richtwerte für die Planung und Ge-
    staltung.* Berlin: Bauinformation, 1976.
Berger, Horst. *4000 km Hauptwanderwege DDR.* Leipzig: VEB Bibliographisches In-
    stitut, 1960.
Blechschmidt, Manfred, and Klaus Walther. *Bergland Mosaik: Ein Buch vom Erzge-
    birge.* Rudolstadt: Greifenverlag, 1978.
Böhm, Karl, and Rolf Dönge. *Unsere Welt von morgen.* Berlin: Verlag Neues Leben,
    1961.
BSG Empor-Löbtau. "Zum Geleit." In *Jahrbuch für Touristik 1954.* Dresden: BSG
    Empor-Löbtau, 1954.

Buggel, Edelfried. *Die Touristik im Massensport.* Kleine Bücherei für den Übungsleiter und Sportlehrer 2. Berlin: Sportverlag, 1957. Reprint, 1961.

Buggel, Edelfried. *Geländesport auf Wanderungen und im Ferienlager.* Berlin: Volk und Wissen Volkseigener Verlag, 1959.

Buggel, Edelfried. *Sport und Touristik in der Familie.* Berlin: Sportverlag, 1977.

Buggel, Edelfried, Armin Umbreit, and Harald Löbe, eds. *Touristik und Wandern in der Feriengestaltung.* Schriften für den Ferienhelfer, Information Nr. 2. Berlin: VEB Verlag Volk und Wissen, 1963.

Carl, Frank Erich. *Erholungswesen und Landschaft: Ein Beitrag zur Planung der Ferienerholung in der DDR.* Berlin: Sektion Städtebau und Architektur, Schriftenreihe Gebiets-, Stadt- und Dorfplanung, 1960.

Carl, Frank Erich. "In Memoriam Reinhold Lingner." *Deutsche Gartenarchitektur* 9, no. 2 (1968): 35–38.

Dehmel, Hans-Henning, and Maximilian Fiedler. *Landschaftsschutz in der DDR: Das sozialistische Landeskulturgesetz in der täglichen Praxis.* Berlin: Verlag Volk und Gesundheit, 1976.

Deutsche Bauakademie. *Landschaft und Planung.* Berlin: Deutsche Bauakademie, 1959.

Drechsel, Erich. "Darum Naturschutz." In *Jahrbuch für Touristik 1954.* Dresden: BSG Empor-Löbtau, 1954.

FDGB. *Zum Freizeitverhalten der Werktätigen.* Berlin: FDGB (Abteilung Kultur), 1968.

FDGB (Freie Deutsche Gewerkschaftsbund). *Freude, Frohsinn, Ferienlager.* Berlin: Verlag Tribüne, 1961.

Fisch, Bernhard. *Sportliches Wandern.* Berlin: Sportverlag, 1977.

Fisch, Bernhard, et al. *Wandern (Sport für alle).* Berlin: Sportverlag, 1983.

Gilsenbach, Reimar. "Die größte DDR der Welt—ein Staat ohne Nationalparke: Des Merkens Würdiges aus meiner grünen Donquichotterie." In *Naturschutz in den Neuen Bundesländern—ein Rückblick,* edited by Regine Auster, 533–546. Berlin: Verlag für Wissenschaft und Forschung, 2001.

Gilsenbach, Reimar. *Wer im Gleichschritt marschiert, geht in die falsche Richtung: Ein biografisches Selbstbildnis.* Berlin: Westkreuz Verlag, 2004.

Gitter, Wolfgang, and Bernhard Wilk. *Lebensfreude, Gesundheit und Leistungsfähigkeit: Körperkultur und Sport in der DDR.* Berlin: Panorama DDR, 1974.

Good Bye, Lenin! Culver City, Calif.: Sony Pictures Classics, 2004.

Grimm, H. "Volksgesundheit in ihrer Abhängigkeit von Natur und Landschaftsschutz." *Sonderdruck aus der Zeitschrift für die gesamte Hygiene und ihre Grenzgebiete* 4, no. 3/4 (1959): 130–145.

Hanke, Helmut. *Freizeit in der DDR.* Berlin: Dietz, 1979.

Heisser Sommer. Directed by Joachim Hasler. 1967. DVD, New York: First Run Features, DEFA Collection, 2001.

Heynert, Horst. *Blühende Bergheimat.* Leipzig: Urania Verlag, 1970.

Heynert, Horst. *Botanische Kostbarkeiten: Zwischen Ostseestrand, Böhmerwald und Tatra; Vegetationsskizzen mitteleuropäischer Landschaften.* Leipzig: Urania Verlag, 1977.

Heynert, Horst. *Das Pflanzenleben des Hohen Westerzgebirges: Ein Beitrag zur Geobotanik des Westerzgebirges.* Dresden: Verlag Theodor Steinkopff, 1964.

Hörning, Willy. *Greifensteingebiet: Thum, Ehrenfriedersdorf, Geyer.* Brockhaus Wanderheft 132. Leipzig: VEB F. A. Brockhaus Verlag, 1961. Reprint, 1970.

KTW (Komitee für Touristik und Wandern). *Campingwegweiser der DDR.* Berlin: Komitee *für Touristik und Wandern,* 1968.

KTW. *Handbuch für den Fahrten und Wanderleiter.* Berlin: Sportverlag, 1968.

KTW. *Leistungsbuch für das Touristenabzeichen der DDR.* Berlin: Komitee für Touristik und Wandern, 1964.

Lange, Eberhardt. *Campinghygiene und Erholung.* Berlin: VEB Verlag Volk und Gesundheit, 1974.

Lingner, Reinhold. *Landschaftsgestaltung.* Berlin: Kulturbund, 1952.

Lingner, Reinhold, and Frank Erich Carl. *Landschaftsdiagnose der DDR.* Berlin: VEB Verlag Technik, 1957.

Ministerium für Umweltschutz und Wasserwirtschaft. *Der Sozialistische Landeskultur Umweltschutz.* Berlin: Staatsverlag, 1978.

Möller, Otto. *Die Umgestaltung der Natur in der Sowjetunion.* Berlin: Verlag der Nation,1952.

Schweitzer, Otto. "Über Landschaftsplanungen in der Sächsischen Schweiz." In *Berichte des Arbeitskreises zur Erforschung der S. Schweiz in der Geographischen Gesellschaft der DDR (Sektion Dresden),* edited by Karl Andrä, 116–141.Pirna: Rat der Kreis Pirna, 1963.

Statistisches Jahrbuch der DDR 1974. Berlin: Staatsverlag, 1974.

Statistisches Jahrbuch der DDR 1979. Berlin: Staatsverlag, 1979.

Weinitschke, Hugo, ed. *Landschaft, Erholung und Naturschutz: Eine Auswahl von Referaten des Landschaftstages des DKB 1966.* Berlin: Kulturbund, 1967.

Wiedemann, Kurt. "Die 'Sächsische Schweiz' als künftiger Nationalpark der Deutschen." In *Jahrbuch für Touristik 1955/56,* 11–28. Dresden: BSG Empor-Löbtau, 1956.

Wille, Hermann Heinz. *Silbernes Erzgebirge.* Dresden: Sachsenverlag, 1958.

Wille, Hermann Heinz. *Vom Kahleberg zum Fichtelberg: Wanderfahrt durchs Erzgebirge.* Leipzig: VEB F. A. Brockhaus Verlag, 1971.

Zühlke, Dietrich. *Zwischen Zwickauer Mulde und Geyerschem Wald.* Berlin: Akademie Verlag, 1980.

SECONDARY SOURCES

Allen, Garland E. "Julian Huxley and the Eugenical View of Human Evolution." In *Julian Huxley: Biologist and Statesman of Science,* edited by C. Kenneth Waters and Albert Van Helden, 193–222. Houston: Rice University Press, 1992.

Allinson, Mark. *Politics and Popular Opinion in East Germany, 1945–68.* Manchester: Manchester University Press, 2000.

Andrews, David L., and Stephen Wagg, eds. *East Plays West: Sport and the Cold War.* London: Routledge, 2007.

Ansorg, Leonore. *Kinder im Klassenkampf: Die Geschichte der Pionierorganisation von 1948 bis Ende der fünfziger Jahre.* Berlin: Akademie Verlag, 1997.

Applegate, Celia. *A Nation of Provincials: The German Idea of Heimat.* Berkeley: University of California Press, 1990.

Augustine, Dolores L. *Red Prometheus: Engineering and Dictatorship in East Germany, 1945–1990.* Cambridge, Mass.: MIT Press, 2007.

Auster, Regine. *Landschaftstage: Kooperative Planungsverfahren in der Landschaftsentwicklung—Erfahrungen aus der DDR.* Forum Wissenschaft Studie 38. Marburg: Bund demokratischer Wissenschaftlerinnen und Wissenschaftler (BdWi) Verlag, 1996.

Auster, Regine. "Landschaftstage und Landschaftspflegepläne." In *Naturschutz in den Neuen Bundesländern—ein Rückblick,* edited by Regine Auster, 475–516. Berlin: Verlag für Wissenschaft und Forschung, 2001.

Auster, Regine, ed., *Naturschutz in den Neuen Bundesländern—ein Rückblick.* Berlin: Verlag für Wissenschaft und Forschung, 2001.

Auster, Regine, and Hermann Behrens. *Landschaft und Planung in den neuen Bundesländern: Rückblicke.* Berlin: Verlag für Wissenschaft und Forschung, 1999.

Austermühle, Theo. "Der DDR Sport im Lichte der Totalitarismus." *Sozial- und Zeitgeschichte des Sports* 11, no. 1 (1997): 28–51.

Badstübner-Peters, Evemarie. "'Lassen wir sie tanzen . . .': Nachkriegsjugend und moderne Freizeitkultur in SBZ und früher DDR." In *Aber nicht im Gleichschritt: Zur Entstehung der FDJ,* edited by Helga Gotschlich et al., 66–78. Berlin: Metropol, 1997.

Bagger, Wolfgang. "1945–1995: 40 Jahre DDR–50 Jahre Naturfreunde? 14 Thesen zur Diskussion." *Grüner Weg 31a: Zeitschrift des Studienarchivs Arbeiterkultur und Ökologie* 10 (January 1996): 75–78.

Bagger, Wolfgang. "Vom Weiterleben der Naturfreundeidee—Das Beispiel Bockwitz." *Grüner Weg 31a: Zeitschrift des Studienarchivs Arbeiterkultur und Ökologie* 10 (January 1996): 47–52.

Baranowski, Shelley. *Nazi Empire: German Colonialism and Imperialism from Bismarck to Hitler.* Cambridge: Cambridge University Press, 2011.

Baranowski, Shelley. *Strength through Joy: Consumerism and Mass Tourism in the Third Reich.* Cambridge: Cambridge University Press, 2004.

Baranowski, Shelley, and Ellen Furlough, eds. *Being Elsewhere: Tourism, Consumer Culture, and Identity in Modern Europe and North America.* Ann Arbor: University of Michigan Press, 2001.

Barkan, Elazar. "The Dynamics of Huxley's Views on Race and Eugenics." In *Julian Huxley: Biologist and Statesman of Science,* edited by C. Kenneth Waters and Albert Van Helden, 230–237. Houston: Rice University Press, 1992.

Barloesius, Eva. *Naturgemässe Lebensführung: Zur Geschichte der Lebensreform um die Jahrhundertwende.* Frankfurt am Main: Campus Verlag, 1997.

Bashford, Alison. "Population, Geopolitics, and International Organizations in the Mid Twentieth Century." *Journal of World History* 19, no. 3 (2008): 327–347.

Baudrillard, Jean. "Consumer Society." In *Selected Writings,* edited by Mark Poster, 32–59. Stanford: Stanford University Press, 2001.

Bauer, Ludwig "Zur Arbeit der Sektion Landeskultur und Naturschutz der Akademie der Landwirtschaftswissenschaften." In *Umweltschutz in der DDR: Analysen und Zeitzeugenberichte*, edited by Hermann Behrens and Jens Hoffmann, 3: 63–68. Munich: oekom verlag, 2007.

Baur, Jürgen, Giselher Spitzer, and Stephan Telschow. "Der DDR-Sport als gesellschaftliches Teilsystem." *Sportwissenschaft* 27, no. 4 (1997): 369–390.

Behrens, Hermann. "Das gesellschaftliche Umfeld der Landschaftsdiagnose und ihre Bedeutung aus der Sicht angrenzender Fachgebiete." In *Die Landschaftsdiagnose der DDR: Zeitgeschichte und Wirkung eines Forschungsprojekts aus der Gründungsphase der DDR*, edited by Olaf Hiller, 51–71. Berlin: Technische Universität Berlin, 2002.

Behrens, Hermann. "Das Institut für Landesforschung und Naturschutz (ILN) und die Biologischen Stationen." In *Umweltschutz in der DDR: Analysen und Zeitzeugenberichte*, edited by Hermann Behrens and Jens Hoffmann, 3:68–72. Munich: oekom verlag, 2007.

Behrens, Hermann. "Die ersten Jahre—Naturschutz und Landschaftspflege in der SBZ/DDR von 1945 bis Anfang der 60er Jahre." In *Naturschutz in den Neuen Bundesländern—ein Rückblick*, edited by Regine Auster, 15–86. Berlin: Verlag für Wissenschaft und Forschung, 2001.

Behrens, Hermann. "Landeskultur als Naturgeschehen auf höherer Ebene: Georg Bela Pniower (1896–1960) und der Naturschutz." In *Naturschutz hat Geschichte: Grussworte und Festrede des Bundespräsidenten anlässlich der Eröffnung des Museums zur Geschichte des Naturschutzes am 12. März 2002; Beiträge der Fachtagung "Naturschutz hat Geschichte vom 13. März 2002*, edited by Bernd Kreuter, 227–244. Essen: Klartext Verlag, 2003.

Behrens, Hermann. "Landschaftstage in der Deutschen Demokratischen Republik—am Beispiel des Bezirks Neubrandenburg." In *Natur- und Umweltschutz nach 1945: Konzepte, Konflikte, Kompetenzen*, edited by Franz-Josef Brüggemeier and Jens Ivo Engels, 62–86. Frankfurt am Main: Campus Verlag, 2005.

Behrens, Hermann. "Landschaft und Planung in der SBZ/DDR bis 1961 unter besonderer Berücksichtigung der 'Landschaftsdiagnose der DDR.'" In *Landschaft und Planung in den neuen Bundesländern: Rückblicke*, edited by Regine Auster and Hermann Behrens, 57–86. Berlin: Verlag für Wissenschaft und Forschung, 1999.

Behrens, Hermann. "Naturschutz und Landeskultur in der Sowjetischen Besatzungszone und in der DDR: Ein historischer Ueberblick." In *Die Veränderung der Kulturlandschaft: Nutzungen-Sichtweisen-Planungen*, edited by Günter Bayerl and Torsten Meyer, 221–22. Münster: Waxmann, 2003.

Behrens, Hermann. *Von der Landesplanung zur Territorialplanung: Zur Entwicklung der räumlichen Planung in der SBZ/DDR von 1945 bis Anfang der 60er Jahre.* Forum Wissenschaft Studien 41. Marburg: Bund demokratischer Wissenschaftlerinnen und Wissenschaftler (BdWi) Verlag, 1997.

Behrens, Hermann, and Jens Hoffmann, eds. *Umweltschutz in der DDR: Analysen und Zeitzeugenberichte.* Vols. 1–3. Munich: oekom verlag, 2007.

Belasco, Warren James. *Americans on the Road: From Autocamp to Motel, 1910–1945.* Baltimore: Johns Hopkins University Press, 1997.

Beleites, Michael. *Altlast Wismut: Ausnahmezustand, Umweltkatastrophe und das San-*

ierungsproblem im deutschen Uranbergbau. Frankfurt am Main: Brandes und Apsel, 1992.

Beleites, Michael. *Pechblende: Die Uranbergbau in der DDR und seiner Folgen*. Wittenberg: Kirchliche Forschungsheim, 1988.

Bender, Barbara. "Introduction: Landscape—Meaning and Action." In *Landscape: Politics and Perspectives*, edited by Barbara Bender, 1–17. Oxford: Berg, 1995.

Benton, Ted. *The Greening of Marxism*. New York: Guilford, 1996.

Berthold-Bond, Daniel. "Hegel and Marx on Nature and Ecology." *Journal of Philosophical Research* 22 (1997): 145–179.

Bess, Michael. *The Light-Green Society: Ecology and Technological Modernity in France, 1960–2000*. Chicago: University of Chicago Press, 2003.

Bessel, Richard, and Ralph Jessen, eds. *Die Grenzen der Diktatur: Staat und Gesellschaft in der SBZ/DDR*. Göttingen: Vandenhoeck und Ruprecht, 1996.

Betts, Paul. "The Twilight of the Idols: East German Memory and Material Culture." *Journal of Modern History* 72, no. 3 (September 2000): 731–765.

Betts, Paul. *Within Walls: Private Life in the German Democratic Republic*. Oxford: Oxford University Press, 2010.

Betts, Paul, and Katherine Pence, eds. *Socialist Modern: East German Everyday Culture and Politics*. Ann Arbor: University of Michigan Press, 2008.

Blackbourn, David. *The Conquest of Nature: Water, Landscape, and the Making of Modern Germany*. New York: W. W. Norton, 2006.

Boardman, Robert. *International Organization and the Conservation of Nature*. Bloomington: Indiana University Press, 1981.

Boardman, Robert. *The International Politics of Bird Conservation: Biodiversity, Regionalism, and Global Governance*. Northampton, Mass.: Edward Elgar, 2006.

Bock, Gisela. *Zwangssterilisation im nationalsozialismus*. Opladen: Westdeutscher Verlag, 1986.

Bonhomme, Brian. "A Revolution in the Forests? Forest Conservation in Soviet Russia, 1917–1925." *Environmental History* 7, no. 3 (July 2002): 411–434.

Bourdieu, Pierre. *Distinction: A Social Critique of the Judgment of Taste*. Cambridge, Mass.: Harvard University Press, 1984.

Bourdieu, Pierre. *The Logic of Practice*. Cambridge: Polity, 1990.

Brain, Stephen. *Song of the Forest: Russian Forestry and Stalinist Environmentalism, 1905–1953*. Pittsburgh: University of Pittsburgh Press, 2011.

Bren, Paulina. "Weekend Getaways: The *Chata,* the Tramp, and the Politics of Private Life in Post-1968 Czechoslovakia." In *Socialist Spaces: Sites of Everyday Life in the Eastern Bloc,* edited by David Crowley and Susan E. Reid, 123–140. Oxford: Berg, 2002.

Brooks, Jeffrey. *Thank You, Comrade Stalin! Soviet Public Culture from Revolution to Cold War*. Princeton: Princeton University Press, 2000.

Bruce, Gary. *The Firm: The Inside Story of the Stasi*. Oxford: Oxford University Press, 2010.

Brüggemeier, Franz-Josef, Mark Cioc, and Thomas Zeller, eds. *How Green Were the Nazis? Nature, Environment, and Nation in the Third Reich*. Athens: Ohio University Press, 2005.

Brüggemeier, Franz-Josef, and Jens Ivo Engels, eds. *Natur- und Umweltschutz nach 1945: Konzepte, Konflikte, Kompetenzen.* Frankfurt am Main: Campus Verlag, 2005.

Buchsteiner, Thomas. "Arbeiter und Tourismus." PhD diss., Eberhard-Karls-Universität-Tübingen, 1984.

Bütow, Martin. "Abenteuerurlaub Marke DDR: Camping." In *Endlich Urlaub! Die Deutschen reisen,* edited by Haus der Geschichte, 101–105. Bonn: Haus der Geschichte, 1996.

Buggel, Edelfried, and Klaus Rohrberg. "Wurde der Volkssport in der DDR vernachlässigt?" *Beiträge zur Sportgeschichte* 14 (2002): 40–44.

Bunce, Michael. *The Countryside Ideal: Anglo-American Images of Landscape.* London: Routledge, 1994.

Buss, Wolfgang. "Das 'Komitee für Tourismus und Wandern' als ein Teil des DDR-Sportsystems, 1956–1975." Unpublished conference paper from the private collection of Joachim Schindler, September 1997.

Buss, Wolfgang, and Christian Becker, eds. *Der Sport in der SBZ und frühen DDR: Genese, Strukturen, Bedingungen.* Schorndorf: Hofmann, 2001.

Chaney, Sandra. "For Nation and Prosperity, Health and a Green Environment: Protecting Nature in West Germany, 1945–1970." In *Nature in German History,* edited by Christof Mauch, 93–118. New York: Berghahn Books, 2004.

Chaney, Sandra. *Nature of the Miracle Years: Conservation in West Germany, 1945–1975.* New York: Berghahn Books, 2008.

Chaney, Sandra. "Protecting Nature in a Divided Nation: Conservation in the Two Germanys, 1945–1972." In *Germany's Nature: Cultural Landscapes and Environmental History,* edited by Thomas Lekan and Thomas Zeller, 220–243. New Brunswick, N.J.: Rutgers University Press, 2005.

Christoffersen, Leif E. "IUCN: A Bridge-Builder for Nature Conservation." *Green Globe Yearbook,* 1997, 59–69.

Cioc, Mark. *The Rhine: An Eco-Biography, 1815–2000.* Seattle: University of Washington Press, 2002.

Closmann, Charles. "Legalizing a Volksgemeinschaft: Nazi Germany's Reich Nature Protection Law of 1935." In *How Green Were the Nazis? Nature, Environment, and Nation in the Third Reich,* edited by Franz-Josef Brüggemeier, Mark Cioc, and Thomas Zeller, 18–42. Athens: Ohio University Press, 2005.

Confino, Alon. *The Nation as a Local Metaphor: Württemberg, Imperial Germany, and National Memory, 1871–1918.* Chapel Hill: University of North Carolina Press, 1997.

Confino, Alon. "Traveling as a Culture of Remembrance: Traces of National Socialism in West Germany, 1945–1960." *History and Memory* 12, no. 2 (2000): 92–121.

Confino, Alon, and Rudy Koshar. "Regimes of Consumer Culture: New Narratives in Twentieth-Century German History." *German History* 19, no. 2 (2001): 135–161.

Conrad, Sebastian. *Globalisation and the Nation in Imperial Germany.* Cambridge: Cambridge University Press, 2010.

Conrad, Sebastian, and Sorcha O'Hagan. *German Colonialism: A Short History.* Cambridge: Cambridge University Press, 2012.

Crew, David F., ed. *Consuming Germany in the Cold War.* Oxford: Berg, 2004.

Cronon, William. "The Trouble with Wilderness, or Getting Back to the Wrong Nature." In *Uncommon Ground: Rethinking the Human Place in Nature*, edited by William Cronon, 69–90. New York: W. W. Norton, 1996.

Crowley, David, and Susan Emily Reid, eds. *Pleasures in Socialism: Leisure and Luxury in the Eastern Bloc*. Evanston, Ill.: Northwestern University Press, 2010.

Crowley, David, and Susan Emily Reid, eds. *Socialist Spaces: Sites of Everyday Life in the Eastern Bloc*. Oxford: Berg, 2002.

Crowley, David, and Susan Emily Reid, eds. *Style and Socialism: Modernity and Material Culture in Post-war Eastern Europe*. Oxford: Berg, 2000.

Cullather, Nick. *The Hungry World: America's Cold War Battle against Poverty in Asia*. Cambridge, Mass.: Harvard University Press, 2010.

Cullather, Nick. "Miracles of Modernization: The Green Revolution and the Apotheosis of Technology." *Diplomatic History* 28, no. 2 (2004): 227–254.

Dähmlow, Anja, and Viola Haertel. "Verreisen kann jeder, Zelten ist Charaktersache." In *Wunderwirtschaft: DDR-Konsumkultur in den 60er Jahren*, edited by Neue Gesellschaft für Bildende Kunst, 152–155. Cologne: Böhlau, 1996.

Darby, Wendy Joy. *Landscape and Identity: Geographies of Nation and Class in England*. Oxford: Berg, 2000.

Daunton, Martin, and Matthew Hilton. "Material Politics: An Introduction." In *The Politics of Consumption: Material Culture and Citizenship in Europe and America*, edited by Martin Daunton and Matthew Hilton. Oxford: Berg, 2001.

Davis, Belinda J. *Home Fires Burning: Food, Politics, and Everyday Life in World War I Berlin*. Chapel Hill: University of North Carolina Press, 2000.

De Certeau, Michel. *The Practice of Everyday Life*. Translated by Steven Rendall. Berkeley: University of California Press, 1984. Originally published as *L'Invention du quotidian* (Paris: Union générale d'éditions, 1980).

DeBardeleben, Joan. *The Environment and Marxism-Leninism: The Soviet and East German Experience*. Boulder: Westview, 1985.

DeBardeleben, Joan. "'The Future Has Already Begun': Environmental Damage and Protection in the GDR." In *The Quality of Life in the GDR*, edited by Marilyn Rueschemeyer and Christiane Lemke, 144–164. Armonk, N.Y.: M. E. Sharpe, 1989.

Deese, R. S. "The New Ecology of Power: Julian and Aldous Huxley in the Cold War Era." In *Environmental Histories of the Cold War*, edited by John McNeill and Corinna R. Unger, 279–300. Washington, D.C.: German Historical Institute, 2010.

de Grazia, Victoria. "Changing Consumption Regimes in Europe, 1930–1970: Comparative Perspectives on the Distribution Problem." In *Getting and Spending: European and American Consumer Societies in the Twentieth Century*, edited by Susan Strasser, Charles McGovern, and Matthias Judt, 59–84. Washington, D.C.: German Historical Institute; Cambridge: Cambridge University Press, 1998.

de Grazia, Victoria. *The Culture of Consent: Mass Organization of Leisure in Fascist Italy*. Cambridge: Cambridge University Press, 1981.

de Grazia, Victoria, ed. *The Sex of Things: Gender and Consumption in Historical Perspective*. Berkeley: University of California Press, 1996.

Dennis, Mike, and Jonathan Grix. *Sport under Communism: Behind the East German "Miracle.'"* Houndmills: Palgrave Macmillan, 2012.

Diemer, Sabine. "Reisen zwischen politischem Anspruch und Vergnügen: DDR-Bürgerinnen und–Bürger Unterwegs." In *Endlich Urlaub! Die Deutschen reisen*, edited by Haus der Geschichte, 83–92. Bonn: Haus der Geschichte, 1996.

Dix, Andreas. "Nach dem Ende der 'Tausend Jahre': Landschaftsplanung in der Sowjetischen Besatzungszone und frühen DDR." In *Naturschutz und Nationalsozialismus*, edited by Joachim Radkau and Frank Uekötter, 331–362. Frankfurt am Main: Campus Verlag, 2003.

Dominick, Raymond H. "Capitalism, Communism, and Environmental Protection: Lessons from the German Experience." *Environmental History* 3, no. 3 (July 1998): 311–332.

Dominick, Raymond H. *The Environmental Movement in Germany: Prophets and Pioneers, 1871–1971*. Bloomington: Indiana University Press, 1992.

Downs, Laura Lee. *Childhood in the Promised Land: Working-Class Movements and the Colonies de Vacances in France, 1880–1960*. Durham: Duke University Press, 2002.

Drayton, Richard. *Nature's Government: Science, Imperial Britain, and the "Improvement" of the World*. New Haven: Yale University Press, 2000.

East Side Story. Directed by Dana Ranga. DVD, Kino Video, 1997.

Edelman, Robert. *Serious Fun: A History of Spectator Sports in the USSR*. New York: Oxford University Press, 1993.

Eley, Geoff. "The Unease of History: Settling Accounts with the East German Past." *History Workshop Journal* 57 (2004): 175–201.

Engeln, Ralf. *Uransklaven oder Sonnensucher? Die Sowjetische AG Wismut in der SBZ/DDR 1946–1953*. Essen: Klartext Verlag, 2001.

Engels, Jens Ivo. *Naturpolitik in der Bundesrepublik: Ideenwelt und politische Verhaltensstile in Naturschutz und Umweltbewegung 1950–1980*. Paderborn: Schöningh, 2006.

Epstein, Catherine. "East Germany and Its History since 1989." *Journal of Modern History* 75, no. 3 (September 2003): 634–666.

Evans, Richard. *Death in Hamburg: Society and Politics in the Cholera Years, 1830–1910*. Oxford: Oxford University Press, 1987.

Farmer, Sarah B. "Symbols That Face Two Ways: Commemorating the Victims of Nazism and Stalinism at Buchenwald and Sachsenhausen." *Representations* 49 (Winter 1995): 97–119.

Fenemore, Mark. "The Limits of Repression and Reform: Youth Policy in the Early 1960s." In *The Workers' and Peasants' State: Communism and Society in East Germany under Ulbricht, 1945–1971*, edited by Patrick Major and Jonathan Osmond, 171–89. Manchester: Manchester University Press, 2002.

Fenemore, Mark. *Sex, Thugs, and Rock 'n' Roll: Teenage Rebels in Cold-War East Germany*. New York: Berghahn Books, 2007.

Feshbach, Murray, and Alfred Friendly. *Ecocide in the USSR: Health and Nature under Siege*. New York: Basic Books, 1992.

Fibich, Peter, and Joachim Wolschke-Bulmahn, "Planungsideen des Wiederaufbaus: Der Tiergartenstreit zwischen Reinhold Lingner und Walter Rossow," *Garten und Landschaft* 3 (2003): 26–30

Fitzpatrick, Sheila. *Everyday Stalinism: Ordinary Life in Extraordinary Times*. Oxford: Oxford University Press, 1999.

Foster, John Bellamy. *Marx's Ecology: Materialism and Nature*. New York: Monthly Review Press, 2000.

Foster, John Bellamy. "Marx's Theory of Metabolic Rift: Classical Foundations for Environmental Sociology." *American Journal of Sociology* 105, no. 2 (September 1999), 366–405.

Fox, Stephen. *The American Conservation Movement: John Muir and His Legacy*. 1981. Reprint, Madison: University of Wisconsin Press, 1985.

Frevert, Ute. "Herren und Helden: Vom Aufstieg und Niedergang des Heroismus im 19 und 20 Jahrhundert." In *Erfindung des Menschen: Schöpfungsträume und Körperbilder 1500–2000*, edited by R. van Dülmen, 323–44. Vienna: Böhlau, 1998.

Fuchs, Ruth, and Klaus Ullrich. *Lorbeerkranz und Trauerflor: Aufstieg und "Untergang" des Sportwunders DDR*. Berlin: Dietz, 1990.

Fulbrook, Mary. *Anatomy of a Dictatorship: Inside the GDR, 1949–1989*. Oxford: Oxford University Press, 1995.

Fulbrook, Mary. *The People's State: East German Society from Hitler to Honecker*. New Haven: Yale University Press, 2005.

Fulbrook, Mary. "Retheorising 'State' and 'Society' in the GDR." In *The Workers' and Peasants' State: Communism and Society in East Germany under Ulbricht, 1945–1971*, edited by Patrick Major and Jonathan Osmond, 280–298. Manchester: Manchester University Press, 2002.

Gandert, Klaus-Dietrich. "Georg Bela Pniower—sein Leben und Wirken für die Garten- und Landeskultur." In *Landschaft und Planung in den neuen Bundesländern—Rückblicke*, edited by Regine Auster and Hermann Behrens, 221–235. Berlin: Verlag für Wissenschaft und Forschung, 1999.

Gaus, Günter. *Wo Deutschland liegt*. Munich: Hoffmann und Campe, 1983.

Gensichen, Hans-Peter. "Umweltverantwortung in einer betonierten Gesellschaft: Anmerkungen zur kirchlichen Umweltarbeit in der DDR 1970 bis 1990." In *Natur- und Umweltschutz nach 1945: Konzepte, Konflikte, Kompetenzen*, edited by Franz-Josef Brüggemeier and Jens Ivo Engels, 287–304. Frankfurt am Main: Campus Verlag, 2005.

Gensichen, Hans-Peter. "Zur Geschichtsschreibung der kirchlichen Umweltbewegung in der DDR." In *Umweltschutz in Ostdeutschland und Osteuropa: Bilanz und Perspektiven*, edited by Fritz Brickwedde, 181–191. Osnabrück: Steinbacher, 1998.

Geyer, Michael. "Germany, or the Twentieth Century as History." *South Atlantic Quarterly* 96, no. 4 (1997): 663–702.

Goodbody, Axel, ed. *The Culture of German Environmentalism: Anxieties, Visions, Realities*. New York: Berghahn Books, 2002.

Goodbody, Axel. "'Es Stirbt das Land an seinen Zwecken': Writers, the Environment, and the Green Movement in the GDR." *German Life and Letters* 47, no. 3 (July 1994): 325–336.

Görlich, Christopher. *Urlaub vom Staat: Tourismus in der DDR*. Cologne: Böhlau, 2012.

Gorsuch, Anne E. *All This Is Your World: Soviet Tourism at Home and Abroad after Stalin*. Oxford: Oxford University Press, 2011.

Gorsuch, Anne E. "'There's No Place Like Home': Soviet Tourism in Late Stalinism." *Slavic Review* 62, no. 4 (Winter 2003): 760–785.

Gorsuch, Anne E. *Youth in Revolutionary Russia: Enthusiasts, Bohemians, Delinquents*. Bloomington: Indiana University Press, 2000.

Gorsuch, Anne E., and Diane P. Koenker, eds. *Turizm: Leisure, Travel, and Nation Building in Russia, the USSR, and Eastern Europe*. Ithaca: Cornell University Press, 2006.

Gotschlich, Helga, ed. *"Links und links und Schritt gehalten . . .": Die FDJ; Konzepte—Ablaeufe—Grenzen*. Berlin: Metropol, 1994.

Gotschlich, Helga, Katharina Lange and Edeltraud Schulze, eds. *Aber nicht im Gleichschritt: Zur Entstehung der FDJ*. Berlin: Metropol, 1997.

Grandits, Hannes, and Karin Taylor, eds. *Yugoslavia's Sunny Side: A History of Tourism in Socialism (1950s–1980s)*. Budapest: Central European University Press, 2010.

Greiner, Johann. "Frank Erich Carl—Mitautor der Landschaftsdiagnose der DDR." In *Die Landschaftsdiagnose der DDR: Zeitgeschichte und Wirkung eines Forschungsprojekts aus der Gründungsphase der DDR*, edited by Olaf Hiller, 131–136. Berlin: Technische Universität Berlin, 2002.

Greiner, Johann. "Planung von Erholungsgebieten im Institut für Städtebau der Bauakademie." In *Die Landschaftsdiagnose der DDR: Zeitgeschichte und Wirkung eines Forschungsprojekts aus der Gründungsphase der DDR*, edited by Olaf Hiller, 243–246. Berlin: Technische Universität Berlin, 2002.

Gröning, Gert, ed. *Planung in Polen im Nationalsozialismus*. Berlin: Hochschule der Künste, 1996.

Gröning, Gert. "Soziale Praxis statt ökologischer Ethik: Zum Gesellschafts- und Naturverständnis der Arbeiterjugendbewegung." In *Jahrbuch des Archivs der Deutschen Jugendbewegung 1984–1985 15*, 201–252. Burg Ludwigstein: Das Archiv der deutschen Jugendbewegung, 1986.

Gröning, Gert, and Joachim Wolschke-Bulmahn. *Grüne Biographien: Biographisches Handbuch zur Landschaftsarchitektur des 20 Jahrhunderts in Deutschland*. Berlin: Patzer Verlag, 1997.

Gröning, Gert, and Joachim Wolschke-Bulmahn. *Liebe zur Landschaft: Drang nach Osten*. Munich: Minerva, 1986.

Gronow, Jukka. *Caviar with Champagne: Common Luxury and Ideals of the Good Life in Stalin's Russia*. Oxford: Berg, 2003.

Grosser, K. H. "Professor Hermann Meusel zum Gedenken." *Naturschutz und Landschaftspflege in Brandenburg* 3 (1997): 109.

Grossman, Atina. *Reforming Sex: The German Movement for Birth Control and Abortion Reform, 1920–1950*. Oxford: Oxford University Press, 1995.

Grotum, Thomas. *Die Halbstarken: Zur Geschichte einer Jugendkultur der 50er Jahre*. Frankfurt am Main: Campus Verlag, 1994.

Grove, Richard. *Green Imperialism : Colonial Expansion, Tropical Island Edens, and the Origins of Environmentalism, 1600–1860*. Cambridge: Cambridge University Press, 1995.

Grundmann, Reiner. *Marxism and Ecology*. Oxford: Clarendon, 1991.

Guha, Ramachandra. *Environmentalism: A Global History*. New York: Longman, 2000.

Günther, Dagmar. *Wandern und Sozialismus: Zur Geschichte des Touristenvereins "Die Naturfreunde" im Kaiserreich und in der Weimarer Republik*. Hamburg: Verlag Dr. Kovac, 2003.

Hage, Ghassan. "The Spatial Imaginary of National Practices: Dwelling-Domesticating/Being-Exterminating." *Environment and Planning D: Society and Space* 14 (1996): 463–485.

Hager, Thomas. *The Alchemy of Air: A Jewish Genius, a Doomed Tycoon, and the Scientific Discovery That Fed the World but Fueled the Rise of Hitler.* New York: Harmony Books, 2008.

Halbrock, Christian. "Beginn einer eigenständigen Umweltbewegung in der DDR." In *Störenfried: DDR-Opposition, 1986–1989,* edited by Wolfgang Rüddenklau, 43–51. Berlin: BasisDruck, 1992.

Hall, Marcus. *Earth Repair: A Transatlantic History of Environmental Restoration.* Charlottesville: University of Virginia Press, 2005.

Harsch, Donna. "Society, the State, and Abortion in East Germany, 1950–1972." *American Historical Review* 102, no. 1 (1997): 53–84.

Hau, Michael. *The Cult of Health and Beauty in Germany: A Social History, 1890–1930.* Chicago: University of Chicago Press, 2003.

Haus der Geschichte, ed. *Endlich Urlaub! Die Deutschen reisen.* Bonn: Haus der Geschichte, 1996.

Hays, Samuel P. *Beauty, Health, and Permanence: Environmental Politics in the United States, 1955–1985.* Cambridge: Cambridge University Press, 1987.

Hays, Samuel P. *Conservation and the Gospel of Efficiency: The Progressive Conservation Movement, 1890–1920.* Cambridge, Mass.: Harvard University Press, 1959.

Heineman, Elizabeth. "Gender Identity in the Wandervögel Movement." *German Studies Review* 12, no. 2 (May 1989): 249–270.

Heldmann, Philipp. *Herrschaft, Wirtschaft, Anoraks: Konsumpolitik in der DDR der Sechzigerjahre.* Göttingen: Vandenhoeck und Ruprecht, 2004.

Heldmann, Philipp. "Negotiating Consumption in a Dictatorship: Consumption Politics in the GDR in the 1950s and 1960s." In *The Politics of Consumption: Material Culture and Citizenship in Europe and America,* edited by Martin Daunton and Matthew Hilton, 185–202. Oxford: Berg, 2001.

Hermand, Jost. *Grüne Utopien in Deutschland: Zur Geschichte des ökologischen Bewusstseins.* Frankfurt am Main: Fischer, 1991.

Herrmann, Bernhard. *Arbeiterschaft, Naturheilkunde, und der Verband Volksgesundheit 1880–1918.* Frankfurt am Main: Peter Lang, 1990.

Hiller, Olaf. "Daten und Fakten zum Ablauf, zur Unterbrechung und Wiederaufnahme des Forschungsauftrages Landschaftsdiagnose der fünf Länder der DDR." In *Die Landschaftsdiagnose der DDR: Zeitgeschichte und Wirkung eines Forschungsprojekts aus der Gründungsphase der DDR,* edited by Olaf Hiller, 83–109. Berlin: Technische Universität Berlin, 2002.

Hiller, Olaf, ed. *Die Landschaftsdiagnose der DDR: Zeitgeschichte und Wirkung eines Forschungsprojekts aus der Gründungsphase der DDR.* Berlin: Technische Universität Berlin, 2002.

Hinsching, Jochen, ed. *Alltagssport in der DDR.* Aachen: Meyer und Meyer Verlag, 1998.

Hobusch, Erich. "Naturfreunde auf dem Weg zum Kulturbund, 1945–1953." *Grüner Weg 31a: Zeitschrift des Studienarchivs Arbeiterkultur und Ökologie* 10 (January 1996): 68–71.

Hoffmann, Detlef, ed. *Das Gedächtnis der Dinge: KZ-Relikte und KZ-Denkmaler, 1945–1995.* Frankfurt am Main: Campus Verlag, 1998.

Holdgate, Martin. *The Green Web: A Union for World Conservation.* London: Earthscan, 1999.

Holzl, Richard. "Historicizing Sustainability: German Scientific Forestry in the Eighteenth and Nineteenth Centuries." *Science as Culture* 19, no. 4 (2010): 431–460.

Hong, Young-sun. "Cigarette Butts and the Building of Socialism in East Germany." *Central European History* 35, no. 3 (2002): 327–344.

Hübl, Erich. "In memoriam Hermann Meusel." *Verhandlungen der Zoologisch-Botanischen Gesellschaft in Österreich* 135 (1998): 381–384.

Hübner, Peter. "Die FDJ als politische Organisation und sozialer Raum." In *"Links und links und Schritt gehalten . . .": Die FDJ; Konzepte—Ablaeufe—Grenzen*, edited by Helga Gotschlich, 58–69. Berlin: Metropol, 1994.

Hübner, Peter. "Die Zukunft war gestern: Soziale und mentale Trends in der DDR-Industriearbeiterschaft.'" In *Sozialgeschichte der DDR*, edited by Hartmut Kaelble et al., 171–187. Stuttgart: Klett-Cotta, 1994.

Hübner, Peter. *Konsens, Konflikt, Kompromiss. Soziale Arbeiterinteressen und Sozialpolitik in der SBZ/DDR 1945–1970*. Berlin: Akademie Verlag, 1995.

Huinink, Johannes and Karl Ulrich Mayer, eds., *Kollektiv und Eigensinn: Lebensverläufe in der DDR und danach*. Berlin: Akademie Verlag, 1995.

Husband, William B. "'Correcting Nature's Mistakes': Transforming the Environment and Soviet Children's Literature, 1928–1941." *Environmental History* 11, no. 2 (April 2006): 300–318.

Jacoby, Karl. *Crimes against Nature: Squatters, Poachers, Thieves, and the Hidden History of American Conservation*. Berkeley: University of California Press, 2001.

Jäger, E., and E. G. Mahn. "Hermann Meusel—ein Nachruf." *Hercynia* 30 (1997): 153–154.

Jarausch, Konrad H. "Beyond Uniformity: The Challenge of Historicizing the GDR." In *Dictatorship as Experience: Towards a Socio-cultural History of the GDR*, edited by Konrad Jarausch, 3–16. New York: Berghahn Books, 1999.

Jarausch, Konrad H. "Care and Coercion: The GDR as Welfare Dictatorship." In *Dictatorship as Experience: Towards a Socio-cultural History of the GDR*, edited by Konrad Jarausch, 47–72. New York: Berghahn Books, 1999.

Jarausch, Konrad H., ed. *Dictatorship as Experience: Towards a Socio-cultural History of the GDR*. New York: Berghahn Books, 1999.

Jarausch, Konrad, and Michael Geyer. *Shattered Past: Reconstructing German Histories*. Princeton: Princeton University Press, 2003.

Jarvis, Robin. *Romantic Writing and Pedestrian Travel*. New York: St. Martin's, 1997.

Jensen, Erik. *Body by Weimar: Athletes, Gender, and German Modernity*. Oxford: Oxford University Press, 2010.

Jeschke, Lebrecht. "Naturschutz der Wendezeit in der DDR." In *Naturschutz hat Geschichte: Grussworte und Festrede des Bundespräsidenten anlässlich der Eröffnung des Museums zur Geschichte des Naturschutzes am 12. März 2002; Beiträge der Fachtagung "Naturschutz hat Geschichte vom 13. März 2002*, edited by Bernd Kreuter, 245–253. Essen: Klartext Verlag, 2003.

Jessen, Ralph. "Diktatorische Herrschaft als kommunikative Praxis: Ueberlegungen zum Zusammenhang von 'Bürokratie' und Sprachnormierung in der DDR-Geschichte." In *Akten, Eingaben, Schaufenster: Die DDR und ihre Texte; Erkundungen zu Herrschaft und Alltag*, edited by Alf Lüdtke and Peter Becker, 57–75. Berlin: Akademie Verlag, 1997.

Johnson, Molly Wilkinson. *Training Socialist Citizens: Sports and the State in East Germany*. Leiden: Brill, 2008.

Jones, Merrill E. "Origins of the East German Environmental Movement." *German Studies Review* 16, no. 2 (May 1993): 235–264.

Josephson, Paul R. *Resources under Regimes: Technology, Environment, and the State*. Cambridge, Mass.: Harvard University Press, 2004.

Judson, Pieter. "'Every German Visitor Has a *Völkisch* Obligation He Must Fulfill': Nationalist Tourism in the Austrian Empire, 1880–1918." In *Histories of Leisure*, edited by Rudy Koshar, 147–168. Oxford: Berg, 2002.

Judt, Matthias, Charles McGovern, Susan Strasser, eds. *Getting and Spending: European and American Consumer Societies in the Twentieth Century*. Cambridge: Cambridge University Press, 1998.

Kaelble, Hartmut, Jürgen Kocka, and Hartmut Zwahr, eds. *Sozialgeschichte der DDR*. Stuttgart: Klett-Cotta, 1994.

Kaiser, Monika. *Machtwechsel von Ulbricht zu Honecker: Funktionsmechanismen der SED-Diktatur in Konfliktsituationen 1962 bis 1972*. Berlin: Akademie Verlag, 1997.

Kaiser, Monika. "Reforming Socialism? The Changing of the Guard from Ulbricht to Honecker during the 1960s." In *Dictatorship as Experience: Towards a Sociocultural History of the GDR*, edited by Konrad Jarausch, 325–340. New York: Berghahn Books, 1999.

Kaminsky, Annette. *Illustrierte Konsumgeschichte der DDR*. Erfurt: Landeszentrale für politische Bildung Thüringen, 1999.

Kaminsky, Annette. *Kaufrausch: Die Geschichte der ostdeutschen Versandhäuser*. Berlin: Ch. Links, 1998.

Kaminsky, Annette. *Wohlstand, Schönheit, Glück: Kleine Konsumgeschichte der DDR*. Munich: Beck, 2001.

Kappeler, Manfred. "Jugendverbände in Deutschland: Zwischen Selbstbestimmungswünschen von Jugendlichen und Funktionalisierungsabsichten von Erwachsenen." In *Aber nicht im Gleichschritt: Zur Entstehung der FDJ*, edited by Helga Gotschlich et al., 9–20. Berlin: Metropol, 1997.

Karlsch, Rainer, and Zbynek Zeman. *Urangeheimnisse: Das Erzgebirge im Brennpunkt der Weltpolitik, 1933–1960*. Berlin: Ch. Links, 2002.

Kluge, Ulrich. *Vierzig Jahre Agrarpolitik in der Bundesrepublik Deutschland*. Hamburg: P. Parey, 1989.

Kneip, Rudolf. *Wandervogel ohne Legende: Die Geschichte eines pädagogischen Phänomens*. Heidenheim: Südmarkverlag Fritsch, 1984.

Knigge, Volkhard. "Die Gedenkstätte Buchenwald: Vom provisorischen Grabdenkmal zum Nationaldenkmal." In *Die Nacht hat zwölf Stunden, dann kommt schon der Tag: Antifaschismus, Geschichte und Neubewertung*, edited by Claudia Keller and literaturWERKstatt Berlin, 309–331. Berlin: Aufbau, 1996.

Knigge, Volkhard. "Vom Reden und Schweigen der Steine: Zu Denkmalen auf dem Gelände ehemaliger nationalsozialistischer Konzentrations- und Vernichtungslager." In *Fünfzig Jahre danach: Zur Nachgeschichte des Nationalsozialismus*, edited by Sigrid Weigel and Birgit Erdle, 193–234. Zürich: vdf Hochschulverlag AG an der ETH Zürich, 1996.

Knoth, Nikola. "Eine 'grüne' SED? Aus dem Protokoll einer ZK-Sekretariatssitzung." *Beiträge zur Geschichte der Arbeiterbewegung* 35, no. 4 (1993): 72–79.

Knoth, Nikola. "'Ich war Bergmann, was wird nun?' Die Niederlausitzer Braunkohlenregion aus umwelthistorischer Sicht." *WerkstattGeschichte* 3 (1992): 27–32.

Knoth, Nikola. "Umwelt: Auf den Spuren einer Erfahrung im sozialistischen Revier." In *Historiche DDR-Forschung: Aufsätze und Studien*, edited by Jürgen Kocka, 233–244. Berlin: Akademie Verlag, 1993.

Kocka, Jürgen. "Die Geschichte der DDR als Forschungsproblem. Einleitung." In *Historiche DDR-Forschung: Aufsätze und Studien*, edited by Jürgen Kocka, 9–26. Berlin: Akademie Verlag, 1993.

Kocka, Jürgen. "Eine durchherrschte Gesellschaft." In *Sozialgeschichte der DDR*, edited by Hartmut Kaelble et al., 547–553. Stuttgart: Klett-Cotta, 1994.

Kocka, Jürgen. "The GDR: A Special Kind of Modern Dictatorship." In *Dictatorship as Experience: Towards a Socio-cultural History of the GDR*, edited by Konrad Jarausch, 17–26. New York: Berghahn Books, 1999.

Koenker, Diane P. "Travel to Work, Travel to Play: On Russian Tourism, Travel, and Leisure." *Slavic Review* 62, no. 4 (Winter 2003): 657–665.

Komarov, Boris. *The Destruction of Nature in the Soviet Union*. White Plains, N.Y.: M. E. Sharpe, 1980.

König, Gudrun M. *Eine Kulturgeschichte des Spazierganges: Spuren einer bürgerlichen Praktik 1780–1850*. Vienna: Böhlau, 1996.

Kopstein, Jeffrey. *The Politics of Economic Decline in East Germany, 1945–1989*. Chapel Hill: University of North Carolina Press, 1997.

Kopytoff, Igor. "The Cultural Biography of Things: Commoditization as Process." In *The Social Life of Things: Commodities in Cultural Perspective*, edited by Arjun Appadurai, 64–91. Cambridge: Cambridge University Press, 1986.

Körner, Stefan. "Kontinuum und Bruch: Die Transformation des naturschützerischen Aufgabenverständnisses nach dem Zweiten Weltkrieg." In *Naturschutz und Nationalsozialismus*, edited by Joachim Radkau and Frank Uekötter, 405–434. Frankfurt am Main: Campus Verlag, 2003.

Kosek, Jake. *Understories: The Political Life of Forests in Northern New Mexico*. Durham: Duke University Press, 2006.

Koshar, Rudy. "Germans at the Wheel: Cars and Leisure Travel in Interwar Germany." In *Histories of Leisure*, edited by Rudy Koshar, 215–232. Oxford: Berg, 2002.

Koshar, Rudy. *German Travel Cultures*. Oxford: Berg, 2000.

Koshar, Rudy. *Germany's Transient Pasts: Preservation and National Memory in the Twentieth Century*. Chapel Hill: University of North Carolina Press, 1998.

Koshar, Rudy. *From Monuments to Traces: Artifacts of German Memory, 1870–1990*. Berkeley: University of California Press, 2000.

Koshar, Rudy, ed. *Histories of Leisure*. Oxford: Berg, 2002.

Kotkin, Stephen. *Magnetic Mountain: Stalinism as a Civilization*. Berkeley: University of California Press, 1995.

Kott, Sandrine. "Everyday Communism: New Social History of the German Democratic Republic." *Contemporary European History* 13, no. 2 (2004): 233–247.

Kramer, Thomas. "Die DDR der fünfziger Jahre im Comic *Mosaik*: Einschienenbahn, Agenten, Chemieprogramm." In *Akten, Eingaben, Schaufenster: Die DDR und ihre*

Texte; Erkundungen zu Herrschaft und Alltag, edited by Alf Lüdtke and Peter Becker, 167–188. Berlin: Akademie Verlag, 1997.

Krenz, Gerhard. *Notizen zur Landwirtschaftsentwicklung in den Jahren 1945–1990: Erinnerungen und Bekenntnisse eines Zeitzeugen aus dem Bezirk Neubrandenburg.* Schwerin: Ministerium für Landwirtschaft und Naturschutz des Landes Mecklenburg-Vorpommern, 1996.

Kreuter, Bernd, ed. *Naturschutz hat Geschichte: Grussworte und Festrede des Bundespräsidenten anlässlich der Eröffnung des Museums zur Geschichte des Naturschutzes am 12. März 2002; Beiträge der Fachtagung "Naturschutz hat Geschichte vom 13. März 2002.* Essen: Klartext Verlag, 2003.

Krüger, Michael, and Kai Reinhart. "Funktionen des Sports im modernen Staat und in der modernen Diktatur." *Historical Social Research* 32, no. 1 (2007): 43–77.

Kruse, Judith. "Nische im Sozialismus." In *Endlich Urlaub! Die Deutschen reisen*, edited by Haus der Geschichte, 106–111. Bonn: Haus der Geschichte, 1996.

Landsman, Mark. *Dictatorship and Demand: The Politics of Consumerism in East Germany.* Cambridge, Mass.: Harvard University Press, 2005.

Laqueur, Walter. *Young Germany: A History of the German Youth Movement.* New Brunswick, N.J.: Transaction Books, 1984.

Last, George. *After the "Socialist Spring": Collectivisation and Economic Transformation in the GDR.* New York: Berghahn Books, 2009.

Lekan, Thomas. *Imagining the Nation in Nature: Landscape Preservation and German Identity, 1885–1945.* Cambridge, Mass: Harvard University Press, 2003.

Lekan, Thomas. "A "Noble Prospect": Tourism, Heimat, and Conservation on the Rhine, 1880–1914." *Journal of Modern History* 81, no. 4 (December 2009): 824–858.

Lekan, Thomas. "Regionalism and the Politics of Landscape Preservation in the Third Reich." *Environmental History* 4, no. 3 (July 1999): 384–404.

Lekan, Thomas, and Thomas Zeller, eds., *Germany's Nature: Cultural Landscapes and Environmental History.* New Brunswick, N.J.: Rutgers University Press, 2005.

Lidtke, Vernon. *The Alternative Culture: Socialist Labor in Imperial Germany.* New York: Oxford University Press, 1985.

Lindenberger, Thomas. "Alltagsgeschichte und ihr möglicher Beitrag zu einer Gesellschaftsgeschichte der DDR." In *Die Grenzen der Diktatur: Staat und Gesellschaft in der SBZ/DDR*, edited by Richard Bessel and Ralph Jessen, 298–325. Göttingen: Vandenhoeck und Ruprecht, 1996.

Lindenberger, Thomas. "Everyday History: New Approaches to the History of the Post-war Germanies." In *Divided Past: Rewriting Post-war German History*, edited by Christoph Klessmann, 11–42. Oxford: Berg, 2001.

Lindenberger, Thomas, ed. *Herrschaft und Eigen-Sinn in der Diktatur: Studien zur Gesellschaftsgeschichte der DDR.* Cologne: Böhlau, 1999.

Linse, Ulrich. "Die 'freie Natur' als Heimat: Naturaneignung und Naturschutz in der älteren Naturfreundebewegung." In *Hundert Jahre Kampf um die Freie Natur*, edited by Jochen Zimmer, 63–77. Essen: Klartext Verlag, 1991.

Linse, Ulrich. "Lebensformen der bürgerlichen und proletarischen Jugendbewegung." In *Jahrbuch des Archivs der Deutschen Jugendbewegung 1978–1981* 10, 24–55. Burg Ludwigstein: Das Archiv der deutschen Jugendbewegung, 1981.

Litz, Patrick. *Der Beitrag des Sports zur Entfaltung der sozialistischen Persönlichkeit in der DDR*. Berlin: Weissensee Verlag, 2007.

Liulevicius, Vejas G. *The German Myth of the East*. New York: Oxford University Press, 2009.

Löfgren, Orvar. *On Holiday: A History of Vacationing*. Berkeley: University of California Press, 1999.

Lorenz, Jürgen. "Warum gab es in der DDR keine Naturfreunde?" *Arbeiterkultur und Ökologie: Rundbrief* 2 (1992): 30–31.

Lorenz, Klaus-Peter. "Auf dem Hohnstein." *Grüner Weg 31a: Zeitschrift des Studienarchivs Arbeiterkultur und Ökologie* 11 (June 1997): 3–11.

Lorenz, Klaus-Peter. "Kontinuitäten mit Fragezeichen. Von wann auf wann?" *Arbeiterkultur und Ökologie: Rundbrief* 2 (1992): 12–13.

Lorenz, Klaus-Peter. "Neuaufbau des Sports in Dresden." *Grüner Weg 31a: Zeitschrift des Studienarchivs Arbeiterkultur und Ökologie* 9 (First Quarter, 1995): 50–51.

Lovell, Stephen. "Soviet Exurbia: Dachas in Postwar Russia." In *Socialist Spaces: Sites of Everyday Life in the Eastern Bloc*, edited by David Crowley and Susan E. Reid, 105–122. Oxford: Berg, 2002.

Lovell, Stephen. *Summerfolk: A History of the Dacha, 1710–2000*. Ithaca: Cornell University Press, 2003.

Lower, Wendy. *Nazi Empire-Building and the Holocaust in Ukraine*. Chapel Hill: University of North Carolina Press, 2007.

Lüdtke, Alf. "'Helden der Arbeit'—Mühen beim Arbeiten: Zur missmutigen Loyalität von Industriearbeitern in der DDR." In *Sozialgeschichte der DDR*, edited by Hartmut Kaelble et al., 188–213. Stuttgart: Klett-Cotta, 1994.

Lüdtke, Alf. *Herrschaft als sozialer Praxis: Historische und sozio-anthropologische Studien*. Göttingen: Vandenhoeck und Ruprecht, 1991.

Lüdtke, Alf, and Peter Becker, eds. *Akten, Eingaben, Schaufenster: Die DDR und ihre Texte; Erkundungen zu Herrschaft und Alltag*. Berlin: Akademie Verlag, 1997.

Lury, Celia. *Consumer Culture*. New Brunswick, N.J.: Rutgers University Press, 1996.

MacCannell, Dean. *The Tourist: A New Theory of the Leisure Class*. New York: Schocken Books, 1989.

MacDonald, Kenneth Iain. "IUCN: A History of Constraint." Accessed July 9, 2010. http://perso.cpdr.ucl.ac.be/maesschalck/MacDonaldInstitutional_Reflexivity_and_IUCN-17.02.03.pdf.

Madley, Benjamin. "From Africa to Auschwitz: How German South West Africa Incubated Ideas and Methods Adopted and Developed by the Nazis in Eastern Europe." *European History Quarterly* 35, no. 3 (July 2005): 429–464.

Mählert, Ulrich. *Blaue Hemden, Rote Fahnen: Die Geschichte der Freien Deutschen Jugend*. Opladen: Leske und Budrich,1996.

Maier, Charles. *Dissolution: The Crisis of Communism and the End of East Germany*. Princeton: Princeton University Press, 1997.

Major, Patrick, and Jonathan Osmond, eds. *The Workers' and Peasants' State: Communism and Society in East Germany under Ulbricht, 1945–1971*. Manchester: Manchester University Press, 2002.

Manser, Roger. *Failed Transitions: The Eastern European Economy and Environment since the Fall of Communism*. New York: New Press, 1993.

Marx, Karl. *Capital*, vol. 1. New York: Vintage, 1976.

Marx, Karl. *Capital*, vol. 3. London: Lawrence and Wishart,1959.

Marx, Karl. *The Communist Manifesto*. Boston: Bedford/St. Martin's, 1999.

Mauch, Christof, ed. *Nature in German History*. New York: Berghahn Books, 2004.

Mazower, Mark. *Hitler's Empire: How the Nazis Ruled Europe*. New York: Penguin, 2008.

McCormick, John. *Reclaiming Paradise: The Global Environmental Movement*. Bloomington: Indiana University Press, 1989.

McNeill, John. *Something New under the Sun: An Environmental History of the Twentieth-Century World*. New York: W. W. Norton, 2000.

McNeill, John, and Corinna R. Unger, eds. *Environmental Histories of the Cold War*. Washington, D.C.: German Historical Institute; Cambridge: Cambridge University Press, 2010.

Merkel, Ina. "Consumer Culture in the GDR, or How the Struggle for Antimodernity Was Lost on the Battleground of Consumer Culture." In *Getting and Spending: European and American Consumer Societies in the Twentieth Century*, edited by Susan Strasser, Charles McGovern, and Matthias Judt, 281–300. Washington, D.C.: German Historical Institute; Cambridge: Cambridge University Press, 1998.

Merkel, Ina. "Der aufhaltsame Aufbruch in die Konsumgesellschaft." In *Wunderwirtschaft: DDR-Konsumkultur in den 60er Jahren*, edited by Neue Gesellschaft für Bildende Kunst, 8–20. Cologne: Böhlau, 1996.

Merkel, Ina. "'. . . in Hoyerswerda leben jedenfalls keine so kleinen viereckigen Menschen': Briefe an das Fernsehen der DDR." In *Akten, Eingaben, Schaufenster: Die DDR und ihre Texte; Erkundungen zu Herrschaft und Alltag*, edited by Alf Lüdtke and Peter Becker, 279–310. Berlin: Akademie Verlag, 1997.

Merkel, Ina. *Utopie und Bedürfnis: Die Geschichte der Konsumkultur in der DDR*. Cologne: Böhlau, 1999.

Merkel, Ina, and Felix Mühlberg. "Eingaben und Öffentlichkeit." In *"Wir sind doch nicht die Mecker-Ecke der Nation": Briefe an das DDR-Fernsehen*, edited by Ina Merkel, 11–46. Cologne: Böhlau, 1998.

Miller, Daniel, ed. *Acknowledging Consumption*. London: Routledge, 1995.

Miller, Daniel. *Car Cultures*. Oxford: Berg, 2001.

Miller, Shawn William. *An Environmental History of Latin America*. New York: Cambridge University Press, 2007.

Mincyte, Diana. "Everyday Environmentalism: The Practice, Politics, and Nature of Subsidiary Farming in Stalin's Lithuania." *Slavic Review* 68, no. 1 (Spring 2009): 31–49.

Mitman, Gregg. *Breathing Space: How Allergies Shape Our Lives and Landscapes*. New Haven: Yale University Press, 2007.

Mitman, Gregg. "In Search of Health: Landscape and Disease in American Environmental History." *Environmental History* 10, no. 2 (April 2005): 184–210.

Moorhouse, H. F. *Driving Ambitions: An Analysis of American Hot-Rod Enthusiasm*. Manchester: Manchester University Press, 1991.

Moranda, Scott. "Camping in East Germany: Making 'Rough' Nature More Comfortable." In *Pleasures in Socialism: Leisure and Luxury in the Eastern Bloc*, edited by David Crowley and Susan E. Reid, 197–218. Evanston, Ill.: Northwestern University Press, 2010.

Moranda, Scott. "East German Nature Tourism, 1949–1961: In Search of a Common Destination." In *Turizm: The Russian and East European Tourist under Capitalism and Socialism*, edited by Anne E. Gorsuch and Diane Koenker, 266–280. Ithaca: Cornell University Press, 2006.

Moranda, Scott. "Maps, Markers, and Bodies: Hikers Constructing the Nation in German Forests." *The Nationalism Project*, December 1, 2000. http://www.nationalismproject.org/articles/Moranda/moranda.html.

Moranda, Scott. "Nature as a Scarce Consumer Commodity: Vacationing in Communist East Germany." In *From Heimat to Umwelt: New Perspectives on German Environmental History*, edited by Frank Zelko and Stephen J. Scala, 103–119. GHI Bulletin Supplement 3.Washington, D.C.: German Historical Institute, 2006.

Moranda, Scott. "Towards a More Holistic History? Historians and East German Everyday Life." *Social History* 35, no. 3 (August 2010): 330–339.

Mosse, George. *Nationalism and Sexuality: Respectability and Abnormal Sexuality in Modern Europe*. New York: Howard Fertig, 1985.

Nadav, Daniel S. *Julius Moses (1868–1942) und die Politik der Sozialhygiene in Deutschland*. Gerlingen: Bleicher, 1985.

Nash, Linda. *Inescapable Ecologies: A History of Environment, Disease, and Knowledge*. Berkeley: University of California Press, 2006.

Nash, Roderick. *Wilderness and the American Mind*. New Haven: Yale University Press, 2001.

Nelson, Arvid. *Cold War Ecology: Forests, Farms, and People in the East German Landscape, 1945–1989*. New Haven: Yale University Press, 2005.

Neubert, Ehrhart. *Geschichte der Opposition in der DDR*. Berlin: Ch. Links, 1998.

Niemann, Heinz. *Hinterm Zaun: Politische Kultur und Meinungsforschung in der DDR; Die geheimen Berichte an das Politbüro der SED*. Berlin: Edition Ost, 1995.

Niemann, Heinz. *Meinungsforschung in der DDR*. Cologne: Bund Verlag, 1993.

Noack, Christian. "Coping with the Tourist: Planned and 'Wild' Mass Tourism on the Soviet Black Sea Coast." In *Turizm: The Russian and East European Tourist under Capitalism and Socialism*, edited by Anne E. Gorsuch and Diane Koenker, 281–304. Ithaca: Cornell University Press, 2006.

Nowak, Kerstin. "Errinerung an Reinhold Lingner: Pionier der Landschaftsdiagnose." *Garten und Landschaft* 9 (1991): 7–8.

Overesch, Manfred. *Buchenwald und die DDR, oder die Suche nach Selbstlegitimation*. Göttingen: Vandenhoeck and Ruprecht, 1995.

Palmowski, Jan. "Building an East German Nation: The Construction of a Socialist Heimat, 1945–1961." *Central European History* 37, no. 3 (2004): 365–399.

Palmowski, Jan. *Inventing a Socialist Nation: Heimat and the Politics of Everyday Life in the GDR, 1945–1990*. Cambridge: Cambridge University Press, 2009.

Paul, Reimar. *Das Wismut Erbe: Geschichte und Folgen des Uranbergbaus in Thüringen und Sachsen*. Göttingen: Verlag der Werkstatt, 1991.

Pence, Katherine. "Schaufenster des sozialistischen Konsums: Texte der ostdeutschen 'consumer culture.'" In *Akten, Eingaben, Schaufenster: Die DDR und ihre Texte; Erkundungen zu Herrschaft und Alltag*, edited by Alf Lüdtke and Peter Becker, 91–118. Berlin: Akademie Verlag, 1997.

Pence, Katherine. "'You as a Woman Will Understand:' Consumption, Gender, and the

Relationship between State and Citizenry in the GDR's Crisis of 17 June 1953." *German History* 19, no. 2 (2001): 218–252.

Perkins, John H. *Geopolitics and the Green Revolution: Wheat, Genes, and the Cold War.* New York: Oxford University Press, 1997.

Petrone, Karen. *Life Has Become More Joyous, Comrades: Celebrations in the Time of Stalin.* Bloomington: Indiana University Press, 2000.

Pierau, Ralf. *Urlaub, Klappfix, Ferienscheck: Reisen in der DDR.* Berlin: Eulenspiegel, 2003.

Poiger, Uta. *Jazz, Rock, and Rebels: Cold War Politics and American Culture in a Divided Germany.* Berkeley: University of California Press, 2000.

Port, Andrew. *Conflict and Stability in the German Democratic Republic.* Cambridge: Cambridge University Press, 2007.

Poutrus, Patrice. *Die Erfindung des Goldbroilers: Über den Zusammenhang zwischen Herrschaftssicherung und Konsumentwicklung in der DDR.* Cologne: Böhlau, 2002.

Rabinbach, Anson. *The Human Motor: Energy, Fatigue, and the Origins of Modernity.* Berkeley: University of California Press, 1992.

Radkau, Joachim. *Nature and Power: A Global History of the Environment.* Washington, D.C.: German Historical Institute; Cambridge: Cambridge University Press, 2008.

Radkau, Joachim. "Wood and Forestry in German History: In Quest of an Environmental Approach." *Environment and History* 2 (1996): 63–76.

Radkau, Joachim, and Frank Uekötter, eds. *Naturschutz und Nationalsozialismus.* Frankfurt am Main: Campus Verlag, 2003.

Rauch, Thilo. *Die Ferienkoloniebewegung: Zur Geschichte der privaten Fürsorge im Kaiserreich.* Wiesbaden: Deutscher Universitäts Verlag, 1992.

Riemer, Wolfgang. *Wahre Geschichten um Stülpner Karl.* Taucha: Tauchaer Verlag, 1993.

Rink, Dieter. "Ausreiser, Kirchengruppen, Kulturopposition und Reformer: Zu Differenzen und Gemeinsamkeiten in Opposition und Widerstand in der DDR in den 70er und 80er Jahren." In *Zwischen Verweigerung und Opposition: Politischer Protest in der DDR 1970–1989,* edited by Detlef Pollack and Dieter Rink, 54–77. Frankfurt am Main: Campus, 1997.

Rink, Dieter. "Environmental Policy and the Environmental Movement in East Germany." *Capitalism, Nature, Socialism* 13, no. 3 (2002): 73–91.

Riordan, James. *Sport in Soviet Society: Development of Sport and Physical Education in Russia and the USSR..* Cambridge: Cambridge University Press, 1977.

Rösler, Markus. "Nationalparkinitiativen in der DDR bis zur Wende 1989." In *Landschaft und Planung in den neuen Bundesländern: Rückblicke,* edited by Regine Auster and Hermann Behrens, 547–560. Berlin: Verlag für Wissenschaft und Forschung, 1999.

Roesler, Jörg. "Die Produktionsbrigaden in der Industrie der DDR. Zentrum der Arbeitswelt?" In *Sozialgeschichte der DDR,* edited by Hartmut Kaelble et al., 144–70. Stuttgart: Klett-Cotta, 1994.

Roesler, Jörg. *Zwischen Plan und Markt: Die Wirtschaftsreform 1963–1970 in der DDR.* Berlin: Verlag Weltarchiv, 1991.

Rohkrämer, Thomas. *Eine andere Moderne? Zivilisationskritik, Natur und Technik in Deutschland 1880–1933.* Paderborn: Schöningh, 1999.

Rollins, William H. *A Greener Vision of Home: Cultural Politics and Environmental Reform in the German Heimatschutz Movement, 1904–1918*. Ann Arbor: University of Michigan Press, 1997.

Ross, Chad. *Naked Germany: Health, Race, and the Nation*. Oxford: Berg, 2005.

Ross, Corey. *Constructing Socialism at the Grass-Roots: The Transformation of East Germany, 1945–1965*. New York: St. Martin's, 2000.

Ross, Corey. *The East German Dictatorship: Problems and Perspectives in the Interpretation of the GDR*. London: Arnold; New York: Cambridge University Press, 2002.

Rothman, Hal. *Devil's Bargain: Tourism in the Twentieth-Century American West*. Lawrence: University of Kansas Press, 1998.

Rubin, Eli. "The Order of Substitutes: Plastic Consumer Goods in the *Volkswirtschaft* and Everyday Domestic Life in the GDR." In *Consuming Germany in the Cold War*, edited by David F. Crew, 87–120. Oxford: Berg, 2004.

Rubin, Eli. *Synthetic Socialism: Plastics and Dictatorship in the German Democratic Republic*. Chapel Hill: University of North Carolina Press, 2008.

Rüddenklau, Wolfgang, ed. *Störenfried: DDR-Opposition, 1986–1989*. Berlin: Basis-Druck, 1992.

Sabrow, Martin. *Geschichte als Herrschaftsdiskurs: Der Umgang mit der Vergangenheit in der DDR*. Cologne: Böhlau, 2000.

Sachs, Wolfgang. *For the Love of the Automobile*. Berkeley: University of California Press, 1992.

Schaarschmidt, Thomas. *Regionalkultur und Diktatur: Sächsische Heimatbewegung und Heimat-Propaganda im Dritten Reich und in der SBZ/DDR*. Cologne: Böhlau, 2004.

Schindler, Joachim. "Dresden 1945." *Grüner Weg 31a: Zeitschrift des Studienarchivs Arbeiterkultur und Ökologie* 9 (First Quarter, 1995): 47–49.

Schindler, Joachim. "ETB in Dresden." *Arbeiterkultur und Ökologie: Rundbrief* 2 (1992): 13–23.

Schindler, Joachim. "Naturfreunde auf dem Weg zur Sektion Touristik—Versuch einer Dokumentation." *Grüner Weg 31a: Zeitschrift des Studienarchivs Arbeiterkultur und Ökologie* 10 (January 1996): 79–108.

Schindler, Joachim. "Rote Bergsteiger: Wahrheit und Legende." *Grüner Weg 31a: Zeitschrift des Studienarchivs Arbeiterkultur und Ökologie* 14 (June 2000): 17–33.

Schindler, Joachim. *Zur Entwicklung von Wandern und Bergsteigen in der Sächsischen Schweiz sowie zur Arbeit touristischer Organisationen Dresdens von 1945 bis 1953*. Dresden: Joachim Schindler, 1999.

Schmitz, Jakob. "Naturfreunde und Wegebezeichnung." *Rheinisches Land: Nachrichten des Gaues Rheinland in Touristin-Verein "Die Naturfreunde"* 7 (1926): 152.

Schröter, Erasmus, ed. *Bild der Heimat: Die Echt-Foto-Postkarten aus der DDR*. Berlin: Schwarzkopf und Schwarzkopf, 2002.

Schwartz, Michael. *Sozialistische Eugenik: Eugenische Sozialtechnologien in Debatten und Politik der deutschen Sozialdemokratie, 1890–1933*. Bonn: Dietz, 1995.

Scott, James C. *Seeing Like a State: How Certain Schemes to Improve the Human Condition Have Failed*. New Haven: Yale University Press, 1998.

Selbach, Claus-Ulrich. "Reise nach Plan: Der Feriendienst des Freien Deutschen

Gewerkschaftsbundes." In *Endlich Urlaub! Die Deutschen reisen,* edited by Haus der Geschichte, 65–76. Bonn: Haus der Geschichte, 1996.

Semmens, Kristin. *Seeing Hitler's Germany: Tourism in the Third Reich.* Houndmills: Palgrave Macmillan, 2005.

Shapiro, Judith. *Mao's War against Nature: Politics and the Environment in Revolutionary China.* Cambridge: Cambridge University Press, 2001.

Skyba, Peter. "Die FDJ im Tauwetter; Tauwetter in der FDJ." In *"Links und links und Schritt gehalten . . .": Die FDJ; Konzepte—Ablaeufe—Grenzen,* edited by Helga Gotschlich, 206–226. Berlin: Metropol, 1994.

Skyba, Peter. "Sozialpolitik als Herrschaftssicherung." In *Der Schein der Normalität: Alltag und Herrschaft in der SED-Diktatur,* edited by Clemens Vollnhals and Jürgen Weber, 39–80. Munich: Olzog, 2002.

Smil, Vaclav. *Enriching the Earth: Fritz Haber, Carl Bosch, and the Transformation of World Food Production.* Cambridge, Mass.: MIT Press, 2004.

Snyder, Timothy. *Bloodlands: Europe between Hitler and Stalin.* New York: Basic Books, 2010.

Soluri, John. *Banana Cultures: Agriculture, Consumption, and Environmental Change in Honduras and the United States.* Austin: University of Texas Press, 2005.

Sonnenfeld, David A. "Mexico's 'Green Revolution,' 1940–1980: Towards an Environmental History." *Environmental History Review* 16, no. 4 (1992): 28–52.

Spode, Hasso. "Fordism, Mass Tourism, and the Third Reich: The 'Strength through Joy' Seaside Resort as an Index Fossil." *Journal of Social History* 38, no. 1 (2004): 127–155.

Spode, Hasso, ed. *Goldstrand und Teutonengrill: Kultur- und Sozialgeschichte des Tourismus in Deutschland, 1945 bis 1989.* Institut für Tourismus—FU Berlin, Berichte und Materialien 15. Berlin: W. Moser, Verlag für Universitäre Kommunikation, 1996.

Spode, Hasso, ed. *Zur Sonne, Zur Freiheit! Beiträge zur Tourismusgeschichte.* Berlin: Freie Universität Berlin Institut für Tourismus, 1991.

Stachura, Peter. *German Youth Movement, 1900–1945: An Interpretative and Documentary History.* New York: St. Martin's, 1981.

Standley, Michelle A. "The Cold War, Mass Tourism, and the Drive to Meet World Standards at East Berlin's TV Tower Information Center." In *Touring beyond the Nation: A Transnational Approach to European Tourism,* edited by Eric G. E. Zuelow, 215–240. Farnham, Surrey: Ashgate, 2011.

Steege, Paul. *Black Market, Cold War: Everyday Life in Berlin, 1946–1949.* New York: Cambridge University Press, 2007.

Steinbrinker, Heinrich. "Der Geist der Gemeinschaft: Wechselwirkungen zwischen Arbeiterjugendbewegung und 'bürgerlicher' Jugendbewegung bis 1933." In *Jahrbuch des Archivs der Deutschen Jugendbewegung 1978–1981* 10,7–23. Burg Ludwigstein: Das Archiv der deutschen Jugendbewegung, 1981.

Steiner, Andre. *Die DDR-Wirtschaftsreform der sechziger Jahre: Konflikt zwischen Effizienz- und Machtkalkül.* Berlin: Akademie Verlag, 1999.

Steiner, Andre. "Dissolution of the Dictatorship over Needs? Consumer Behavior and Economic Reform in East Germany in the 1960s." In *Getting and Spending: European and American Consumer Societies in the Twentieth Century,* edited by Susan

Strasser, Charles McGovern, and Matthias Judt, 167–85. Cambridge: Cambridge University Press, 1998.

Stern, Klaus. *Wirkung der grossflächigen Landbewirtschaftung in der DDR auf Flora, Fauna und Boden.* Osteuropastudien der Hochschulen des Landes Hessen 174. Berlin: Duncker und Humblot, 1990.

Stokes, Raymond G. *Constructing Socialism Technology and Change in East Germany, 1945–1990.* Baltimore: Johns Hopkins University Press, 2000.

Stokes, Raymond G. "Plastics and the New Society: The German Democratic Republic in the 1950s and 1960s." In *Style and Socialism: Modernity and Material Culture in Post-war Eastern Europe,* edited by David Crowley and Susan E. Reid, 65–80. Oxford: Berg, 2000.

Stokes, Raymond G. "In Search of the Socialist Artifact: Technology and Ideology in East Germany, 1945–1962." *German History* 15, no. 2 (1997): 221–239.

Stoltzfus, Nathan. "Public Space and the Dynamics of Environmental Action: Green Protest in the German Democratic Republic." *Archiv für Sozialgeschichte* 43 (2003): 385–403.

Sunseri, Thaddeus. "Reinterpreting a Colonial Rebellion: Forestry and Social Control in German East Africa, 1874–1915." *Environmental History* 8, no. 3 (July 2003): 430–451.

Sutter, Paul. "Reflections: What Can U.S. Environmental Historians Learn from Non--U.S. Environmental Historiography?" *Environmental History* 8, no. 1 (January 2003), 109–29.

Taylor, Karin. *Let's Twist Again: Youth and Leisure in Socialist Bulgaria.* Vienna: Lit, 2006.

Taylor, Karin. "My Own Vikendica—Holiday Cottages as Idyll and Investment." In *Yugoslavia's Sunny Side: A History of Tourism in Socialism (1950s–1980s),* edited by Hannes Grandits and Karin Taylor, 171–210. Budapest: Central European University Press, 2010.

Thöns, Kerstin. "Jugendpolitik in der DDR Zwischen Staatlichem Erziehungsanspruch und Selbstgestaltungsinteresse: Untersucht am Beispiel des 'sozialistischen Jugendverbandes' FDJ (1958 bis 1965)." In *"Links und links und Schritt gehalten . . .": Die FDJ; Konzepte—Ablaeufe—Grenzen,* edited by Helga Gotschlich, 227–241. Berlin: Metropol, 1994.

Timm, Annette. "The Legacy of Bevölkerungspolitik: Venereal Disease Control and Marriage Counselling in Post-World War II Berlin." *Canadian Journal of History* 33, no. 2 (1998): 173–214.

Tucker, Richard P. *Insatiable Appetite: The United States and the Ecological Degradation of the Tropical World.* Lanham, Md.: Rowman and Littlefield, 2007.

Uekötter, Frank. "Eine ökologische Ära? Perspektiven einer neuen Geschichte der Umweltbewegungen." *Zeithistorische Forschungen* 9, no. 1 (January 2012): 108–114.

Uekötter, Frank. *The Green and the Brown: A History of Conservation in Nazi Germany.* Cambridge: Cambridge University Press, 2006.

Urry, John. *Sociology beyond Societies: Mobilities for the Twenty-First Century.* London: Routledge, 2000.

Urry, John. *The Tourist Gaze: Leisure and Travel in Contemporary Societies.* London: Sage, 1990.

Valencius, Conevery Bolton. *The Health of the Country: How American Settlers Understood Themselves and Their Land.* New York: Basic Books, 2002.

Vollnhals, Clemens, and Jürgen Weber, eds. *Der Schein der Normalität: Alltag und Herrschaft in der SED-Diktatur.* Munich: Olzog, 2002.

von Richthofen, Esther. *Bringing Culture to the Masses: Control, Compromise, and Participation in the GDR.* New York: Berghahn Books, 2009.

von Richthofen, Esther. "Normalisierung der Herrschaft? Staat und Gesellschaft in der DDR 1961–1979; Kulturelle Massenarbeit in Betrieben und Massenorganisationen im Bezirk Potsdam." In *Das war die DDR: DDR-Forschung im Fadenkreuz von Herrschaft, Aussenbeziehungen, Kultur und Souveränität*, edited by Heiner Timmermann, 573–591. Münster: LIT Verlag, 2005.

Wächter, Eva. "'An der lauten Stadt vorüberziehen!' Naturfreundejugend 1918—1933, zwischen Jugendbewegung und Jugendpflege." In *Wir sind die grüne Garde: Geschichte der Naturfreundejugend*, edited by Heinz Hoffman and Jochen Zimmer, 13–62. Essen: Klartext Verlag, 1986.

Wallace, Anne. *Walking, Literature, and English Culture: The Origins and Uses of Peripatetic in the Nineteenth Century.* Oxford: Oxford University Press, 1993.

Walter, Franz, Viola Denecke, and Cornelia Regin, eds. *Sozialistische Gesundheits und Lebensreform Verbände.* Bonn: Friedrich Ebert Stiftung, 1991.

Warren, Louis. *The Hunter's Game: Poachers and Conservationists in Twentieth-Century America.* New Haven: Yale University Press, 1997.

Waters, C. Kenneth. "Introduction: Revising Our Picture of Julian Huxley." In *Julian Huxley: Biologist and Statesman of Science*, edited by C. Kenneth Waters and Albert Van Helden, 1–30. Houston: Rice University Press, 1992.

Waters, C. Kenneth, and Albert van Helden, eds. *Julian Huxley: Biologist and Statesman of Science.* Houston: Rice University Press, 1992.

Weder, Heinrich. *Sozialhygiene und Pragmatische Gesundheitspolitik in der Weimarer Republik am Beispiel des Sozial und Gewerbehygnikers Beno Chajes, 1880–1938.* Husum: Matthiesen Verlag, 2000.

Weindling, Paul. *Health, Race, and German Politics between National Unification and Nazism, 1870–1945.* Cambridge: Cambridge University Press, 1989.

Weiner, Douglas R. *A Little Corner of Freedom: Russian Nature Protection from Stalin to Gorbachev.* Berkeley: University of California Press, 1999.

Weiner, Douglas R. *Models of Nature: Ecology, Conservation, and Cultural Revolution in Soviet Russia.* Bloomington: University of Indiana Press, 1988. Reprint, Pittsburgh: University of Pittsburgh Press, 2000.

Wierling, Dorothee. "Der Staat, die Jugend und der Westen: Texte zu Konflikten der 1960er Jahre." In *Akten, Eingaben, Schaufenster: Die DDR und ihre Texte; Erkundungen zu Herrschaft und Alltag*, edited by Alf Lüdtke and Peter Becker, 223–240. Berlin: Akademie Verlag, 1997.

Wierling, Dorothee. "Die Jugend als innerer Feind. Konflikte in der Erziehungsdiktatur der sechziger Jahre." In *Sozialgeschichte der DDR*, edited by Hartmut Kaelble et al., 404–425. Stuttgart: Klett-Cotta, 1994.

Weitz, Eric D. *Creating German Communism, 1890–1990: From Popular Protests to Socialist State.* Princeton: Princeton University Press, 1997.

Williams, John A. "'The Chords of the German Soul Are Tuned to Nature': The Movement to Preserve the Natural Heimat from the Kaiserreich to the Third Reich." *Central European History* 29, no. 3 (1996): 339–384.

Williams, John A. *Steeling the Young Body: Official Attempts to Control Youth Hiking in Germany, 1913–1938*. Occasional Papers in German Studies 12. Edmonton: University of Alberta, 1997.

Williams, John A. *Turning to Nature in Germany: Hiking, Nudism, and Conservation, 1900–1940*. Stanford: Stanford University Press, 2007.

Williams, Raymond. "Ideas of Nature." In *Problems in Materialism and Culture: Selected Essays*, 67–85. London: Verso, 1980.

Williams, Raymond. "Nature." In *Keywords*. Oxford: Oxford University Press, 1985.

Wilson, Jeffrey K. *German Forest: Nature, Identity, and the Contestation of a National Symbol, 1871–1914*. Toronto: University of Toronto Press, 2011.

Witkowski, Gregory R. "On the Campaign Trail: State Planning and Eigen-Sinn in a Communist Campaign to Transform the East German Countryside." *Central European History* 37, no. 3 (2004): 400–422.

Wolle, Stefan. *Die heile Welt der Diktatur: Alltag und Herrschaft in der DDR 1971–1989*. Berlin: Ch. Links, 1998.

Wolschke-Bulmahn, Joachim. *Auf der Suche nach Arkadien: Zu Landschaftsidealen und Formen der Naturaneignung in der Jugendbewegung und ihrer Bedeutung für die Landespflege*. Munich: Minerva, 1990.

Wonneberger, Günter. "Sowjetische Sportpolitik für die SBZ und DDR." *Grüner Weg 31a: Zeitschrift des Studienarchivs Arbeiterkultur und Ökologie* 10 (January 1996): 53–61.

Wonneberger, Günter. "Studie zur Struktur und Leitung der Sportbewegung in der SBZ/DDR (1945–1961)." In *Der Sport in der SBZ und frühen DDR*, edited by Wolfgang Buss and Christian Becker, 167–247. Schorndorf: Hofmann, 2001.

Wonneberger, Günter. "Zur Sportpolitik in der SBZ von 1945 bis 1949: Unter Betonung der Besatzungspolitik." *Arbeiterkultur und Ökologie: Rundbrief* 2 (1992): 24–29.

Wonneberger, Ingeburg. "Breitensport: Studie zum Breitensport/Massensport in der Sowjetischen Besatzungszone Deutschlands und der DDR (1945–1960)." In *Der Sport in der SBZ und fruehen DDR*, edited by Wolfgang Buss and Christian Becker, 397–464. Schorndorf: Hofmann, 2001.

Worster, Donald. *Nature's Economy: A History of Ecological Ideas*. Cambridge: Cambridge University Press, 1994.

Wright, Angus. *The Death of Ramón González: The Modern Agricultural Dilemma*. Austin: University of Texas Press, 2005.

Wübbe, Irmela. "Landschaftsplanung in der DDR." In *Landschaft und Planung in den neuen Bundesländern—Rückblicke*, edited by Regine Auster and Hermann Behrens, 33–56. Berlin: Verlag für Wissenschaft und Forschung, 1999.

Wübbe, Irmela. *Landschaftsplanung in der DDR: Aufgabenfelder, Handlungsmöglichkeiten und Restriktionen in der DDR der sechziger und siebziger Jahre*. Bonn: Bund Deutscher Landschaftsarchitekten, 1995.

Young, James. *The Texture of Memory*. New Haven: Yale University Press, 1993.

Zatlin, Jonathan. "Ausgaben und Eingaben: Das Petitionsrecht und der Untergang der DDR." *Zeitschrift für Geschichtswissenschaft* 10 (1997): 902–917.

Zatlin, Jonathan. "Consuming Ideology: Socialist Consumerism and the Intershops,

1970–1989." In *Arbeiter in der SBZ-DDR*, edited by Peter Hübner and Klaus Tenfelde, 555–572. Essen: Klartext Verlag, 1999.

Zatlin, Jonathan. *The Currency of Socialism: Money and Political Culture in East Germany*. Washington, D.C.: German Historical Institute, 2007.

Zatlin, Jonathan. "The Vehicle of Desire: The Trabant, the Wartburg, and the End of the GDR." *German History* 14, no. 3 (1997): 358–380.

Zeller, Thomas. *Driving Germany: The Landscape of the German Autobahn, 1930–1970*. New York: Berghahn Books, 2007.

Zeller, Thomas. *Strasse, Bahn, Panorama: Verkehrswege und Landschaftsveränderung in Deutschland von 1930 bis 1990*. Frankfurt am Main: Campus Verlag, 2000.

Zimmer, Jochen, and Wulf Erdmann. *Hundert Jahre Kampf um die freie Natur: illustrierte Geschichte der Naturfreunde*. Essen: Klartext Verlag, 1991.

Zimmerman, Andrew. *Alabama in Africa: Booker T. Washington, the German Empire, and the Globalization of the New South*. Princeton: Princeton University Press, 2010.

Zuelow, Eric G. E, ed. *Touring beyond the Nation: A Transnational Approach to European Tourism*. Farnham, Surrey: Ashgate, 2011.

Zutz, Axel. "Die Landschaftsdiagnose der DDR." *Garten und Landschaft* 3 (2003): 34–37.

Zutz, Axel. "Die Landschaftsdiagnose der DDR." 2003. Accessed August 31, 2004. http://www.garten-landschaft.de.

Zutz, Axel. "'Kranke' und 'gesunde' Landschaft—Anmerkungen zur Kritik des Landschaftsbegriffs bei der Landschaftsdiagnose. " In *Die Landschaftsdiagnose der DDR: Zeitgeschichte und Wirkung eines Forschungsprojekts aus der Gründungsphase der DDR*, edited by Olaf Hiller, 111–119. Berlin: Technische Universität Berlin, 2002.

Index

German Association for Hiking and
    Mountain Climbing (*continued*)
  BSG Empor Löbtau, 39–41
  leisure hiking, 37, 123
  mass forest runs, 37
  Nature and Heimat Friends, proposed
    merger, 39
  orienteering, 36–37, 41
  resistance to athletic tourism, 39
German "average consumer," 11, 17
German Democratic Republic (GDR or
    DDR)
  antifascism, 16, 36–37
  automobiles, 85–86, 88–89, 95, 171–
    72
  bungalows, 135–51
  camping, 79–97
  compared to FRG, 16, 68–69, 150–51
  compared to Third Reich, 16, 50–51
  conservation, 49–70, 107–26, 156–75
  conservation, compared to FRG, 68–
    69
  consumer desires, 79, 81–83, 86–97,
    136–37, 143–51
  continuity, 9–11, 14–17, 52–59, 174,
    181
  debt, 136
  discontinuity, 8, 16–17, 174
  environmental decline, 1, 156–57,
    183–84
  environmental law, 61–62, 68, 107–26
  former Social Democrats, 25, 28–29,
    38–40, 58
  founding, 1, 25
  health crisis, 122–23
  Hippocratic world view, 54
  hyperindustrialization, 13
  inflation, 136
  IUCN membership, 115
  local identity, 80, 89, 92–93
  mainstream consensus, 3, 8, 10–11,
    17, 86, 97, 111, 137, 158, 170–
    71, 183–84
  Malthusianism, 14, 115–16
  nationalism, 65
  new environmentalism, 156–59, 166–
    75
  physical environments and social engi-
    neering, 2
  pollution, 1

  private property 6, 93, 144–48
  repression of environmentalists and
    conservationists, 49–70, 156–75
  repression of leisure organizations,
    25–42
  scarcity, 16, 38, 49, 81, 87, 90, 92,
    150, 159, 170, 184
  social class, 4, 17, 84–86, 144–48
  sport, 25–42, 123
  state-society relations, 8–9, 81
  tourism, 2–7, 10, 27–28, 33–42, 50,
    63, 67, 79–97, 111, 120–26, 135–
    51, 158, 160, 162–63, 166, 181–
    83
  trade networks, 16
  uranium mining, 92
German Gymnastic and Sports League
    (DTSB), 33–41
  competition, 35
  tourism, 35–36
  See also sport and athletic competition
Gesellschaft für Natur und Umwelt. *See*
    Society for Nature and Environment
Geyer, 91–93, 95–97, 138
Geyer, Michael, 11, 17
Gilsenbach, Reimar, 66, 109, 112, 124–
    25, 161, 164, 166–67, 175
Glacken, Clarence, 108
GNU (Gesellschaft für Natur und Um-
    welt). *See* Society for Nature and
    Environment
Goodbye, Lenin! (film), 135, 137
Gorbachev, Mikhail, 156
Görlich, Christopher, 9, 41, 81–82, 182
Great Britain, 85
Green Ecology Network the Ark, 169
Green Party, 157
Green Revolution, 115–16
Greifenbach Reservoir, 91–97, 136–38,
    140–48, 183
  automobiles, 95
  bungalows, 97, 140–48
  campgrounds, 95, 143–48
  camping, 143–48
  Christian groups, 94
  consumer desires, 95–96
  customer service, 96
  draining, 94–95
  environmental decline, 95
  farmers, 92